*Being Born of God:*

The Role and Significance of Baptism
in Becoming a Christian

Chad Sychtysz

© 2014 Chad Sychtysz
All rights reserved. No part of this book may be
reproduced in any form
without the written permission of the publisher.

Published by
Spiritbuilding Publishing
15591 N. State Rd. 9
Summitville, IN 46070


Printed in the United States of America
BORN OF GOD
by Chad Sychtysz

ISBN: 978-0-9829811-5-3




Spiritual "equipment" for the contest of life.

# Acknowledgements

THE PRODUCTION OF THIS BOOK was largely a private effort, at least until a working manuscript had been written. At that point, other people became involved—some to refine what was written, others to check my theology (so to speak), and still others to critique the manuscript's "readability." I want to thank all these people, and especially Jeff Archer (a fellow minister of the gospel) and Leigh Hubbard for reading through the entire manuscript and offering valuable comments, corrections, and recommendations. I also am deeply appreciative of Carl "Mac" McMurray at *Spiritbuilding Publishing* for continuing to support my writing ministry through his own endeavors. Jamey Hinds, who has done the layout for several of my books, also deserves my heartfelt appreciation for his making my work (literally) look better than when it started. And of course there are friends and family, including my church "family," who offer all kinds of encouragement and support—I thank you. I especially want to thank my wife, Honey, for always being there, no matter when and no matter what.

# Table of Contents

**Introduction** . . . . . . . . . . 3

**Part One: What The Bible Actually Teaches On Baptism**
   Chapter 1: Admission Into Christ's Church . . . . 15
   Chapter 2: You Must Be Born Again Church . . . . 34
   Chapter 3: Instruction And Implementation . . . . 51
   Chapter 4: Washing Away Your Sins . . . . . 69
   Chapter 5: Separation And Identification . . . . 90
   Chapter 6: The Sign Of The Covenant . . . . . 104
   Chapter 7: The One Baptism . . . . . . 119

**Part Two: Challenges To Baptism**
   Chapter 8: The Thief On The Cross . . . . . 136
   Chapter 9: Hypothetical Arguments . . . . 144
   Chapter 10: Infant Baptism . . . . . . 159
   Chapter 11: The Doctrine Of Calvinism . . . . 186
   Chapter 12: The Doctrine Of "Faith Only" . . . . 207
   Chapter 13: The "When" Factor . . . . . 223
   Chapter 14: Common Questions About Baptism . . . 243

**Endnotes** . . . . . . . . . . 281

Scripture taken from the NEW AMERICAN STANDARD BIBLE®,
Copyright © 1960, 1962, 1963, 1968, 1971, 1972, 1973,
1975, 1977, 1995 by The Lockman Foundation.
Used by permission.

# Introduction

*But as many as received Him, to them He gave the right to become children of God, even to those who believe in His name, who were born, not of blood nor of the will of the flesh nor of the will of man, but of God.*
John 1:12-13

"Born of God." This phrase brings to mind wonderful things: cleansing, forgiveness, renewal, hope, acceptance, fellowship, love, and salvation itself. This is intentional, since God knows that your soul truly hungers for all of these things.

We have all been born of humankind, and most of us have become disappointed and disillusioned with this birth. It is not just what we have been born *into* that has caused this, but also what we ourselves have done to our own innocence. The world is filled with sin and all the consequences *of* sin, but our own "world"—the sphere of our individual lives—has also been corrupted with *our* sin. Being born of God provides the redemption that we have been seeking. Our new birth in God through Christ gives us more than just forgiveness of our sins; it also makes it possible for us to have communion with God Himself.

But *how* is a person born of God (or, "born again")? And *when* does this happen? The concept of one's spiritual rebirth, as well as the occasion of that rebirth, is straightforward and uncomplicated: you die to your old life, and you are born into a new life with God. In being born *of* God, you become identified *with* God. In this process, you "die" to sin and walk in newness of life with Christ. Simply put, being born of God is the process by which you are made a Christian. A Christian is one who is "in Christ," having been spiritually enlightened, saved by grace, made a partaker of the Holy Spirit, and "tasted the good word of God" (cf. Hebrews 6:4). He or she is, indeed, a child of God. One who is *not* born of God, however, has not yet become a Christian and remains a captive of "the corruption that is in this world" (cf. 2 Peter 1:4).

The method of becoming a child of God is extremely important to Him; therefore it must also be extremely important to you. But because it *is* so important to Him, you can be sure that His revealed instruction on the matter is very clear and not left to subjective opinions, including yours or mine. A subject so crucial to our salvation cannot possibly be ambiguous or open to various interpretations—all of which are presumed to be equally valid. It is impossible for us to teach divergent and contradictory methods of being born of God and yet somehow all end up "in Christ" as legitimate children of God.

So then, where are you personally in all of this? Have *you* been born of God—and if so, *how* and *when* did this happen? My purpose for asking is not to question your sincerity, for I already assume you are sincere. I cannot imagine someone reading a book like this who believes that he is insincere. But no one is saved or justified by God based upon sincerity alone. God has provided the plan for *how* and *when* to be born of Him; your responsibility is to conform to this plan to the very best of your ability. What we will cover from here forward may or may not support what *you* did, but it will provide biblical information on what a person *must* do in order to be born of God.

The proposition of this book is that **the New Testament teaches that we cannot be born of God—that is, we cannot**

**become Christians—apart from being baptized *into* Christ.** Baptism marks the occasion of one's conversion to Christ; it symbolizes the death and new birth of the soul that comes to God. Baptism is not a mere ceremonial rite performed *after* one's conversion to Christ; it is a critical necessity *of* that conversion. Even if you have already been baptized into Christ, you would do well to broaden your understanding of this subject. Since everything about your fellowship with God depends upon your having been born of Him, this experience ought to have a profound effect on that fellowship.

Yet, despite all that the New Testament has to say on this—which is more than many people realize—baptism remains at the center of religious controversy. In fact, it is not an exaggeration to say that water baptism is perhaps one of the most misunderstood, misrepresented, and divisive subjects in the religious world today. Strong disagreement over how to *become* a Christian creates a fundamental division among believers. This division prevents us from going forward with any other religious dialogue: if we cannot agree on how to *be* born of God, then we cannot resolve disagreements beyond this step. Instead, we are divided over whether everyone who *claims* to be born of God really *is* born of Him.

The controversy over baptism largely centers around three major topics: the *role* of baptism in conversion; whether or not baptism is *essential* to salvation; and then *who* can be baptized. Every self-proclaimed Christian religion seems to have its own version of teaching on baptism. Hardly any of these religions are passive on the subject: either you accept its view on baptism, or you cannot be a part of that religion. In some cases, water baptism is a prerequisite for membership in a congregation *apart from* its connection to one's "born again" experience.

Adding to the controversy over baptism is the fact that not everyone is on the same page as to what the word actually means. In the Bible, "baptism" is a word transliterated (rather than translated) from the original Greek text in which the New Testament was written. The word that the New Testament writers used, by inspiration of the Holy Spirit, is the exact same word which we have adopted into our English language today. In order to understand what the apostles meant, we have to appeal to the words they used in the language *and* context that they wrote. We cannot give contemporary meanings to ancient words and come up with an accurate representation of what was originally meant. Thus, whatever "baptism" meant to those who wrote it by inspiration of the Holy Spirit is *precisely* what it must mean to us who (allegedly) practice it.[1]

In the original (Koine) Greek of the New Testament, "baptism" always meant the same thing: immersion in (something); a whelming (of water, trials, etc.); to make fully wet; specifically, immersion in water as a religious rite as commanded by Christ and His apostles.[2] Baptism *never* meant pouring or sprinkling; none of the examples of baptism in the New Testament support such interpretations.[3] Pouring of water was introduced centuries after the church began in order to accommodate those on their deathbeds who wanted to be baptized but were deemed too sick or frail to do so.[4] Sprinkling of water likely was adopted from the ancient practice of sprinkling blood as a means of consecration (as in Exodus 24:8, Hebrews 9:19-22). We will assume that these methods came about with the best of intentions, but having the best of intentions is not interchangeable with *obedience to the command*. Uzzah had the best of intentions when he put out his hand to steady the ark of the covenant during its transport to Jerusalem, yet God struck him dead for irreverence (1 Samuel 6:3-8). Naaman also had the best of intentions when he expected Elisha to perform some great ceremony in order to heal his leprosy, yet he never would have been cleansed until he did what the prophet told him to do—namely, dip himself seven times in the Jordan River (2 Kings 5:1-14). And Apollos had the best of intentions in preaching his limited knowledge of Jesus that he learned through John the Baptist, yet when he was confronted with a fuller understanding of this message he was obligated to preach this instead (Acts 18:24-28). Obedience to God's commands has always been more important than one's feelings or intentions.

Likewise, there are many people today who—with the best of intentions—believe that they have been born of God and thus saved through a means that God never revealed, the apostles never taught, and the early church never practiced. These people may support the practice of baptism itself, but they believe it is something to be taken care of *after* one's conversion, not an essential part *of* conversion. This reduces baptism to a mere ceremonial act rather than a necessary requirement of those who wish to be born of God.

It is true that baptism is rich with symbolism; it is *not* true that, because it *is* symbolic, it is therefore optional, expendable, or something other than an act of obedience to God. Baptism emulates Christ's death, burial, and resurrection. But He actually died, whereas the believer's death is symbolic; He actually rose from His actual death, whereas the believer is raised in a spiritual context; and so on. Nonetheless, if Christ (through His Word) commands a person who believes in Him to be baptized, then baptism is something *required* of that person and cannot be reduced to anything less than this.

Commandments need only to be obeyed, not questioned or interpreted.

    The act of baptism is not, however, a mere act of commandment-keeping. It is an illustration of spiritual resurrection, spiritual redemption, and the hope for a future with God. Baptism is nearly always mentioned (from Acts 2 forward) in direct connection with forgiveness, union with Christ, identity with Christ, membership in Christ's spiritual church, cleansing of the human conscience (from the guilt of sin), and calling upon the name of God for salvation. Every time a Christian partakes of communion (the Lord's Supper) he is reminded of the day of his conversion when *his* sins were forgiven because of Christ's atoning death on the cross. In having *died* with Christ, the believer now *lives* with Him; in having died to sin, the believer now lives to God. The great transaction of when he became a "new creature" (cf. 2 Corinthians 5:17) was not merely something he felt in his heart, but was a real and historical event. Having died *with* Christ in baptism, the believer can now know that he will receive eternal life according to God's promises (cf. 1 John 5:13).

    There are not a variety of "faiths" or gospels taught in the New Testament, but only one. Likewise, there is only "one baptism" (Ephesians 4:5) that is required of you, not several, and not one *of* several. We cannot all claim "One gospel!" but have different (and contradictory) practices *of* that gospel. Likewise, we cannot all claim "One baptism!" but have different (and contradictory) practices of or beliefs about baptism. One author writes, "If a church's *practice* is different from the practice of the church in the New Testament, it is likely that its *doctrine* is also different from first-century Christianity."[5] He means this in an ideal sense, as when the early Christians actually *did* what they were *instructed*. But the point still remains: variant practices will not legitimately arise from a singular instruction.

Believers are not divided on *every* biblical subject, however.[6] On several significant points, most of those who call themselves Christians are in agreement. We know that we have sinned against God; we also know that God has provided in His Son the remedy for the self-inflicted sabotage of our spiritual well-being. We know that we need Christ's redemption, and that our redemption is ultimately secured through His blood offering on the cross. In other words, we know that we need to be saved, and that this salvation is not predicated upon what we do for God, but what God does for us. We all teach about the grace of God, and we all believe that those who trust in that grace we will be with the Lord in the hereafter.

It is at this point that we begin to diverge in our beliefs, and baptism is a key part *of* that divergence. On one hand, most will be willing to admit the *significance* of baptism. One denominational author, for example sums this up well: "We can agree that baptism is commanded by our Lord Jesus Christ … and thus should never be treated as trivial. Put simply, baptism is important, and this is why we must be serious about it: baptism is bound up with Christ and his gospel, and this connection makes it important for all who wish to be faithful to Jesus."[7] Yet, while most people understand baptism itself to be "important," many of these also believe that the necessity, timing, and method *of* baptism are not important or are deemed altogether expendable.

Some believe that, since God's grace is what saves us, therefore we need to do *nothing* in order to save ourselves. Others believe that God's grace leads us to having faith in Him, rather than the obedience of our faith being that which initiates the salvation of our souls. Thus, baptism is not designed to call upon the name of the Lord, but is something done after one has already been "saved." Others believe that they were saved when they called upon Jesus for salvation, but that this calling did not involve any "works" on their part. And there are many who simply listen to the words of their pastors and clergymen rather than reading the New Testament themselves.

Part of the problem, then, is that not everyone is coming to the table empty-handed, so to speak. Instead, many strive to defend their predetermined traditional practice or persuasion of belief. The Baptist, for example, seeks to defend the Baptist position concerning baptism. He cites Scripture, he argues passionately, he believes sincerely. Despite this, he comes *to* the table—and plans to leave *from* the table—as a Baptist, and not as an objective student of God's Word. The Catholic defends infant baptism because he is a Catholic, not because of what is written in the New Testament (because there is *nothing* written of this in the New Testament). The Mormon defends his "baptism for the dead" (cf. 1 Corinthians 15:29) because that has become a doctrinal practice of Mormonism. The Presbyterian begins his approach as a Calvinist, and thus is already convinced of the Doctrine of Predestination before he ever dives into the doctrine of baptism.

Someone will argue, of course, that I am coming to the table with my *own* religious baggage and bias. In the sense that I am human, I cannot help but do this. But must we defend baptism (or any other subject of the gospel of Christ) in the context of a certain religious affiliation, or is it possible to understand baptism as God *revealed* it to us in His Word? It is my firm belief that baptism *can* and *must* be understood objectively, not in the existing framework of one's personal beliefs or denominational system.[8] Otherwise, the very definition of "Christian"—and thus, being "born of God"—is reduced to each person's opinion of what this means and how it is achieved. We can call this religion if we want to, but it is not the Christianity that Paul and others preached in the beginning. We cannot claim to be keepers of the New Testament pattern while simultaneously ignoring or violating it.

Baptism is not expected of people *after* they have been born of God. Rather, the New Testament instructs those who are *not* born of God how to *become* born of Him—that is, how to become *Christians*. This instruction also expounds upon this subject in order for those who *are* Christians to better understand their fellowship with Christ *in light of* their baptism. This better knowledge is then expected to be taught by believers to those who have yet to obey God. The entire gospel message was written *not* to make a person a denominationalist, non-denominationalist, or (as is increasingly popular) "un-denominationalist."[9] It was written so that we can put our faith—and thus, our souls—in the hands of God's Son for the purpose of "eternal life" (cf. John 20:31).

My own "position," if it can be called a position at all, is simply this: God's Word trumps all man-made or denominational teachings, regardless of what they are, who came up with them, how long they have been around, or how earnestly they are maintained. If God requires believers to be baptized in order to become Christians, then this must be the clear and inescapable conclusion of His revealed Word, this is what must be taught by all those who represent Him, and this will be what I defend. (The same must be true if God does *not* require believers to be baptized.) Upon examination of the evidence, I am confident that the honest and sincere person will come to a clearer understanding of God's teaching on salvation—and the role of baptism in that salvation. If one truly wishes to be born of God, then he or she will discover how this is to be done by following the apostolic pattern of the New Testament.

What you believe about God and your relationship with Him must be based upon His revealed truth if indeed you wish to be "approved" by Him (cf. 2 Timothy 2:15). A belief system that is based on anything else will lead to spiritual ruin. Thus, whatever you believe—regardless if you are presently in agreement with me or not—I respectfully challenge you to examine the biblical evidence for yourself and see how your own beliefs compare to what God actually teaches. If you are truly a believer, then you will choose to comply with whatever God has said. Jesus Himself said, "If you love Me, you will keep My commandments" (John 14:15). This is as true with commandments concerning baptism as it is for anything else for which He has instructed us.

# Part One:
## What the Bible Actually Teaches on Baptism

# Chapter One:
# Admission into Christ's Church

*See how great a love the Father has bestowed on us,
that we would be called children of God; and such we are. For
this reason the world does not know us,
because it did not know Him.*
1 John 3:1

Before talking about being "born of God," one must understand the reason why we *need* to be born of God. A person who does not believe that he is lost certainly will not understand the importance of being saved. Likewise, one who believes that his present situation—being born of *man*—will sufficiently prepare him for the afterlife will not be interested in being born of *God*. If one does not sufficiently understand his problem, then he will not see the need for a solution. We are not covering this information because you are necessarily unaware of it, but simply so that we can build a common foundation in order to move onto other things.

The apostle Paul wrote, "You were dead in your trespasses and sins, in which you formerly walked according to the course of this world …" (Ephesians 2:1-2). By "dead," Paul means separated from God's fellowship, not completely incapacitated.[10] Nowhere in the New Testament does it say that one who is "dead" to God is completely unable to *hear, believe,* and *respond to* the gospel of Christ. Quite the opposite: Paul preached *in order that* people would hear, believe, and call upon the Lord for salvation (see Acts 26:16-18, Ephesians 4:17-20, Colossians 1:5-7, et al). The one who has sinned against God is thus separated from His fellowship; he becomes a "sinner."

The end result of this separation, provided the breach is never reconciled, will be that person's spiritual ruin—his "death" in the final and permanent sense.[11] Left to ourselves, we are unable to rectify this situation. A corrupted soul simply cannot escape its own corrupted state of being, since that soul is limited and trapped by its own circumstances.

Christ *can* restore our fellowship with God, however, since He has not succumbed to our own affliction (sin) *and* He wields the life-giving power and authority of God Himself. The process by which He brings a person out of his state of spiritual "death" to God is called regeneration [lit., the process of being made alive again]. Thus, in the conversion *from* his sinful state and *into* fellowship with God, this person is forgiven of his sins, sanctified by God's Spirit, and presented before God as "holy and blameless and beyond reproach" by Jesus Christ (cf. Colossians 1:21-22). He is in fact born of God. The result of this great transaction is that he has become a *Christian*, whereas before he was simply a sinner. The gospel message is preached for this very objective (see 1 Timothy 1:15-16).

Just because Christ is the *Source* of regeneration does not mean, however, that nothing is required of the one who wishes to be "made alive" to God. Peter declared, "It shall be that everyone who calls on the name of the Lord will be saved" (Acts 2:21). One who is separated from God can indeed call upon Him for salvation—in fact, he cannot be saved unless or until he does so. Christ is the One who brings him back to life—and thus restores his fellowship with God—and makes him one of His own. Christ never does this against one's own will, or without one's full knowledge and consent. There is nothing in Scripture that even hints that Christ regenerates those who do not themselves *choose* to be regenerated.

The sanctuary of regenerated souls is the spiritual body of believers known to us in Scripture as Christ's church (Colossians 1:18). Those who are born of God are made members of this church by Christ Himself, since He is its head and presides over it with full authority. In other words, those who are born of God are never rogue Christians who "go at it alone" in whatever manner they deem appropriate (or convenient), but are subject to the One who has made them a part of His church. Just as a Christian wife is to subject herself to her husband—regardless of how archaic this seems to many people today—so the church is subject to Christ (Ephesians 5:23-24). If this is expected of the entire church, then it must be expected of each individual believer within the church.

Admittance into God's fellowship—which is equivalent to one's salvation—is not decided by one's subjective determination. God has not put something as critical as the salvation of one's soul into the hands of mere men, church synods, or denominational officials. Religious *sincerity* cannot be confused with conformity to God's *doctrine*, since sincerity can never be a replacement for obedience. If you wish to be born of God, then you must abide by the terms and conditions that God the Father has laid down for this. No one can come to the Father except through Christ (John 14:6), and no one can be "in Christ" who does not become a Christian.

### What Being "In Christ" Means (and Does Not Mean)

To appreciate what has just been said, we should pull back and look at the big picture. God's love is unconditional: He loves all people no matter what. This does not mean He is happy with every person's decision concerning Him, or that He will automatically save all people. It means that He continues to act in our best interest regardless of what we do or fail to do. God shows kindness to all people—even those who remain in a condemned state of being (Matthew 5:44-45). But in showing such undeserved kindness, He expects more than the sinner's mere acknowledgement of His existence. Instead, He rightly expects a genuine change of heart toward Him that is proved by obedience. "Or do you think lightly of the riches of His kindness and tolerance and patience," the apostle Paul wrote, "not knowing that the kindness of God leads you to repentance?" (Romans 2:4).

Our obedience to God must not be looked upon as some noteworthy effort on our part, or some great favor that we do for Him. Regardless of how much our obedience costs us—in time, effort, and the loss of what must be given up in order to provide it—it is exactly what we should have been doing all along. This is not meant to diminish the difficulty of discipleship; it is meant only to keep things in perspective. "So…when you do all the things which are commanded you, say, 'We are unworthy slaves; we have done only that which we ought to have done'" (Luke 17:10). Even if we lived with perfect obedience after having become Christians, we would still fail to do more than what God has always required of us in the first place.

And yet the fact remains: none of us *has* lived with perfect obedience, "for all have sinned and fall short of the glory of God" (Romans 3:23). Since "all have sinned" and fallen, it is necessary to have our innocence restored if we wish to stand justified before God. Sinful people cannot provide the necessary *effort* or *payment* required to overcome the damage caused by even a single human sin. Having broken a single law of God, we become guilty of transgressing the *entirety* of God's law (James 2:10). However, Christ is the One who makes our justification before God possible.  Christ becomes to the believer everything that the believer has failed to be to God.  As Paul said, "By His doing you are in Christ Jesus, who became to us wisdom from God, and righteousness and sanctification, and redemption" (1 Corinthians 1:30).

A person cannot obtain these blessings on his own, but "in Christ Jesus" they are given to him by God (Ephesians 1:3). The one who is not in Christ, however, stands outside of God's fellowship.  It is critically important, then, to understand exactly what it means to be in Christ.  Being "in Christ" is not to be confused with:

- ❑ *Being a good, moral person (by itself).*  Just because a person thinks he is saved does not make him saved, any more than a person thinking he is an astronaut makes him one.
- ❑ *Feeling saved.*  Salvation is an objective reality; it is not a feeling or an emotion.  Christ did not die on the cross so that people could "feel" forgiveness or redemption.  He died to actually forgive and redeem human souls.
- ❑ *Claiming to be a Christian* (without having complied with the terms and conditions of becoming a Christian). No one is saved because of what he calls himself.  He is saved only because of what he does for God (in faith) and what God does for him (by grace).
- ❑ *Going to church.*  This is often reduced to: "Sitting through a church service in a church building."  Many people place a great deal of reverence on church buildings and religious liturgy, but no one has ever been saved by sitting in a building or participating in a church service.  Salvation is a deeply personal experience, not an institutional one, and certainly not an environmental one.

# Being Born of God

- ❏ *Church membership.* Just because a person is a member of a given congregation does not make him "saved." Furthermore, Christ does not recognize every congregation that invokes His name in what it does. Those churches that stray from the New Testament pattern are told to repent (cf. Revelation 2 – 3), not remain as they are. Straying from the pattern is a sinful action, not an acceptable or harmless one.

Being "in Christ" means being saved: a state of fellowship with God through the redemptive work of His Son. Often, people associate their relationship to God with their personal beliefs or the religious designation they have selected (according to their preferences). Thus, someone will say, "I am a Methodist" or "I am a Catholic"; or, one will say, "I go to this church" or "I go to that church"; or, one might say, "I believe in this religion" or "I believe in that religion." Yet no one is saved because of their affiliation with a particular denomination, congregation, or religion. No one is saved because he adopts a particular name or joins himself to a particular movement. One is saved only when he (or she) comes to God through Christ according to the terms and conditions of His covenant—the gospel of Christ.

The gospel's terms and conditions are the same for every person in every place at any time. The Holy Spirit has revealed what God requires of every person, regardless of human opinions or beliefs to the contrary. Therefore, you will be saved in the same manner as those who were saved in the first century, as recorded in Acts. In coming to God for His salvation, we are all in the same condition: we all have the same problem; we all need the same Savior; we all must obey the same gospel; and we all are born of God and thus made to be "in Christ" through that obedience. No one "in Christ" is superior to anyone else who is "in Christ." In the Lord's church, there is no clergy-laity system; "For you are all sons of God through faith in Christ Jesus" (Galatians 3:26). Being a "son of God"—regardless of your physical gender—means that you can look forward to an inheritance from God in Christ.

## Things that Complicate the Situation

While the situation explained above is really quite clear and straightforward, it is complicated by at least three things: human emotions, ignorance, and doctrines of men.

**Human emotions:** Our human emotions can easily interfere with what God has asked of us. This is especially true in the case of one particular *part* of the born-again experience: water baptism. When it comes to one's belief in God, faith, repentance, or love for the Lord, few people will take issue. When it comes to the necessity of baptism, however, many people in the religious world balk and begin reasoning in a different way than they did with these other things. Instead of using logic and reason, they often switch to another form of thinking—an emotional or subjective one.

Objective reasoning examines relevant evidence, applies sound reasoning, and comes to a natural and (often) inescapable conclusion. Subjective reasoning is always dependent upon how the conclusion (or outcome) will affect the person doing the reasoning. The objective person will allow the argument to go where it must go, and accepts whatever conclusion it draws. The subjective person first asks, "How will this affect me?" or "What outcome do I *want* to have (for myself, someone I care about, or my belief system)?" His argument does not always follow the facts, but often gets derailed along the way because he already disagrees with any undesirable outcome. He may be oblivious to this; he may think, in his mind, that he makes perfect sense; he may be blinded to his error in reasoning. Or worse: he knows that he does *not* make sense, but is so averse to an undesirable outcome that he will accept whatever logical compromises or contradictions are necessary to avoid it.

For example, if a person reads, "Repent and return, so that your sins may be wiped away" (Acts 3:19), he will likely have no problem with this. He will likely reason, "Obviously, repentance is a necessary prerequisite for forgiveness; this makes sense. Besides, whatever God said, I must obey it in order to receive the salvation that He offers." Here is a person who is thinking intelligently and logically. He is using the reasoning ability that God imparted to him when He made him "in His image." He is using discernment—the ability to judge things according to a fixed and transcendent authority or standard—and thus realizes the true nature of his situation. He stands in condemnation before God, and yet God offers him an opportunity to have that situation reconciled through the blood of Christ. Access to His blood requires obedience to His gospel. He knows intuitively that his repentance is a work of human effort, but it is required of God all the same. He places his trust in God to do what He alone can do, but he also realizes that he has a responsibility to fulfill as well. Thus, he willfully repents of his sins in response to the command.

Yet, when he reads, "Repent, and each of you be baptized in the name of Jesus Christ for the forgiveness of your sins" (Acts 2:38), he (like many people) bristles at the idea of baptism. He reasons, "I can accept [performing the work of] repentance, but I do not believe I have to be baptized. That cannot be necessary for me to be 'born again.' Being dunked in water simply cannot be a part of a spiritual re-birth. Therefore, I will not do it. God knows my heart that I am sincere in what I *will* do." Now this person is no longer using the same process as before. Given these two passages that tell him what is necessary to be forgiven *by* God—and thus, is required in order to be born *of* God—he chooses one and rejects (part of) the other. He has no problem with one admission requirement but will not agree to the other. He objectively accepted the conclusion of the first passage but subjectively refuses the conclusion of the other.

What happened? He was doing so well at first, while he was thinking objectively. Yet, something compelled him—something *personal* and *emotional*—to shift to an entirely different form of reasoning. In other words, he allowed something else to get in the way of seeing the simplicity and purity of the gospel (cf. 2 Corinthians 4:3-4, 11:3). This emotional interference could be (and often is) one or more of the following:

- ❑ He wishes to defend a particular *religion* rather than submitting himself to the revealed commandments of God. When these two things are in agreement, he is in agreement; where there is a jarring contradiction, however, his heart lies with the religion he seeks to defend rather than a genuine desire to uphold whatever God has instructed.
- ❑ He wishes to retain his chosen identity rather than be affiliated with people that he does not agree with, has had a bad experience with, or simply dislikes. This is related to the point just discussed. For example, someone in a denominational religion may reject the necessity of baptism *not* for lack of biblical evidence, but because he does not want to lose his identity with those with whom he is comfortable (i.e., his church friends). Or, he does not want to identify with those of whom he does not

have a high opinion (i.e., adherents of a belief system different than his own). Thus, he foregoes obeying the commandment of God *not* because it is unclear to him, but because of personal reasons.

- He believes that numbers are on his side, and is unwilling to challenge the popular majority. This is the "A million [insert: preferred religionists] can't be wrong" argument. This is not a logical or objective conclusion, but a purely subjective one. Ironically, those who use this argument are often oblivious to the fact that it only works when *they* use it. For instance, suppose I am a Baptist and I say, "A million Baptists can't be wrong." Yet, my own religion will not allow for (say) a billion *Muslims* to be saved. What I am actually saying is, "But a billion *other* people *can* be wrong—and I believe they are!" Regardless, millions or billions of people cannot determine what is necessary to redeem the human soul; only God can do this. By appealing to any quantity of people to justify one's position, a person automatically rejects whatever God says to the contrary. It should be noted here that God has never operated by a majority rule, popular vote, or politically-correct system.

- He does not want to offend—or condemn—his friends or family members who refuse to be baptized. This is often communicated in the following way: "If I am baptized for the forgiveness of my sins, then I will judge my [insert: spouse, favorite relative, best friend, admired mentor, or all of the above] to be wrong, and I cannot do that. I believe him [or her] to be good person, and who am I to condemn him?" This perspective misrepresents the situation entirely. Salvation is not about who we do or do not offend; it is about seeking fellowship with God in this life and in the life to come. Basing one's spiritual welfare on someone else's beliefs (or hurt feelings) is not a logical decision but a purely subjective one. If you think about it, this kind of reasoning will prevent a person not only from baptism, but also repentance or anything else God requires of believers. Given this logic, no one will be saved unless *everyone* is saved all at once, since in any other case *someone's* friend or relative will be offended. Yet, if a person chooses to obey God, he is not *willfully* offending or condemning anyone. He is simply doing what all people ought to be doing in response to their Creator. Those who refuse to obey God judge or condemn themselves (John 3:18-21, Acts 13:44-46).

These examples are common, yet they remain indefensible. Refusing to be baptized—or refusing any other clear and explicit command that God has given to us—cannot be justified by such responses. This does not stop people from trying, however. In the end, people are going to do whatever they want. Nonetheless, God has only one method of salvation, and He does not change it to accommodate anyone's emotional position.

**Ignorance:** People may resist baptism because of their emotions, but a second reason may be their ignorance of what the Scriptures actually teach on the subject. In the following chapters, we will examine a number of passages that both directly and indirectly provide instruction and explanation concerning this action. Just because the information is available, however, does not mean that everyone who claims to be a Christian—or who has refused to become one—has read any or all of it. Even though we live in a so-called Information Age, the truth is that people seem to be less *accurately* informed

*Being Born of God* 25

about the most important things in life than ever. Many people have a great deal of knowledge about their computer programs, HDTV, iPhones, and video games, but these things add nothing to their spiritual well-being. Instead of discovering what God has revealed in His Word, many people will simply Google® their religious questions and read what someone else *says* about His Word. This is not only intellectually lazy; it is a contributing factor to the moral decay of our society.

People are not being taught to think for themselves. In fact, people are not being taught to think at all—this is why we have the Internet, calculators, smart phones, GPS navigation, and all sorts of technological gadgetry. "Studying the Bible" is a foreign concept for many people who identify themselves with one (allegedly) Christian religion or another. In order to "[understand] what the will of the Lord is" (Ephesians 5:17), it is necessary to read and meditate upon what He has said. In fact, Paul told the Ephesians that "when you read [his inspired writings] you can understand my insight into the mystery of Christ, which in other generations was not made known to the sons of men, as it has now been revealed to His holy apostles and prophets in the Spirit…" (3:4-5, bracketed words are mine). In other words, we can "read and understand" what God wants us to *know* and *do* in order to have fellowship with Him (cf. 2 Corinthians 1:13). We have more privilege and access to the Word than at any time in human history. Given this, we should be the most spiritually-enlightened people in all of human history. Sadly, this is hardly the case.

When many people read John 3:16, for example—"For God so loved the world, that He gave His only begotten Son, that whoever believes in Him shall not perish, but have eternal life"—they tend to oversimplify that statement. They interpret this to mean, "If I just believe in God, then I will have eternal life." It is the word "just" that complicates things in this case. If there was nothing else to do and nothing else required of us, then to "just believe" would be acceptable and accurate. Yet "believe" in the context of the New Testament necessarily implies "obey" (see John 3:36). Furthermore, to "believe in Him [God's Son]" provides the object of one's belief. Jesus did not say, "Whoever believes that the Son *loves* him," but (in essence), "Whoever *obeys* the Son and thus does whatever He commands." This is supported also in John 14:15, where Jesus said, "If you love Me, you will keep My commandments." No one can truly love Jesus who will not obey Him, and if one will not obey Him then he does not really believe in Him.

    The point is that we cannot take pieces and snippets of Scripture and turn those fragments into an entire belief system. No one gains an accurate knowledge of God by reading a few select verses while refusing to examine others. When it comes to baptism, no one can read one verse on baptism and then claim to have an accurate understanding of what it is or what it does for a person. Likewise, no one can read one (or even several) verses that *omit* baptism and then claim, "See? Baptism isn't here—therefore it is not necessary at all." You cannot discover any of God's doctrines by pointing out what is *not* in a given passage. This is an extremely popular method, however, and even a number of well-respected evangelicals promote it. Yet, it remains illogical and unconvincing and only serves to distract people from the gospel truth. If we were to use that logic elsewhere, we would render faith, repentance, grace, and forgiveness itself completely unnecessary since these things are not mentioned in every passage concerning salvation (such as John 3:16 itself). Such arguments, if we dare to call them arguments at all, do not manifest an honest or diligent study of God's Word, but instead call attention to that person's *lack* of honesty and/or study. (We will revisit this situation when dealing with specific passages later in this book.)

Ignorance can never be offered as an excuse when in fact we are expected to know better *and* God has given all the information we need in one Book. Even in ancient Israel, God did not excuse the ignorance of His people when they should have known better (see Leviticus 5:14-19). "My people are destroyed for lack of knowledge," God told Israel when that people became steeped in idolatry. "Because you have rejected knowledge, I also will reject you from being My priest. Since you have forgotten the law of your God, I also will forget your children" (Hosea 4:6). God has said a great deal about baptism in His Word—again, far more than most people realize—and we have no good reason to be ignorant of His instruction. This is especially true if baptism is directly involved in one's becoming a Christian in the first place.

**Doctrines of men:** A third reason why many people reject baptism (but cling to far less important doctrines) is because of the teachings of men. This is directly related to what was just said concerning ignorance: in not knowing what *God* has said in His Word, many will embrace instead what *men* think they know about God's Word. Not all of this latter knowledge is inaccurate, either; some of my own studies have been greatly enriched through the wisdom and perspectives of biblical scholars and commentators. Yet, listening to such men *instead* of God's Word or *at the expense* of it is a serious error indeed. When Jesus said, "Beware of men" (Matthew 10:17), He was not only talking about those people outside of our church buildings, He was talking about men in general—including those who claim to teach and preach in His name. Any man who cannot authenticate what he teaches with an intelligent appeal to Scripture in its proper context is a man that you ought to avoid. Your soul is far too precious to be swayed by another man's "take" on what you should or should not do.

In my own 30+ years of experience as a Christian, virtually every person that I have talked to who rejected the necessity of baptism did *not* do so through an appeal to Scripture. In nearly every case, such people did so because someone else *told* them what to believe, what to say, and what to do. These people chose to listen to men instead of God; they chose to take someone else's word for what God said rather than read it themselves. Whether or not they did so intentionally (or lazily) is irrelevant. What happened is that they put man-made teachings over and above God's own—and this continues to happen over and over at an alarmingly increasing rate.

Think about what the apostle Paul said: "For I would have you know, brethren, that the gospel which was preached by me is not according to man. For I neither received it from man, nor was I taught it, but I received it through a revelation of Jesus Christ" (Galatians 1:11-12). If Paul's gospel teaches you how to be saved, and this gospel necessarily involves baptism, then you cannot be saved unless you obey that gospel and submit to this command. If some pastor or evangelist today says otherwise, you must choose between listening to *him* or listening to Paul's inspired teaching, since you cannot do both. If you listen to, say, a minister *rather* than Paul, then you are putting your faith in a man and not God.

Not everyone who says "Lord, Lord" actually teaches what the Lord has said to do (cf. Luke 6:46). Simply put, not everyone who *says* he is a Christian actually *is* one. Not everyone who *thinks* he is born of God actually *is*. Whoever attempts to be born of God—and thus, become a Christian—through some means that contradicts the revealed Word *of* God cannot possibly be approved *by* God. If we could be saved by man-made teaching, then we would not need the gospel of Christ. If faith in men (or preachers, man-made churches, or religions) could duplicate or replace one's faith in God, then the Holy Spirit was confused when He revealed to Paul that there is only *one* faith (Ephesians 4:5). This one faith is the belief system that God defined; it is the only one that He recognizes. According to God, there are not many faiths that are all equally-acceptable to Him, but only one. If anyone teaches otherwise, he implies that God is a liar and brings upon himself an awful curse (Galatians 1:8).

Calling upon the name of the Lord for salvation requires absolute honesty with oneself *and* God. This level of honesty is often uncomfortable and may even be painful, but it is critical. Each of us has to ask himself (or herself), "Whom am I trying to please—God, other people, or merely myself?" In John 12:42-43, the apostle John tells of certain Pharisees who actually believed that Jesus was their Messiah, but they would not follow Him "for they loved the approval of men rather than the approval of God." Your salvation is far too important to leave to someone else's approval. If you believe that you *should* be baptized in obedience to God's Word, then you admit that baptism is necessary *for* your salvation. If some friend, relative, colleague, mentor, pastor, or spiritual guru opposes (or scoffs at) your decision, then you must choose between that person and God. "For am I now seeking the favor of men, or of God?

Or am I striving to please men? If I were still trying to please men, I would not be a bond-servant of Christ" (Galatians 1:10)—because it is impossible to do both.

## Summary Thoughts

Jesus declared, "I am the way, and the truth, and the life; no one comes to the Father but through Me" (John 14:6). This "way" is the path of righteousness that leads to life with God (Matthew 7:13-14). Being born of God is the means by which we are put upon that path. God's truth provides the correct information and legitimate authority to explain what being born of God means and how we can become born-again believers. At the same time, this "way" is not one of many ways that a person can find salvation. Jesus' declaration (in John 14:6) is an exclusive, binding, and non-negotiable statement. It allows for zero exceptions; it provides for zero alternatives; it cannot be amended or modified in any way. Correspondingly, there are not many ways to be born of God, but only one. Whatever God says is required for this born-again process excludes all other methods or directions.

Our present study focuses on baptism, but baptism is merely a part of the process of being born of God. It is not the whole of it, and certainly is not a replacement for it. As important as baptism is as an act of faith, it cannot possibly replace what God does for the believer. On the other hand, baptism is not something separate from the conversion process, but is in fact a critical part of it. We are expected to have a balanced understanding on this subject without going to one extreme or the other.

The terms and conditions for admission into Christ's church are laid down by Christ, not you, not me, and not any self-proclaimed Christian religion. Admission into His church is equivalent to becoming a Christian. No one can be a Christian who is not in His church, and no one can enter into His church without submitting to whatever commandments are required of us *for* that admittance. We are not allowed to pick and choose which commandments are agreeable to us or not, since every commandment of God will be agreeable to a genuine believer. Whether or not a person is such a believer will be evident through his actions, not merely his words.

# Chapter 2
# You Must Be Born Again

*Blessed be the God and Father of our Lord Jesus Christ, who according to His great mercy has caused us to be born again to a living hope through the resurrection of Jesus Christ from the dead ...*
1 Peter 1:3

In the early part of Jesus' ministry, a Jewish teacher named Nicodemus confronted Jesus privately in order to ask Him some questions. This man came to see Jesus by night, likely because his fellow Pharisees did not approve of Him. Nicodemus began his discussion with the Lord by acknowledging God's approval of Him through the miracles that He performed. "Rabbi"—a significant address, given that Jesus had not been schooled in the rigorous rabbinic training of His day—"we know that You have come from God as a teacher; for no one can do these signs that You do unless God is with him" (John 3:2). God's approval of Jesus was clearly obvious to the sincere observer through the signs that He performed.

While Nicodemus initiated the discussion, Jesus immediately gave it a certain direction. "Truly, truly, I say to you," He said, "unless one is born again he cannot see the kingdom of God" (John 3:3). "Unless" here means "without exception" or "it cannot be otherwise." Jesus linked being *born again* and *the kingdom of God* with an unbreakable or unchangeable condition: it must be *this way* and no other. If a person desires to "see" (or, become a participant in) the kingdom of God, he *must* be "born again."

## God's Kingdom

To appreciate the full impact of what Jesus just said, we must understand the two major phrases that He used. First, we must understand what "kingdom of God" meant in the context that He used it. In order for there to *be* a kingdom of God, at least four things are required:

- There must be a *kingdom* over which to rule. This domain or realm must be specific and identifiable. No one can rule over an abstract concept or an idea or a figment of their own imagination.
- There must be a *king* who rules over this domain. Someone must be in charge; someone must have the authority *to* rule, or else there cannot be a kingdom. Ultimately, this requires the sovereign authority of a ruler who answers to no one higher than himself.
- This specific kingdom must be *of God*.[12] It is not "of man," since man does not have the power to create or rule over any kingdom more powerful than human ability can control. Since this kingdom is "of God," this necessarily implies that it is spiritual in nature—it is not of this world, not bound by this world, and cannot be destroyed by anything in this world. This is exactly what Jesus later confirmed (John 18:36-37).
- This kingdom must have a *purpose*, since nothing God does is without purpose. There is a *reason* why God has established a kingdom; there is also a reason why Jesus *revealed* this kingdom to us in the way that He did. He did not merely say, "There is a kingdom of God, and you should know this." Rather, He said (in essence), "It is imperative that you enter into the kingdom of God—and I will tell you how to do this." The reason

for this imperative is twofold: first, God wants to be our God and He wants believers (kingdom citizens) to be His people[13]; second, we cannot receive salvation through any other means other than by full citizenship in God's kingdom.

Many Christians will interchange "kingdom of God" with Christ's church, as though the two terms mean exactly the same thing. It is true that these terms are necessarily related: if one is in Christ's church, then he *must* be in God's kingdom (i.e., as a citizen of it). Yet, the interchangeableness of "kingdom" and "church" is not supported by the New Testament, except in the most general sense (as in Colossians 1:13). Jesus never went about telling Jews to enter into His church; but He had much to say about entering into the "kingdom of God." After Christ established His church, the focus of attention shifted from the kingdom to the church. Nonetheless, Jesus' message to Nicodemus was this: the physical kingdom of Israel—the failed and fractured kingdom that the Israelites corrupted through centuries of rebellion and idolatry—would be replaced by a spiritual kingdom that would transcend earthly corruption and false worship. The church thus became the sanctuary of those who believe in this kingdom and worship Christ as its King. But before the church *could* be established, the kingdom had to be put into the charge of the Redeemer who would make this church's existence possible.

The "kingdom of God" has always existed; Jehovah has always been the "King of glory" (Psalm 24:7-10). We cannot assume that Jesus' preaching of the coming kingdom meant that it was something that had never been. Instead, He spoke of a new *phase* or *revelation* of the already-existing and eternal kingdom. Concurrent with the preaching of the kingdom of God was the preaching of Israel's Messiah—the Redeemer of

Jewish prophecy that would come to restore the glory of Israel *and* bring salvation to the ends of the earth (Isaiah 42:1-7, 49:5-6). The kingdom that Jesus preached was very *Jewish* in nature, since it was a direct response to (or fulfillment of) these prophecies given to that people. The kingdom of God that Jesus preached was inseparable from His identity as the Jews' Messiah. Thus, Jesus' proclamation of the kingdom inescapably meant, "Your Messiah is about to rule, as prophesied in the Scriptures" (see Luke 24:44-48).

The kingdom of God was not exclusively for Jews, however. Paul spoke often about universal salvation "in Christ"—salvation irrespective of nationality or ethnicity. Furthermore, Jesus' appointment as King over His Father's entire kingdom extended far beyond His rule over those who are saved. The church is never described as having a king; and the kingdom is never described in the New Testament as having a head, husband, or shepherd. Christ's rule extended over all of Creation—there is nothing exempted from His kingship but the Father Himself (1 Corinthians 15:27-28). Jesus Himself said (after His resurrection), "All authority has been given to Me in heaven and on earth" (Matthew 28:19). This authority is not limited to the church, but is all-inclusive (Colossians 1:15-18). Thus, Christ has all authority over His church; but He also has all authority over anything and everything that has been created—specifically, anything that is not God. However, not all of Creation has (yet) submitted to Christ or acknowledged His kingship. In due time, this will happen (1 Corinthians 15:25-26, Philippians 2:9-11).

### Christ's Church

The church, on the other hand, is a specific and special sanctuary in the midst of all Creation. The church is the spiritual refuge for those who have willingly submitted themselves to the King's authority *and* have accepted responsibility as citizens of His kingdom. To be transferred (or translated) out of the domain of Satan and into the kingdom of God's Son means to change allegiance from one lord to the other (as described in Colossians 1:13-14; see Acts 26:15-18). One who is "in the kingdom" has fellowship with the King and enjoys all the protections, privileges, and blessings of that fellowship. This is different from merely being under Christ's authority, since all of Creation is under His authority, including Satan's own kingdom. Those who are "in Christ" are also "in the kingdom" in the sense that they have a relationship with the King rather than merely having to answer to Him.

We can illustrate this in a visual manner: imagine an earthly kingdom with its king's enormous castle in the middle of it. The only access to the castle is through a moat—in other words, through water—and anyone who comes into the castle must do so through the water. Every person in the kingdom is invited to live in the castle, and those who accept this invitation are regarded as the king's "sons"—in other words, as *family*. However, only a small percentage of people accept this offer and leave their own homes and possessions behind. Those who remain outside the castle are merely servants; they remain under the king's rule, but they do not respect his authority. They submit to him out of necessity, not by choice. Meanwhile, those within the castle receive protection, privileges, and blessings that the people outside the castle will never receive. These people are free from the burdens that those outside the castle must endure (John 8:35-36).

So it is for all those who become members of Christ's spiritual church.[14] We have been called by God through His gospel message to live in fellowship with Him in the sanctuary of believers (Christ's church), which dwells in the center of God's kingdom. We leave everything else behind in order to enter through the water into fellowship with Him. We are made sons of God because of our acceptance of the terms and conditions of this entrance (Galatians 3:26-27, 4:4-7). We enjoy privileged access to the Father as a result of our new and transcendent relationship with His Son. When the church enters into glory in the hereafter, all those who have remained faithful to the King will participate in that grand entrance. Those who refused to enter into this sanctuary will be separated from God forever.

The church is something the believer becomes a part of now; his place in the eternal kingdom of God is something he is guaranteed (based upon the continuance of his faith) but refers to something in the future. If you look up all the passages in Acts and the New Testament epistles, you will see that the kingdom is nearly always something promised, not something one already possesses (so to speak). The kingdom is something the believer inherits—permanently and irrevocably—in the hereafter. In contrast, the church is something a person immediately becomes a part of upon his obedience to the terms and conditions of Christ's gospel. We do not inherit the church, because the church is Christ Himself—His body (Ephesians 1:22-23). However, those who are in His church and who remain "faithful until death" (cf. Revelation 2:10) are made heirs of His kingdom. As heirs of the kingdom of God, we will share in the glory and rule that He exercises over all that has been created.[15]

Thus, the kingdom of God in its ultimate or universal sense refers to Christ's reign over all that has been created. The church, on the other hand, did not exist until Christ built it

(Matthew 16:18), and He could not build it until His authority as King over God's kingdom was established. The reference to Christ sitting down at the right hand of God (Matthew 26:64, Acts 2:33, Romans 8:34, Hebrews 1:3, et al) concerns His having received "all authority" from His Father to rule over His [the Father's] kingdom.[16] The *purpose* for Christ's reign over His Father's kingdom is for Him to serve as the Redeemer for all those who come to Him for salvation. Christ could not redeem a single soul until He had been given "all authority" to do so. To remove a soul's condemnation (Romans 8:1) *and* admit that soul into the sanctuary of believers within the kingdom (Colossians 1:13-14) requires divine authority. Christ received that authority only after He had proven Himself worthy *of* it with His flawless obedience and perfect blood sacrifice.

### The New Birth

We can now return to Jesus' discussion with Nicodemus, since we now have a much better understanding of what Jesus meant when He talked about entering into the kingdom of God. Nicodemus, as a Jew to whom the promise of God's kingdom was given, anticipated his own entrance into this new state of being. What Nicodemus did *not* understand was the manner in which one entered into this kingdom: he must be "born again." Thus, he asked incredulously, "How can a man be born when he is old? He cannot enter a second time into his mother's womb and be born, can he?" (John 3:4). Nicodemus was not being disrespectful, nor was he so dense (as some have accused him) by assuming that re-entering and then being re-born from one's mothers' womb was what Jesus really meant. Instead, he was merely stating the human impossibility of the instruction—in essence, "If what you say is true, then I have no hope."[17] R. C. H. Lenski says on this verse, "This Rabbi from Galilee calmly

## Being Born of God

tells him that he is not yet in the kingdom! ...[And] unless he attains this mysterious new birth, even he shall not 'see' it."[18] Yet, there is hope, and the kingdom is attainable, as we shall see.

Being born again certainly does parallel a natural birthing process. But paralleling a process and exactly duplicating it are two different things. Being born again necessarily requires that a person *sever himself completely* from that to which he was first born, so that he can be born *again* to something entirely new. Thus, in order to be born *again*, one must first *die*. We cannot maintain two separate, concurrent lives; we must have only one life, and this one life must have only one allegiance to one King who leads us in one direction. Thus, we must die to the first life in order to enter into the second. This is spiritual language, not literal, but just because it is spiritual does not mean it is any less real or necessary. Those who are *not* born again cannot enter into the kingdom of God, which means they will lose all hope of life *with* God in the hereafter. There is nothing imaginary or harmless about this latter state of being.

Our first birth was by physical parents into a physical world. Having been born into this world, we immediately became a part of it in a physical way. Even so, we were born as innocent creatures, not sinful ones.[19] Once we sinned against God, however, we corrupted our fellowship with Him and chose instead to have fellowship with the ungodly world. Originally, we identified with the world in a merely physical or biological sense; as sinners, we came to identify with the world in a spiritual sense as well. It is this *identification* or *allegiance* that must be put to death in order for us to enter into the kingdom of God. This carnal, satanic, and defiant attitude is completely incompatible with the heavenly, godly, and holy nature of God's kingdom. In having sinned against God, we entered into the domain of darkness which is controlled by "the prince of the power of the air ... the spirit that is now working in the sons of disobedience" (Ephesians 2:2).

You and I cannot change the fact of our physical birth. We cannot change our parents, physical family, race, ethnicity, skin color, gender, or biological traits. We can, however, change the allegiance of our soul from one master to another. This is what Jesus talked about elsewhere. In Matthew 16:25, for example, He said, "For whoever wishes to save his life will lose it; but whoever loses his life for My sake will find it." Loosely translated, this means, "Whoever wants to retain his old identity with world will lose everything in hereafter; but whoever wants to live with God in hereafter must be born of God in the here-and-now." The one who wishes to "save his life" is the one who refuses to die—and Jesus is not talking about a physical death (because everyone dies, regardless of his moral condition) but the death of one's spiritual allegiance to this world. But the one who "loses His life for My sake" is the one who is willing to *die* to this world in order to *live* for Christ. He is, indeed, re-born into a new life.

Once a person is born again, he is given a new identity. Paul said, "Therefore if anyone is in Christ, he is a new creature; the old things passed away; behold, new things have come" (2 Corinthians 5:17). "In Christ" means, in essence, *being in fellowship with God through one's allegiance to Christ*, the One to whom God the Father has given all authority over His kingdom. Jesus Himself said, "I am the way, and the truth, and the life; no one comes to the Father but through Me" (John 14:6). He could as well have said, "No one will have fellowship with My Father whose heart (or, allegiance) still belongs to this world." Anyone who is a friend of the world is an enemy of

# Being Born of God

God (Romans 8:7-8, James 4:4); if a person is not willing to die *to* the world, then he cannot become a friend of God.

So then, we understand much more now what Jesus said to Nicodemus. Only one crucial question remains, and that is: *how* is one born again in the manner in which He spoke?

## Water and the Spirit

After Nicodemus expressed (what he thought was) the utter impossibility of being born again into the kingdom of God, Jesus gave him new hope. The born-again process is not impossible, but it *does* require divine intervention. In other words, a person cannot be born of God without God Himself doing for that person what he is incapable of doing for himself. At the same time, God does not do *everything*, but requires that the one who seeks His salvation participate in his own born-again experience.

"Truly, truly, I say to you, unless one is born of water and the Spirit he cannot enter into the kingdom of God" (John 3:5). The "unless" here means exactly what it meant in verse 3: it cannot be any other way; there are no exceptions to this. "Born of water" means that *actual water* is involved in one's spiritual re-birth; it cannot be any other way. This is not "spiritual" water, and there is no reason to believe that this is metaphorical "water." There is no other meaning of this phrase in the context of New Testament teaching other than immersion in literal water (as in Jesus' own baptism), which is exactly what "baptism" means. In baptism, one is submerged in water—plunged, in essence, to his death—and buried beneath it. He rises from this watery grave in order to walk in "newness of life" (Romans 6:4). Just as a human child is born of the "water" of his mother's womb, so the child of God is born of water; just as a human child did not have any independent identity until he was physically born, so the child of God had no identity with God (since he became a sinner) until he was born *again*.

It is not surprising to see baptism as an integral part of nearly every conversion account in the Book of Acts. Even those accounts in which it is not mentioned, it is necessarily implied: no one becomes a Christian in any other manner that does not involve water baptism. When Peter said, "Repent, and each of you be baptized in the name of Jesus Christ for the forgiveness of your sins" (Acts 2:38), three thousand Jews responded by repenting and being baptized in water. If they wanted to be forgiven by God, then they needed to be baptized into Christ. In other words, those who heard the gospel preached understood what being "born of water" meant. What first seemed incomprehensible to Nicodemus was finally understood in the clearest of terms. They did not interpret this to be "an outward sign of an inward grace"—a popular teaching today. They did not even *receive* saving grace until they obeyed that which they were told to do. Their baptism was not a sign of what *already* happened, but of what was *in the process* of happening. It demonstrated their change of allegiance from the domain of Satan to the kingdom of God (cf. Acts 26:18).

"Born of water" is *not* something God does for the believer; it is something the believer does for God—i.e., in obedience to God. (I have never seen God miraculously plunge a person underwater—especially without that person's consent!—but I have seen many people be baptized voluntarily in response to the Word of God.) No one can be born again <u>unless</u> he meets this condition: he <u>must</u> be born of water. And if *any* action is required of the believer in order to receive salvation from God, then his salvation is *conditional* and not unconditional. God is not baptized for the believer; rather, the believer—if he wishes to remain a "believer" —must be baptized for God. (By "believer" here, we do not mean yet a "Christian." There is no record in Scripture of *any* Christian being baptized in water. Baptism is not something Christians do to prove that they are believers; rather, it is what believers do in order to become Christians.)

While being born of water is absolutely necessary for the believer to enter into the kingdom of God, it is not the only thing necessary. There is at least one other requirement: he must be "born of ... the Spirit."[20] (The text will not allow this born-again process to be merely a spiritual one, with a lower-case "spirit." Jesus clearly and necessarily means "the Spirit of God" here, and this is supported by the rest of New Testament teaching on the subject of one's conversion to Christ.) It is grammatically and theologically impossible to separate the importance of being "born of water" here from being "born of the Spirit": one is as necessary as the other. The two actions either stand or fall together; no person can claim that either one is sufficient to meet the requirements. And if a person does not meet both requirements, then he *cannot* be a citizen of the kingdom of God. In other words, he remains under Christ's authority and will ultimately answer to Him (2 Corinthians 5:10), but he does not live in fellowship with Him since he has not yet died to his allegiance to his old life.

Just as God does not do what is required of the believer, so the believer cannot do that which is performed only by God. The believer has his own responsibility in his conversion, and God has His; neither party can assume that of the other. Being born "of the Spirit" is God's response to one who calls upon His name for salvation. This "calling" is not something separate from baptism, but baptism itself is the *means* by which it is accomplished (Acts 22:16).

As necessary and instrumental as the Holy Spirit is in one's conversion, He works in seamless conjunction with Christ, not independent of Him. The Spirit of God does not atone for anyone's sins; that responsibility belongs to Christ. But the Spirit is directly involved in sanctifying the believer's soul and transforming him from a sinner into a saint. The Spirit also testifies with the believer's spirit that the things that he [the believer] has done in obedience to God are correct and sincere (Romans 8:16-17). It is the Spirit, after all, who has revealed to us the Word of God; it is by His authority that we have received the instruction to be "born of water and the Spirit." Not surprisingly, all those who are baptized into Christ have done so according to the Spirit of God—by His authority and under His direction. Thus, "For by one Spirit we were all baptized into one body, whether Jews or Greeks, whether slaves or free, and we were all made to drink of one Spirit" (1 Corinthians 12:13). While some commentators have made considerable effort to interpret Paul's words as referring to a "spiritual" baptism (or, the baptism of the Spirit), this is unsupported by either this text or the rest of the New Testament. "By one Spirit" means that *one* Spirit has determined the means by which we come into the *one* body of Christ (His church), which is what Paul specifically addresses in this passage. To "drink" of the Spirit is to internalize (spiritually) the living water of which Jesus spoke, which is the Spirit Himself (John 7:37-39). It means, then, to have the Spirit indwell the faithful Christian (Romans 8:9).

### Born Again to a Living Hope

Peter brings together both ideas in the same way that Jesus did, but from an after-the-fact perspective. "Peter, an apostle of Jesus Christ, to those...who are chosen according to the foreknowledge of God the Father, by the sanctifying work of

*Being Born of God*

the Spirit, to obey Jesus Christ and be sprinkled with His blood: May grace and peace be yours in the fullest measure. Blessed be the God and Father of our Lord Jesus Christ, who according to His great mercy has caused us to be born again to a living hope through the resurrection of Jesus Christ from the dead..." (1 Peter 1:1-3). "Those who are chosen" refers to those who are members of the body of Christ: Christ's *church* has been predestined for glory, and thus all those who are *in* Christ are among the "chosen" because of their inclusion in His church. It is true that God calls us by His gospel (2 Thessalonians 2:13-14); it is not true that everyone who is called responds to that invitation ("Many are called, but few are chosen"—Matthew 22:14). Those who do respond in obedience are added to His church (Acts 2:47); those who do not respond remain in a state of condemnation.

Notice that "obeying" Christ and "sprinkled with His blood" are dependent upon being "born again to a living hope." We cannot separate what Jesus said about being born again from what Peter says in Jesus' words to Nicodemus. In other words, Peter alludes directly to what Jesus said about being reborn as a child of God without restating the procedure. However, he describes more than what Jesus said, especially with regard to the results and benefits of this conversion. Once again, God did not miraculously plunge these believers underwater, but they carried out this command of their own volition. But if they had not submitted to this command, then they could not be born again. At the same time, no one could have been born again until (and if not for) the resurrection of Jesus Christ.

## Summary Thoughts

Our study is intended to provide a better understanding of baptism—what it is, why it is done, and why it is necessary.

However, the believer's objective is not merely to be baptized, but to be *born again*.²¹ Baptism is a means to an end; it is not the "end" in itself. Baptism is an act *of* faith; it is never a replacement *for* faith. God has chosen baptism as the method by which we undergo this spiritual process. Being born *again* necessarily implies being born of *God* rather than being born of one's biological parents. This is exactly what John talks about in his gospel: "But as many as received Him, to them He gave the right to become children of God, even to those who believe in His name, who were born, not of blood nor of the will of the flesh nor of the will of man, but of God" (John 1:12-13). No one can become a child of God who is not born of Him; yet, no one can be born of God who is not born *again* through the means that Jesus described to Nicodemus.

Being born of God encompasses far more than one's initial conversion. The believer must be converted in order to become a Christian. Conversion indicates a different direction; transformation indicates a radical change in one's heart. Conversion takes us down a path that we had not taken before, or from which we had once strayed (as in Matthew 18:1-3); transformation is what we become as we travel down that path. Conversion involves our response to God's commands; transformation is God's work upon the human heart. Yet, God will not transform the one who is not converted, or who resists the very process *of* conversion.

"Born of God" takes in this entire picture: once we become children of God, we increasingly conform to His will and nature. In effect, we become more and more like our Father (Ephesians 5:1). God calls us with His gospel, and we must respond appropriately to this call. God tells us our part in the conversion process, and we must fulfill that part exactly as He

*Being Born of God* 47

said. God reveals to us the path that leads to life, and we must be willing to walk that path and trust that He will take care of us along the way (Matthew 7:13-14, Galatians 5:16-17).[22]

Certainly much more will be said on this entire subject as we continue. For now, it is sufficient to make the point that **born of God = born again = born of water and the Spirit = becoming a Christian.** As we have said, baptism in water is *our part* of our conversion; it does not address the entirety of what happens to our soul *in* conversion. At the same time, if our part is *required* in this process, then the process remains incomplete without it. If it meant nothing else or did nothing else, baptism would still be necessary if indeed God commanded us to perform it. Thus, we are not saved *only* because of our baptism, but we are not saved *without* it, either.

# Chapter Three:
# Instruction and Implementation

*All authority has been given to Me in heaven and on earth. Go therefore and make disciples of all the nations, baptizing them in the name of the Father and the Son and the Holy Spirit, teaching them to observe all that I commanded you ...*
Matthew 28:18-20

According to the apostle Peter, no one could be "born again" except for the resurrection of Christ (1 Peter 1:2-3). Likewise, no one could be born of the Spirit until the Spirit Himself entered into His ministerial work within Jesus' church (John 7:37-39). Jesus' words to Nicodemus (in John 3:1-5), then, anticipated what would be required of believers rather than what was immediately applicable. No one could be born of God until He had finished the necessary work of redemption that made this rebirth possible. This is why many Jews were baptized by John's baptism of repentance (cf. Luke 3:3), but neither Jew nor Gentile was baptized into Christ until after His resurrection from the dead and His ascension to the right hand of God (Acts 2:33).

Not surprisingly, just prior to that time in which men and women would be admitted into His church, Jesus laid down the procedure once again. "All authority has been given to Me in heaven and on earth," He told His apostles after His resurrection. "Go therefore and make disciples of all the nations, baptizing them in the name of the Father and the Son and the Holy Spirit, teaching them to observe all that I commanded you ..." (Matthew 28:18-20).[23] Jesus told Nicodemus that the believer must be "born of water and the

*Being Born of God*

Spirit"; now he tells the apostles that the process of making disciples necessarily includes baptizing them in the name of God the Father, God the Son, and God the Spirit. We can safely conclude that if one is not baptized for this purpose, then he cannot be a disciple of Christ.

### The Process of Becoming Christ's Disciple

Jesus' instruction to His apostles was clear and inescapable. One cannot be made a Christian apart from the teaching of "the message of truth" (Ephesians 1:13-14). Baptism never precedes the hearing of the gospel, but is an inescapable result of that hearing. This demands personal responsibility from the one being taught: whatever he does in response to the gospel message—whether he obeys it or not—is his own conscious decision.

Throughout His preaching, Jesus repeatedly underscored the need for personal responsibility in the case of each person's relationship with God (Matthew 5:20, 7:21-23, and Luke 9:62, for example). Jesus spoke to Jews in order to prepare them for what was to come; we should not think, therefore, that when that time *did* come, He removed all responsibility from the believer and made God entirely responsible for each person's salvation. As we have noted previously, salvation is comprised of two components: the believer's part and God's part. These "parts" are not equal in scope or power, since man's work of faith is hardly comparable to God's work of grace, but both parts are *necessary* in order to achieve the objective of salvation.[24]

Likewise, Jesus made baptism a responsibility of the believer in becoming His disciple. If baptism meant nothing more than immersion in water, then this is still *required* as a demonstration of obedience to what He commanded. James

Coffman writes, "If nothing else appeared in all the Bible relative to the ordinance of baptism, Christ's mention of it in this circumstance would have been more than sufficient to bind it upon all men for all time to come."[25] If someone wishes to call upon the Lord for salvation but has not been baptized, then he has yet to comply with this simple and straightforward command. If a person says, in essence, "But I was saved by asking Jesus into my heart—and then later I was baptized," he manifests not only an ignorance of what Jesus commanded, but he has imagined into Scripture a procedure of which neither Jesus nor His apostles ever spoke. We are not suggesting that that person did not have good intentions, but we have already established that no one is saved based upon good intentions apart from obedience to God's commands. The fact remains that this person has not yet obeyed what Jesus commissioned His apostles—and all believers thereafter—to do. If we truly confess Him to be "Lord" (cf. Luke 6:46), then we must comply with whatever instructions He has given to us.

Baptism is to be carried out "in the name of the Father and the Son and the Holy Spirit," which means that the entire Godhead supports it. **In fact, baptism is the only act we have been commanded to perform in the name of the Father, Son, and Holy Spirit.** One's baptism invokes the Godhead itself to witness, respond, and participate in the conversion of the one who comes to Christ.[26] Curiously, some commentators argue that this "triune formula" (in Matthew 28:19) was not used until a later time in church history, and therefore we should not have expected to see it in Matthew's text. Nonetheless, it conspicuously *is* in the text, even against the expectations of these men. (And it appears that the only ones who seem to have a problem with this are those who have already rejected the

# Being Born of God

necessity of baptism.) Until someone has actual proof that these words are indeed not genuine, we must take Matthew's word over those of his critics.[27]

Jesus' instructions are also repeated in Mark 16:15-16, but with slightly different emphasis: "Go into all the world and preach the gospel to all creation. He who has believed and has been baptized shall be saved; but he who has disbelieved shall be condemned." One would think that this passage, too, would be as clear as crystal in its meaning and instruction. Yet, critics—especially those who have already rejected the necessity of baptism in salvation—have been quick to say that this passage in Mark (from 16:9-20) is not found in all of the extant manuscripts of the New Testament, and therefore is questionable.[28]

While the fact of its omission in some manuscripts must be conceded, whatever is recorded in Mark's passage does not disagree with anything we find elsewhere in the New Testament. This is especially true with regard to the direct link between baptism and salvation: if one truly believes, he will be baptized into Christ's spiritual church; if he does not believe, then neither will he be baptized.[29] If he is baptized in obedience to Christ's gospel—and remains faithful to that confession of faith (see Colossians 1:23)—then he will be saved. Refusal to be baptized is refusal to obey the gospel. This does not mean that baptism is the only act of faith to be considered in one's conversion, but that it is a *required* one. If there are other requirements—and we know that there are—then these will be stated elsewhere with equally-binding authority.

## On the Day of Pentecost

Given their instructions, it is no surprise that the apostles told others to do exactly what they themselves were commanded by Jesus. In Acts 2, we read of Peter's speech to the Jews, their response to Peter, and then Peter's response to them. This is excellent information, since we have the actual implementation of Jesus' instructions to His apostles being transmitted to those who seek reconciliation with God. Notice first what Peter does not say:

- ❑ "Just ask Jesus into your heart to be your personal Savior."
- ❑ "Just say this 'sinner's prayer,' and then Jesus will be your Savior."
- ❑ "Accept Jesus and be saved—and *after* this, you should be baptized to let everyone know of the salvation that you have already received."
- ❑ "You need to repent in order to be forgiven—this is essential!—but baptism is *not* essential."
- ❑ "You do not have to do *anything*: because you are completely dead to God and unable to make any decision concerning your salvation, there is nothing you *can* do to be saved. If you are one of God's elect, you will be saved no matter what; but if you are not, then you will be lost no matter what. Absolutely *no work at all* on your part can contribute to your salvation."

All of these are basic restatements of what denominational teachers have been claiming is the gospel truth about salvation. Yet, none of these accurately communicate what Peter actually said. When it comes to the salvation of your eternal soul, should you trust the words of a denominational preacher, or should you put your faith in the inspired words of an apostle whom Christ Himself commissioned to tell you exactly what to do?

Upon Peter having indicted them for the crucifixion of

## Being Born of God

their own Messiah, the Jews said to him and the rest of the apostles, "Brethren, what shall we do?" (Acts 2:37). They knew they stood condemned before God; how could they now escape that condemnation—was there any recourse? "Peter said to them, 'Repent, and each of you be baptized in the name of Jesus Christ for the forgiveness of your sins; and you will receive the gift of the Holy Spirit'" (Acts 2:38). "Repent" is plural: it is something that is expected of all those who call upon the Lord (cf. 2:21). "Each of you be baptized" is singular: it is something that each person is expected to do in *conjunction* with this repentance.[30] Instead of diminishing baptism in order to emphasize repentance (which is often the case among those who oppose the necessity of baptism), the order is quite the opposite: repentance is a general command, but baptism is a very direct and personal one. Regardless, repentance and baptism are *both* required in order to receive forgiveness *and* the "gift of the Holy Spirit." If nothing else was known about how a person is to seek God's forgiveness, we know this much: he *must* repent of his sins and he *must* be baptized.

Many who believe that "faith only" is required for salvation argue against the necessity of baptism in this passage. Their argument rests almost entirely upon the word "for" (*eis* in the Greek) in the phrase "for the forgiveness of sins."[31] This word, so it is argued, *can* mean "because of"—in other words, a person is baptized *because of* his forgiveness of sins. In fact, one Baptist author has written an entire book to defend this very point. His thesis: since *eis* can have other uses than "for (the purpose of)," therefore Acts 2:38 must be altogether rejected as having anything to do with the necessity of baptism.[32] Yet, of the 1,773 uses of *eis* in the New Testament, *none* of the Bible translators of any reputable translation have rendered this word "because of."³³ More importantly, Peter simply could *not* have said "be baptized because your sins are already forgiven" because Jesus made baptism necessary for being born again, and no one's sins can be forgiven until he has died to the world and begun life anew with God. Repentance is also necessary for this, but is insufficient *by itself* to comply with the instructions given by the Lord and His apostles. The conditions to forgiveness are clearly and unequivocally stated: repentance and baptism. These two conditions cannot be grammatically or theologically separated; they stand or fall together. "Forgiveness of sins" in the gospel's vernacular is a phrase equivalent to "salvation." No one who is saved can be unforgiven by God; anyone who is forgiven by God is also saved by Him (Ephesians 1:7). "The only honest reading [of Acts 2:38] is that baptism is for the *purpose* or *goal* of receiving forgiveness. This meaning is not just warranted but is actually demanded by the context."³⁴

Remarkably, many denominational teachers' responses to Acts 2:38 (and other conversion accounts in Acts) are convoluted and often desperate attempts to avoid the *necessity* of baptism in conversion. For example, one noted evangelical minister says this (on Acts 2:38): "[Baptism] is an important step of obedience for all believers, and should closely follow conversion. In fact, in the early church it was inseparable from salvation, so that Paul referred to salvation as being related to 'one Lord, one faith, one baptism.'"³⁵ By "believers," he means "Christians," but this premise is impossible to defend. The idea or example of an unbaptized Christian is completely foreign to the New Testament.³⁶ Nonetheless, he cannot avoid the inescapable: baptism is *inseparably* linked to salvation. Yet, this man later says that the idea that baptism is required for salvation is a "false teaching."³⁷ This begs the question:

*Being Born of God* 55

how can one teach that baptism is "important," necessary for "obedience," and inseparably linked to salvation, yet at the same time teach that it is a "false teaching" to require it? Such self-refuting doublespeak will be avoided when we approach the subject objectively instead of trying to defend a predetermined religious position.

### The Record in Acts

The New Testament pattern for becoming a Christian is remarkably clear, despite all the interference that man-made religion has created. Jesus provided this clear instruction, and the apostles implemented that instruction in all of their preaching of His gospel. All those who choose to obey the gospel are immediately baptized as a demonstration *of* that obedience. Baptism is not something that Christians do; it is what those who call upon the name of the Lord do in *becoming* Christians. The citations speak for themselves:

- Acts 2:37-41, three thousand people responded to Peter's command to repent and be baptized; as a result, they received forgiveness of sins and were added to the Lord's church (2:47).
- Acts 8:12-13, Philip preached the gospel of Christ to the Samaritans (8:4-5), and many believed *and* were baptized.
- Acts 8:26-39, Philip "preached Jesus" to the Ethiopian; as a result of hearing this good news, this man desired to be baptized. (How could he have learned about baptism, unless this is an essential part of "preaching Jesus"?)
- Acts 9:11-19, the conversion of Saul (Paul) included baptism. Conspicuously, repentance is nowhere mentioned in this account, but no one denies that this

requirement is necessarily implied (and so forth in the following cases).
- ❏ Acts 10:44-48, the conversion of Cornelius (and others) included baptism.
- ❏ Acts 16:14-15, the conversion of Lydia (and others) included baptism.
- ❏ Acts 16:33, the conversion of the Philippian jailor included baptism.
- ❏ Acts 18:8, Crispus and many other Corinthians "were believing and being baptized."
- ❏ Acts 19:1-5, Paul baptized into *Christ* twelve men who had previously only been baptized according to *John's* baptism.

What we see is a consistent agreement between the instruction and its implementation. Those of the "faith only" persuasion have argued that baptism is not mentioned in *every* instance of conversion, and therefore it is not necessary, but only "important." (Please note that these same people remain unconvinced even when baptism *is* specifically mentioned.) We could well apply their logic to other steps of conversion that everyone *does* agree on:
- ❏ Believing is commanded (Acts 16:31), but is not mentioned in every case of conversion. Therefore it must not be necessary for salvation (?).
- ❏ Repentance is commanded, but is not mentioned in *most* cases of conversion. Therefore it also must not be necessary for salvation (?).
- ❏ Faith is not mentioned in *most* cases of conversion. Therefore faith must not be necessary for salvation (?).
- ❏ Sincerity is necessarily implied in one's conversion, yet it is not mentioned in *any* conversion accounts in Acts.

Therefore, sincerity is not necessary for salvation (?). As you can see, the argument only (allegedly) works when it is directed at baptism. Otherwise, it undermines the theology of the one who uses the argument. Once again, baptism is being singled out as the one thing that is *not* required for salvation, even though it is mentioned more often in conversions in Acts than any other obvious requirements. An inconsistent approach to Scripture is necessary, however, in order to support a predetermined agenda.

### The Sum of God's Word

This much is clear: in no *one* passage of Scripture are *all* the necessary requirements for salvation given. We cannot point to any *single* passage and say that this is *all* that needs to be done. None of us is allowed to cite only our favorite passages to the neglect of those that add to them or interpret them differently. When Jesus said that we must be born of water and the Spirit, He did not mean that belief and repentance are expendable or unnecessary. And when Peter commanded that we repent and be baptized in order to be forgiven by God, he did not imply that faith and sincerity are expendable or unnecessary in this process. This is a common-sense and systematic approach to biblical interpretation.

Sadly, when it comes to avoiding baptism, people choose to violate this very simple principle. In a classic example, many Bible teachers cite Romans 10:9-10 as "proof" that baptism is unnecessary for salvation simply because it is not mentioned there. That passage reads: "... If you confess with your mouth Jesus as Lord, and believe in your heart that God raised Him from the dead, you will be saved; for with the heart a person believes, resulting in righteousness, and with the mouth he confesses, resulting in salvation." In camping on this passage, "faith only" proponents hope to exclude or minimize to insignificance all other aspects of obtaining salvation. They assume, too, that Paul meant to give a comprehensive instruction *on* salvation that contradicts what Jesus commanded and Peter implemented—and what Paul himself did in his own obedience to God (Acts 22:16).

If we keep his words in context, nothing that Paul said (in Romans 10:9-10) contradicts what Jesus or Peter taught. Jesus requires that men believe in Him and confess Him in order to be saved (John 3:16, Matthew 10:32). Those who do *not* believe or will *not* confess will face the wrath of God (John 3:36, Matthew 10:33). But Paul's point in Romans 10:9-10 specifically focuses on a particular *aspect* or *dimension* of one's belief and confession. In the full context of that passage (10:1-13), Paul contrasts the Jews' dependence upon their own works of law for salvation rather than putting their full confidence in Christ (10:2-4). Moses taught that perfect righteousness can only be achieved through perfect law-keeping (10:5, cf. Leviticus 18:5). Once a person breaks a law of God, however, he is no longer a law-keeper but a law-breaker, and is guilty of the entire law (James 2:10-11). Thus, Paul says that one's righteousness must be obtained through something (Someone) outside of himself.

"The righteousness based on faith" (10:6) does *not* mean that human works or human efforts are unnecessary. (If it did, then we would not need a gospel to tell us how to live *by* faith, which always requires *doing* things—but we will save this for a later discussion.) What it *does* mean is that the source of one's righteousness must be in Christ rather than in one's personal effort. As Paul said elsewhere, "By His doing you are in Christ Jesus, who became to us wisdom from God, and righteousness

*Being Born of God*

and sanctification, and redemption, so that, just as it is written, 'Let him who boasts, boast in the Lord'" (1 Corinthians 1:30-31). So then, Christ is the One who does for us everything that we cannot do for ourselves with regard to our salvation. This is the essential definition of "grace" as used in the New Testament context of salvation.[38]

But if we need Christ in order for us to be made righteous, how will we access Him? We did not ascend into heaven to bring Him down to us; we did not descend into the earth to bring Him up from His grave. Paul says: our access to Christ and His righteousness is through *faith*, not through human effort. Faith in Christ is predicated upon knowledge; otherwise it is "blind faith" which accomplishes nothing. "'The word is near you, in your mouth and in your heart'—that is, the word of faith which we are preaching" (10:8). This "word of faith" is the gospel of Christ (see 10:17). So then, when one hears the gospel of Christ and (as a result of this knowledge) puts his faith in Christ to save him rather than in himself, he is declared righteous by God. This does not negate works of human faith (including baptism), but puts them in their proper context and gives them their appropriate meaning.

This leads us to the verses in question (10:9-10). "Confess" and "believe" are popularly regarded in the most general sense, as in, "I confess His name!" or "I believe in Jesus!" Yet, Paul indicates a specific *aspect* of belief and a specific *fact* being confessed. The context is very clear on this. "If you confess with your mouth Jesus as Lord" means "I confess that Jesus is *from God*, and therefore I submit to His authority, which is far above my own." "If you believe in your heart that God raised Him from the dead" means "I believe in Jesus' resurrection, and therefore I appeal to His supreme power rather than depend upon my own finite ability." One is saved when he puts his full confidence in Christ's *authority* and His *power*—this is Paul's point in this passage. His point is *not* to limit all the terms and conditions required for entering into a covenant relationship with God. Rather, His point is to contrast one's trust in himself (which will fail him) versus his trust in Christ (who will not disappoint him—10:11).

To cite this passage as a comprehensive explanation of *all* that is required for salvation not only defies common sense, but is an entirely incorrect method of biblical interpretation. In other words, it is illogical as well as unbiblical. If *only* "believing" and "confessing" are required for salvation, then this would nullify the need for repentance, for example. Someone might argue, "But repentance is necessarily implied!" Yes, because repentance is mentioned *elsewhere* in direct connection with one's salvation. But so is baptism—and far more often than repentance—so why not apply the same reasoning? "Because *baptism* is a work, and no one is saved by works!" will be the anticipated reply. Yet, repentance is also a work: Christ does not repent *for you*, but expects you to do this *for Him*. Likewise, believing and confessing are both works: Christ does not believe for you or confess for you—these are actions (works!) that He expects *you* to do as part of *your* salvation. Without believing or confessing (in the context in which Paul defined these in Romans 10:9-10), a person cannot be saved. Thus, while he is not saved merely *because* he believed or confessed, he is not saved *without* these actions, either. This soundly defeats the entire "no human works are necessary in our salvation" theory.

## Summary Thoughts

In the broadest of terms, virtually all those who call themselves Christians are in agreement: the source of our salvation is Christ, not our own effort. Where the path diverges is in the understanding (or placement) of our personal effort in the matter of our own salvation. Paul teaches that our works of faith do have a place and are necessary; "faith only" proponents *want* to say that our works of faith are not necessary because everything depends upon God—but they do not and cannot really practice this. Think about what we have covered so far:

- ❏ Jesus said that, in order to enter the kingdom of God, you must be born of water and the Spirit. One part is your responsibility; the other part is God's responsibility. Which one is more necessary than the other? They are both absolutely required, since without one *or* the other, you cannot enter the kingdom of God. (Just because both are necessary does *not* mean that they are both equal in power; it only means that they are both required to accomplish the given objective.)

- ❏ Jesus said that, in order to become a disciple of His, you must be taught His Word *and* be baptized in the name of the Father, Son, and Holy Spirit. Jesus is not baptized for you; His responsibility is to provide you with necessary teaching *and* regenerate your soul upon your obedience to Him. Your responsibility is to respond obediently to the teaching, which necessarily includes (but is not limited to) baptism.

- ❏ Peter said that, in order to receive God's forgiveness of your sins, you must repent *and* be baptized in the name of Jesus Christ.[39] If you do not repent *and/or* are not baptized in His name, you will not receive God's forgiveness. Christ is not repenting or being baptized for you; these are things that *you* must do for *your* salvation. This does not make your salvation entirely dependent upon your human effort, since it is Christ who has the power of salvation. However, it does mean that your salvation is impossible *without* your human effort.

- ❑ Paul said that you must confess that Jesus came down from heaven—He is God, and has divine authority—*and* you must believe that He rose from the dead—He has divine power, even over death itself. If you *personally* do not perform these acts of faith, then you really do not *have* faith, since "faith" without such confession or belief is no faith at all. Yet, these actions are not done for you, but *you* are expected to do them. If you do not, then you are not saved. Thus, your salvation is conditioned upon your obedience.

The above teachings are not only biblical, but are clear and inescapable. They also render pointless any attempt to remain loyal to one church's teaching over another's.

You may have questions about salvation that have not yet been covered (or that cannot be answered by mere men), but that does not mean you do not have enough information to know what to do. The Book of Acts is filled with accounts of believers who became Christians based upon far less information than you have covered in the book you are reading right now, but it was sufficient information and they all responded the same way. When accompanied by faithful obedience, the correct instruction always leads to the correct implementation. As it was with those early Christians, so it will be with us.

Let's summarize even further. In the few passages we have examined so far, it is clear that your salvation is the result of:

*Being Born of God* 

- Being born again by water *and* the Spirit of God.
- Hearing the Word of Christ *and* acting upon it obediently, *at least* through baptism, in order to become a disciple of Christ.
- Confessing that Jesus has divine authority to pronounce your innocence.
- Believing that Jesus has divine power to rescue you from your spiritual ruin.
- Repenting *and* being baptized into Christ for forgiveness of your sins.

Notice (again) that no single passage provides everything that is needed to be done with regard to salvation. We must put them all together; "The sum of Your word is truth" (Psalm 119:160). While it is true that "whoever believes in Him shall not perish, but have eternal life" (John 3:16), this is a most general prescription, not a specific one. Similarly, the entire Law of Moses was summed up in, "You shall love God with all your heart, soul, and might, and you shall love your neighbor as yourself" (cf. Matthew 22:37-40), but it took Exodus, Leviticus, Numbers, and Deuteronomy for God to expound upon all the particulars of those two commandments.

Again, our purpose here is not to promote baptism as being greater than any other work of faith. Rather, we are discovering—through an honest and objective investigation of Scripture—that baptism is a *required* act of faith. We have much more to say in defense of this, and yet the conclusion will remain the same because the Scriptures are consistent in what they teach.

## Chapter Four:
# Washing Away Your Sins

*Corresponding to that, baptism now saves you—not the removal of dirt from the flesh, but an appeal to God for a good conscience—through the resurrection of Jesus Christ, who is at the right hand of God ...*
1 Peter 3:21-22

Water is one of the most diverse and amazing substances on earth. All life on earth is dependent upon water. About 70% of the earth is covered with water, and your body is comprised of about the same percentage of water. "In the beginning," the world was literally engulfed in water. God separated the waters of the earth so as to allow dry land to appear (Genesis 1:1-10). Thus, "by the word of God the heavens existed long ago and the earth was formed out of water and by water" (2 Peter 3:5). Just as a child emerges from the watery womb of its mother, the earth once emerged from the watery womb of God's initial creation. Both situations define a birth experience.

Water figured prominently in the cleansing rituals of the Law of Moses. The bronze laver of the tabernacle was placed between the bronze altar and the entrance to the holy tent so that the priests could wash their hands and feet before entering into the tabernacle or ministering to the altar (Exodus 30:18-21). Ordination of the high priest, however, required a washing of one's entire body with water before putting on his priestly garments and being anointed with holy oil (Leviticus 8:6). In a very real sense, the washing of water served as a point of *separation* between his two lives: the one that belonged to himself before he was ordained as a priest, and the one that belonged to God.[40]

Likewise, water was part of the ritual cleansing of a man who once had leprosy—a generic term for any infectious or corruptive skin disease—but then became healed. On behalf of this man, two "clean" birds were offered in his ritual purification. The priest killed one bird in "living" or running water; the other was dipped in water and blood and then set free (Leviticus 14:4-7). After this, the man himself was completely shaved, his clothes washed, and his entire body bathed in water. This bathing in water served as a historical point of his re-introduction into the Israelite community from which he had previously been alienated due to his leprosy. In other words, this procedure served to *separate* the man's disease-ridden life from the new life that he enjoyed thereafter. After this ritual was completed—a seven-day process altogether—he was, in effect, a new man, and we could say that he indeed walked in newness of life.

Likewise, water was an integral part of the cleansing of an Israelite who had been contaminated with coming into contact with a dead human body. This cleansing process is often called the red heifer ordinance, since it required the sacrifice of a flawless red heifer (Numbers 19). The heifer was to be slain and burned entirely upon the bronze altar, and its ashes put in a "clean place." Whenever an Israelite was contaminated by any contact with a corpse, he could be ritually cleansed through a mixture of these ashes and water. In such a case, this "water for impurity" was sprinkled upon the one being cleansed, while the one who sprinkled him with this water was required to bathe himself in water for his own ritual purity. Similarly, any Israelite who was contaminated with human blood (of menstruation), a seminal discharge (Leviticus 15), eating an animal that died naturally (17:15), or touching an unclean animal (22:5-6) had to be ceremonially cleansed through bathing in water. In each case, the water not only served as a cleansing agent, but the washing event itself served as a point of separation between being *unfit* to serve God and being *fit* or *prepared* to serve Him.

We should not think of "ritual" or "ceremonial" actions as being any less important than, say, the Ten Commandments themselves. While these prescriptions were ritualistic, they were still *required* by Law, and one's failure to abide by them made him a law-breaker and not a law-keeper.[41] Thus, the observance of ritual laws and "signs" of God's covenant with Israel were just as important as any of the moral laws that Israel was required to obey.

### The Water of Cleansing

Through His perfect life and His uncorrupted blood offering, Jesus Christ fulfilled the entire Law of Moses.[42] In having fulfilled "the Law," He also fulfilled all the types, figures, and shadows of the Law—including all of its ritual feasts, cleansings, and holy days (Colossians 2:16-17). In fact, the entire Law itself was only "a shadow of the good things to come and not the very form of things" (Hebrews 10:1), and thus could not fulfill what was *ultimately* required for cleansing any man of his corruption. Water cannot cleanse a man's conscience any more than animal blood can cleanse a man's soul (9:13-14, 10:4).[43] However, water continues (in the *new* covenant) to serve as a symbol of purification and (as illustrated in the case of Christ's own baptism) a separation from one life to another.

A person loses his innocence when he acquires carnal knowledge through his conscious and deliberate sin against God's holy nature. Like Adam and Eve's consumption of the forbidden fruit, so every person thereafter has given away his innocence for a taste of the world. In so doing, that person becomes corrupted *by* the world; in essence, he becomes a man *of* the world (as opposed to being merely born *into* the world). In this spiritual identification with the world, he relinquishes the purity and fellowship that he once enjoyed with his Creator. The corruption of his soul (through his act of disobedience) is likened to—but far more serious than—the ceremonial uncleanness explained in the Law of Moses. Ritual uncleanness under the Law was not considered *sin*, but did render the Israelite unfit for participating in further service to God. The only way that his uncleanness became *sinful* was if he failed to address it through ritual purification. One who is an alien sinner, however, is "dead" to God (Ephesians 2:1). He is not merely in need of healing, but needs to be brought back to life—i.e., he needs to be reconciled with the Giver of Life.

What the two scenarios have in common, however, is the need for *water* in the remedial process. We have already examined the use of water in the purification rites of those Israelites who became "unclean." They remained unclean until (or unless) they underwent the water-cleansing procedure dictated by the Law. But one who has become a sinner is also "unclean"—not just in a symbolic manner, but in a real and perilous one. His uncleanness will lead to the ruin of his soul, until (or unless) he addresses that uncleanness in the water-cleansing procedure dictated by the gospel of Christ.[44]

## Water Is Necessary in Conversion

Water "cleanses," but only in that it is involved at all, not because it is removing actual filth from the person who is washed in it (1 Peter 3:21). In other words, the water did not make the Israelite "clean" because of any magical or healing properties of the water itself; he was made "clean" because in faith he *obeyed the commandment of God* regarding his purification. Likewise, the believer is not *literally* cleansed of his sins by water, because water cannot cleanse sins. There are no healing or reconciliatory properties in the *water itself* in either case. (The centuries-old use of "sacrament" to define the rite of baptism does imply the mysterious work of God, and some have taken this to mean virtually the *magical* work of God.) Water itself does not provide any physical or spiritual healing effects; baptism itself cannot regenerate the soul. The water of baptism is not "holy water" filled with special or magical qualities. Baptism does not serve as a kind of amulet designed to protect the believer against all harm. Baptism is not an act of exorcism of demonic forces that have entered into one's heart. Such are some of the myths and superstitions of those who import pagan religion, supernaturalism, and subtle forms of sorcery into the gospel of Christ.

Only the blood of Christ is able to take away the sins of the world (John 1:29, Ephesians 1:7). Nothing can take the place of this blood—not water, ritualism, churchgoing, sincerity, good intentions, good feelings, a "sinner's prayer," or any other such notion. On the other hand, *access* to the blood is through the believer's obedience, and the *medium* that God has chosen to express this obedience is at least (but not limited to) immersion in water. Thus, the believer is made "clean," so to speak, when in faith he *obeys the commandment of God*. And God's command is that he be baptized in the name of Christ for the forgiveness of his sins (Acts 2:38).

Thus, water is used as a cleansing agent, but only in a spiritual or symbolic manner. But as we said earlier, just because something is ritual or symbolic does not mean it is

## Being Born of God

optional, or that one can forego it without sinning against God. If God *commands* the symbol, then it is a *violation* of the commandment not to observe or participate in it. The sabbath, for example, was a "sign" of the covenant between God and Israel, yet Israel was charged with sin when they failed to observe properly that "sign" (Ezekiel 20:12, 16). Likewise, baptism is a symbol of one's cleansing of his sins—in essence, his uncleanness—but it is not offered as a suggestion or an option, but a command: "Go therefore… baptizing them…" (Matthew 28:19); "And he [Peter] ordered them to be baptized in the name of Jesus Christ" (Acts 10:48). It is impossible to seek God's favor—and especially His forgiveness—while simultaneously resisting the very thing He says is required to *obtain* that favor or forgiveness.

So then, with the purification rites of the Law of Moses in mind, we will consider several passages in which this water-cleansing concept is incorporated into the gospel of Christ. (These are not presented in the order that they appear in the New Testament.)

- "Now why do you delay? Get up and be baptized, and wash away your sins, calling on His name" (Acts 22:16). These are the words spoken to Saul (a.k.a. Paul) after Jesus blinded him on the road to Damascus. While some clever (but unconvincing) interpretations have been given to this passage in order to avoid associating water baptism with either "washing away sins" or "calling" on the name of the Lord, the passage is actually quite simple and straightforward. It teaches thus:
  - Saul was himself instructed to be baptized. He did not consider it unnecessary, as some have assumed, but willingly submitted to it as a matter

of obedience to Christ's gospel. "Be baptized" was not something that Saul did after the fact of his conversion, but was a necessary *part* of it.

- Baptism is not only a demonstration of one's *obedience* but is also necessary for his *forgiveness*. The "washing away" is figurative language, since only the blood of Christ can truly remove sins; yet it is appropriate because the sinner-turned-believer must undergo a ritual cleansing process that symbolizes what Christ is doing for his soul. There is no way—grammatically, logically, or biblically—to escape this conclusion in this passage. Furthermore, this instruction exactly matches what Peter told the Jews on the day of Pentecost (Acts 2:38).

- Baptism is required in order to "call upon His name." This expression means to petition God's help for that which is beyond the scope of human ability.[45] To call upon God's name means to put complete trust in His ability to save, but it also necessarily demands obedience to whatever God says to do with *regard* to that salvation. Peter quoted the prophet Joel on the day of Pentecost: "And it shall be that everyone who calls on the name of the LORD will be saved" (Acts 2:21). At the end of the sermon, Peter told them *how* to call upon that name: "Repent, and let each of you be baptized … for the forgiveness of your sins." God called them through His gospel message (2:39); three thousand people called upon God with their obedience to His instruction by being baptized

(2:41). Saul's experience was no different than theirs: both the instruction and the response were the same.

- If Saul had not been baptized, then his sins could not have been "washed away"—i.e., they could not have been forgiven. And if Saul had never been baptized, he could not have called upon the name of the Lord for salvation, since this is the means the *Holy Spirit* has chosen by which people do this. All said, Saul could not have become a Christian unless or until he complied with these instructions. Yet, the instructions given to Saul were no different than those given to anyone else seeking God's salvation.

❑ In Ephesians 5:24-26, Paul taught that the church—the bride of Christ—is subject to Christ, and that Christ has sanctified His church, "having cleansed her by the washing of water with the word." The direct connection between water and sanctification should seize our attention. The church *as a single entity* is not washed with water; it has been immersed in a different sense—in the Holy Spirit. Yet, each soul that is added *to* Christ's church is added through the same process: he (or she) is "washed" with water for all the reasons stated above in Saul's conversion. This washing is symbolic in nature, but this fact does not render it optional or expendable. If the church—which is comprised only of individual souls that have obeyed the gospel of Christ—can only be sanctified through water, then without water it remains unsanctified and thus unfit to serve as Christ's bride.

- "With the word" has led some to assume that "washing" here is merely a figure of speech and not an actual rite to be performed. This view also assumes that "the word" is what cleanses us, and is often based upon Jesus' words to His disciples: "You are already clean because of the word which I have spoken to you" (John 15:3). But the contexts of the two passages are completely different. In John 15, Christ's disciples had not yet been given the command to go and make disciples through baptism. Also, that context has to do with their preparedness for bearing fruit in their ministry to Him; it is not addressing the means of becoming part of His church or entering into the kingdom of God. The two scenarios use common words, but are not interchangeable.
- "With the word" refers instead to *the source of authority*, just as "by one Spirit" does in 1 Corinthians 12:13. In other words, the "washing"—and thus sanctifying—of Christ's church is in full compliance with the Holy Spirit-revealed Word of God which has instructed this method in the first place.[46] The church is not "washed" according to tradition, man-made doctrines, or any such thing; it is "washed" because Christ required this for His most special bride. Only in this way could He present His bride to His Father as "holy and blameless." (See Colossians 1:22, where Paul uses the same language but with reference to individual believers rather than the entire church.)

- Once again, we see that each believer—and, subsequently, the entire church—comes to Christ *through the water*. It is through the symbolic rite of being "washed" or cleansed with water that one identifies with Christ. Just as water was used to prepare the Levitical priests for service, allowed for the newness of life of a man healed of his leprosy, and provided ritual cleansing for all those who had become "unclean," so water continues to serve as an agent of cleansing for those who call upon God's name for salvation.

❑ "Corresponding to that, baptism now saves you—not the removal of dirt from the flesh, but an appeal to God for a good conscience—through the resurrection of Jesus Christ…" (1 Peter 3:21). Peter defines the "that" to which baptism corresponds in the previous verse: Noah and his family "were brought safely through the water" in the ark. The ark itself prefigures Christ's own church as a refuge or sanctuary specifically prepared by God for the purpose of saving lives. Noah built the ark, whereas Christ built His church; yet both were built according to God's divine plan and authority. Water serves as a means of separation between those *outside* the ark (who were destroyed by water) and those *within* the ark (who were saved through the water). Likewise, in the gospel plan, water separates a person's identification from *those who will be destroyed* and *those who will be saved*. No one comes into Christ's church except through the water, just as Noah could not be saved unless God had brought him safely through the water. If Noah had disobeyed God's commands to build the ark and then seek refuge in it, you can be certain that he also would have been destroyed by water instead of saved through it.[47] Likewise, if a person today refuses to obey God's command to seek refuge in Christ's church, he will be destroyed rather than saved.

- "Corresponding to that" means "in like figure" or "in a parallel thought." The two situations—Noah's and ours—are not interchangeable, but they do share important similarities. Noah's life was spared "through the water," but nothing is said of his soul. Yet, Peter draws upon that figure to speak of our soul's salvation, not that of our physical lives. The one is an analogy of the other, not a point-for-point comparison.
- "Baptism now saves you" is impossible to interpret accurately except in the context in which it is used. Peter is talking about *the salvation of your soul*—and he links baptism directly to this salvation. As real and necessary as Christ's own resurrection from the dead is for your salvation, so is your resurrection (so to speak) from the watery burial of baptism. If Christ was not raised from the dead, baptism is rendered pointless and "you are still in your sins" (cf. 1 Corinthians 15:17).[48] But as it is, Christ *has* been raised, and you must be raised *with* Him in the likeness of His own death, burial, and resurrection. We understand that the *act* of baptism itself is not the power that saves us, for it is God's power that saves (Romans 1:16). But this power is only extended to those who believe and obey Him. We are saved *by* God's grace, but we are not saved *apart from*

human faith (Ephesians 2:8); "faith without works is dead" (James 2:26).

- "Not the removal of dirt from the flesh, but an appeal to God for a good conscience"—this explains exactly what Peter means. Baptism *is* a washing, but not for the body; it is instrumental in the cleansing of the soul. Sin and rebellion corrupt the human conscience: we know that we have sinned, and we know that we stood condemned when we did this. Through our obedience to God's commands—specifically in this case, the command to be baptized—we call upon His name and receive the cleansing of our conscience. The blood of Christ is the *actual* healing agent of our conscience (Hebrews 9:13-14), which is what God "applies" to us.

- Since "baptism now saves you," then one's *refusal* to be baptized cannot possibly save that person. Similarly, one's claim to be "saved" *prior* to being baptized also does not work, since it contradicts Peter's clear and unmistakable teaching on this subject. Once again, it is not baptism alone that brings about salvation, for we know that this only addresses one aspect of what is required—yet it *is required* nonetheless. A person cannot stand before God with a clear (or cleansed) conscience if he has willfully refused to do what God has asked in order to have his conscience cleared.

❏ "... Let us draw near with a sincere heart in full assurance of faith, having our hearts sprinkled clean from an evil conscience and our bodies washed with pure water" (Hebrews 10:22). One should read the entire passage (10:1-22) to get the full impact of what the writer is presenting. Our focus, however, is the method by which we can "enter the holy place by the blood of Jesus" (10:19). This is not something we can do—not for ourselves or for anyone else. We are unable to enter into the heavenly throne room of God and present ourselves literally before Him—which is what the writer describes—but Jesus did this for us (see 9:11-12). We cannot "draw near" to God apart from the divine work and intercession of His Son. But *because* of His intercession (and our "sincere heart"), we ought to have "full assurance of faith" that this is being done for us.

- Yet, there is something that both parties—the one wishing to "draw near" and God Himself—must do. God's work is to sprinkle clean the conscience of the one who calls upon His name for salvation. This "sprinkling" is an allusion to what Moses did upon outlining God's covenant with Israel at Mount Sinai (Exodus 24:1-8). After the elders of Israel agreed to the terms and conditions of this covenant ("All the words which the LORD has spoken we will do!"), Moses took the blood from the offerings made at that time and sprinkled half of it on the altar upon which those offerings were made. The other half he sprinkled upon the people themselves and said, "Behold the blood of the covenant, which the LORD has made with you in accordance with all these words." Thus, the sprinkling of blood upon the *heart* of one who comes to God refers to that person's induction into

### Being Born of God

God's fellowship through *covenant* (see Hebrews 9:15-22). Just as Moses spelled out the terms and conditions of the first covenant at Sinai, so Christ and His apostles have spelled out these for the "new covenant" of the gospel.

- One cannot enter into covenant with God without obeying the terms and conditions of that covenant. He also cannot enter into covenant with God unless (or until) the blood of the covenant *sacrifice* has been applied to that person's soul. But there is at least one other specific condition that must be met: the one wishing to draw near to God in covenant must have his body "washed with pure water." This is a ritual cleansing, not a literal one. In other words, Peter has already explained (in 1 Peter 3:21) that this is not for the cleansing of the body, but the cleansing of one's conscience. No one can enter into covenant with God with a *guilty* conscience; this is something that must be cleansed at the time that the covenant is made.

- In baptism, the believer's former allegiance to the world is severed, since he has died to this. Just as Israel was no longer a slave nation to Egypt once they entered into covenant with God, so the believer is no longer a slave to sin once he is sprinkled with the blood of Christ. As we cited earlier, "to obey Jesus Christ and be sprinkled with His blood" is the method by which we enter into God's covenant of salvation (1 Peter 1:2). "To obey" necessarily indicates that our salvation is conditional: it is not something that just happens to us; it is something that we actively seek. Our obedience demonstrates sincerity and confidence in God's ability to save us. One who is not yet been "washed" has not yet fulfilled *his* part in the covenant-making process. This means that he does not yet *have* a covenant relationship with God.

❏ "But when the kindness of God our Savior and His love for mankind appeared, He saved us, not on the basis of deeds which we have done in righteousness, but according to His mercy, by the washing of regeneration and renewing by the Holy Spirit, whom He poured out upon us richly through Jesus Christ our Savior..." (Titus 3:4-6).

- This passage so closely parallels Ephesians 2:8-9 that we can easily use the one to interpret the other. In both passages, the emphasis is placed upon the Godhead—God the Father, God the Son, and God the Spirit—as the source of all salvation. Yet, neither passage excludes human effort; they simply show that effort to be incomparable to divine effort. In other words, Paul is not saying in either case that *nothing* is required of the believer, but that what God provides *for* the believer is far greater than what the believer can ever provide for God or himself. Both passages teach that we are saved by grace through faith—that is, divine grace that is *in response to* human faith (Hebrews 10:38).

- Those who are decidedly against the necessity of baptism put the two phrases—"washing of regeneration" and "renewing by the Holy Spirit"—together as one interchangeable thought. In other words, they want the Holy Spirit to be directly responsible for *both* the "washing" and "renewing." This puts *all* the work of salvation upon God, and *none* of it upon the person needing it. But this does not work, grammatically, biblically, or theologically. We are saved "by grace ... through faith" (Ephesians 2:8); in a parallel thought, we are renewed by the Holy Spirit but not apart from the "washing of regeneration." The only reference that "washing" has with regard to salvation in the New Testament is *baptism in water*. Those who claim that this is "Holy Spirit baptism" must first read that conclusion into the text, because it is not natural to the context; secondly, they must explain exactly what they *mean* by this. It is convenient to defer to a "spiritual baptism" to avoid a literal one; it is quite another thing to have this answer actually make sense. It is true that the Spirit is "poured out upon us" (Titus 3:6), but only as a *result* of the "washing" and "renewing," not as a *definition* of those actions.[49]

- There is no disagreement between what Jesus said in John 3:5 and what Paul wrote in Titus 3:5:

    **Born of water = washing of regeneration**
    **[Born of] the Spirit = renewing of the Spirit**

    One is an act of human faith; the other is an act of divine power; yet *both* are necessary in order to be *born of God*. Thus, both parts are necessary and, when coupled together, achieve the desired objective:

**Born of water + [born of] the Spirit
= entrance into the kingdom**
*or*
**Washing of regeneration + renewing of the Spirit
= salvation**

No one would deny that entrance into the kingdom of God is something different than the salvation of the human soul. Thus, two things equal to the same thing are also equal to each other: becoming a citizen of the kingdom of God is equal to becoming a Christian.

❑ "Or do you not know that the unrighteous will not inherit the kingdom of God? … Such were some of you; but you were washed, but you were sanctified, but you were justified in the name of the Lord Jesus Christ and in the Spirit of our God" (1 Corinthians 6:9, 11).

- In what case is "washed" used in the New Testament in the context of salvation? It consistently refers to that person's *water baptism* into Christ—not for a physical cleansing, but as an appeal to God for a "good conscience" (cf. 1 Peter 3:21).
- We might ask rhetorically: which of these actions—"washed," "sanctified," or "justified"—is expendable or unnecessary? They are *all* necessary. This does not mean that they are all equal in power or scope, but that is not what "necessary" implies. A man's contribution to the conception, gestation, and birth of a child is

minimal in comparison to a woman's, but *both parties are absolutely necessary* in order for a child to be born. Likewise, what the believer does to prove that he *is* a believer in God is infinitesimally small in comparison to the incomprehensible work of God's saving grace, yet *both parts are absolutely necessary* in order for one to be born of Him.

Once again, we see water used as the means by which a person comes to God for salvation—thus, in one's conversion to Christ. It is through the water that the believer calls upon the name of God, identifies with Christ's church (His bride), is actually saved, has his conscience cleansed, demonstrates his faith in God's power, and enters into a covenant of salvation with God. Removing water baptism from the conversion process fails to carry out the process altogether. Relegating baptism to an after-the-fact demonstration of faith undermines the very purpose *for* baptism in the first place. Baptism is not only a part of the conversion process; it is a necessary and significant one. "*Every single Bible passage* that says anything at all about the meaning of baptism represents it in some way as the time when God bestows His saving grace upon the sinner."[50]

## Summary Thoughts

God has chosen water to symbolize one's ritual cleansing of his uncleanness so that he can enter into fellowship with Him. While other requirements also exist to obtain this fellowship (under the Law of Moses as well as the gospel of Christ), this one element is critical. Under the Law of Moses, if an Israelite was "unclean," then he could not be made "clean" apart from a ritual cleansing with water. Under the gospel of Christ, one who has an unclean conscience cannot have this cleansed apart from a ritual cleansing with water (i.e., baptism).

Water does not take the place of blood—and that was never the point—but God does not ask for us to provide blood, either. He has provided the only blood necessary for the cleansing of our heart and conscience: the blood of His Son, which is the blood of God's covenant with us (Matthew 26:27-28). He only asks that we be obedient to the terms and conditions of this covenant. If God had asked us to be immersed in tomato juice or buttermilk in order to access this blood, hopefully we would comply. How much easier and more practical it is that He has asked us only to be immersed in water! Yet, even with the simplicity of this command, many people still offer all kinds of resistance against it.

The six passages that we have examined above not only teach but also demand that the believer *does something* in order to obtain his own salvation. This does not and cannot mean that what he does *by itself* obtains salvation, for this is impossible. The sin-corrupted human soul cannot be redeemed by works of the sinner himself: sin never makes one holy, but holiness is itself corrupted by sin.[51] What it *does* mean, however, is that no one is saved against his own will, apart from his own faith, and without his own expressed obedience *of* that faith. In comparison to what He does for us, God has not asked much in return, yet what He *does* ask is essential to our covenant relationship with Him.

## Chapter Five:
# Separation and Identification

*For you are all sons of God through faith in Christ Jesus.*
*For all of you who were baptized into Christ have*
*clothed yourselves with Christ.*
Galatians 3:26-27

You are likely familiar with the account of Israel's exodus from Egypt (Exodus 13 – 14). After the tenth plague—the death of all the first-born males in Egypt—the Israelites left that nation and headed toward the land of Canaan. They were led by God's presence through a pillar of cloud by day and a pillar of fire by night. Shortly after they left, however, Pharaoh had a change of heart and decided to go and retrieve his nation of slave laborers, and thus he pursued them with his army. This put Israel in the middle of two formidable obstacles: the impassable Red Sea on one side and the entire Egyptian army and its chariots on the other.

What God did for Israel at that point has become one of the most memorable events in all of human history. First, He put the pillar of cloud between Israel and Egypt, and at night this pillar provided light for Israel but darkness for the Egyptians. Then, He parted the Red Sea for the Israelites to cross it throughout the night, and they walked between two literal walls of water to the other side.[52] Finally, He allowed Pharaoh's army to pursue Israel through the parted sea, but then closed the water upon those men and drowned them.[53]

The apostle Paul draws upon this very event: "For I do not want you to be unaware, brethren, that our fathers were all under the cloud and all passed through the sea; and all were baptized into Moses in the cloud and in the sea" (1 Corinthians 10:1-2). "The cloud" refers to the cloudy/fiery pillar that accompanied Israel during their entire sojourn in the wilderness, from the time they left Egypt to the time they crossed the Jordan River into the Promised Land (Exodus 40:36-38). Israel was "baptized" into the cloud in that they were surrounded or whelmed by God's presence. Likewise, Israel was "baptized" in the sea when they walked between the two walls of water—in essence, when they passed literally *through* the sea. Through these two experiences—which really was *one* experience with two different elements—all of Israel was "baptized into Moses."

This is important, not just because the word "baptized" is used, but because of what was accomplished as a *result* of this baptism. The Red Sea represented a type of *death* to what Israel used to be: no longer would they be a mass of slaves to Egypt; after passing through the sea, they were in essence "born again" as a new nation with an exclusive identity and (in time) a land of their own. Similarly, they would no longer serve Pharaoh, but would become a nation that served God alone and no one else. As God told them at Mount Sinai, "Now then, if you will indeed obey My voice and keep My covenant, then you shall be My own possession among all the peoples, for all the earth is Mine; and you shall be to Me a kingdom of priests and a holy nation" (Exodus 19:5-6).

In a very real sense, the water itself provided the specific point of reference for this great transition: the Israel that entered *into* the sea was not the same nation that came *out* of the sea. The situation had irreversibly and forever changed.[54] Before its "baptism," Israel identified with four hundred years of life (and slavery) in Egypt, not really knowing who Jehovah was. After its "baptism," Israel identified exclusively with Jehovah and His servant Moses. "Baptized into Moses" indicates Israel's recognition of Moses as God's prophet and lawgiver. In fact, no greater authority among men would be over Israel until the time when God raised up a prophet *like* Moses but superior to him in every respect (Deuteronomy 18:15-19). This, of course, is a direct prophecy of Christ Himself (Acts 3:22-25).

## A New Life in Christ

One theme keeps repeating itself throughout Scripture: the Holy Spirit's use of water as a means of *separation* as well as *identification*. We can draw upon Jesus' own baptism to make the point, even though His baptism was not for the same purpose as ours. Jesus' baptism was not for purification, since He had no sins of which to be purified. However, in submitting to baptism, Jesus identified with those who were indeed baptized by John as a sign of their genuine repentance (Luke 3:3). His baptism also served as the defining event between His life on earth prior to His messianic ministry and the ministry itself. In this way, baptism permanently separated the two parts of His life. Indeed, the apostles themselves recognized that His earthly ministry began with His baptism by John and ended with His resurrection from the dead (Acts 1:21-22). Thus, Jesus' baptism was necessary "to fulfill all righteousness" (Matthew 3:15)—in other words, to participate rightly or properly in the plan that God had put in place from the beginning.

Similarly, water serves to separate the believer's former allegiance to the world and his new allegiance to Christ. This separation is necessary in order for the believer to make a new identification—one that is no longer with the sinful world, but now is with God Himself. Just as Jesus was baptized "to fulfill all righteousness," so the believer is baptized for this same reason—because it is the right and proper thing to do.

This separation and identification is exactly that to which Paul refers in Galatians 3:26-27: "For you are all sons of God through faith in Christ Jesus. For all of you who were baptized into Christ have clothed yourselves with Christ." Notice how Paul links *faith* with *baptism*, since baptism is an act *of* faith, and not something independent of it.[55] Just as Israel was baptized into Moses in the presence of God *and* "through the sea," so the believer is baptized into Christ in the presence of God's Holy Spirit *and* in water. Just as Israel died to its former life and identification with Egypt, so the believer "dies" (*in* baptism, and not prior to it) to his former life and his identification with the godless world. After Israel passed through the sea, that nation belonged to God and heeded the words of His servant, Moses; after the believer is baptized, he belongs to God and heeds the words of His Son, Jesus Christ (see Hebrews 3:1-6).

Upon passing through the water, so to speak, we are no longer merely biological children of our parents. Far more importantly than this, "now we are children of God" (cf. 1 John 3:1-2). Being "sons of God" indicates not only a change in allegiance from the world to Christ, but also our qualification as heirs of the kingdom of God (Galatians 4:4-7, Ephesians 1:13-14, Colossians 1:12, et al). "Through faith" means that we acted *in* faith, just as Noah, Abraham, Moses, and all the other men and women of old who "by faith" did something to *demonstrate* their faith (Hebrews 11). One who claims to have faith but does nothing has only an idea in his head, but there is no substance to it. The believer cannot just "accept Jesus into his heart" to separate himself from the world and identify with Christ; he must be *baptized* in order to do this. This is what "for all of you who were baptized" means. It also means that those who are *not* baptized for this very purpose have not yet properly demonstrated their faith.

"For all of you who were baptized into Christ have clothed yourselves with Christ." To be "naked" or "unclothed" in Scripture usually means to be vulnerable, unprepared, and ashamed (as in 2 Corinthians 5:4). To be improperly clothed is no better, since a person is still unfit for service to God (as in Zechariah 3:1-7). To be properly clothed, however, means to be fit, prepared, and ready to serve. In Jesus' parable of the wedding feast, for example, the man who was cast into outer darkness was clothed, but not with the garments that the king had provided him [implied] (Matthew 22:11-14). It is extremely important to God that we be properly "clothed" or prepared for our presentation before Him. Christ can present us before the Father only if we have been cleansed of our sins, our conscience has been cleared, and we are properly attired (so to speak) for that occasion.

To be "clothed" with Christ also means to be identified with Him. Anyone who wears the king's clothes represents the king *and* is obviously in his favor (as in Esther 6:6-11). In being clothed with Christ, however, we are not merely putting on something that belongs to Him, or to which He has given us, but we are putting on Christ Himself. As Paul said, "It is no longer I who live, but Christ lives in me" (Galatians 2:20). In coming into Christ, we retain all of our faculties and decision-making control, but we voluntarily subject ourselves to His authority. In having submitted to the King, we become citizens of the kingdom of God. In dying to our allegiance to the world, we are born of God. In coming *out* of the world, we are brought *into* Christ's church.

Those who regard baptism as an after-the-fact demonstration of faith fail to understand the necessary implication of Paul's words in Galatians 3:27. If *through* baptism we are "clothed" with Christ, then it stands to reason that *without* baptism we remain unclothed of Him—which is another way of saying that we have no identity with Him at all. If left in that condition, we will be like the man at the wedding feast who wanted to share in the celebration, but refused to do what was required on *his* part for this.[56] Indeed, we ought to be preparing for the greatest wedding feast of all time: the eternal union of Christ and His "bride," the church (Revelation 19:7-9). If the apostle Paul says that baptism is *necessary* to prepare for that celebration, then you can be certain that those who refuse to be baptized will not share in it.

In being clothed with Christ, we must first remove all the "clothes" that belonged to the world (or someone else). We lose our own identity in order to take on His; we abandon all other allegiances in order to submit to His authority. Having separated ourselves from the world, we can now be fit and prepared to serve Him in His kingdom. But it is *water* that provides the point of reference for that separation. Just as the Israelites came through the water in order to prepare for their entrance into the Promised Land, so the believer today must come through the water in order to prepare for his entrance into the heavenly kingdom.

### A Necessary Point of Reference

We cited *part* of Paul's statement in Galatians 2:20 earlier, but here is the full verse: "I have been crucified with Christ; and it is no longer I who live, but Christ lives in me; and the life which I now live in the flesh I live by faith in the Son of God, who loved me and gave Himself up for me." One thing is clear:

we must *die* with the Lord in order to be *united* with Him. "For if we died with Him, we will also live with Him" (2 Timothy 2:11)—which means that if we have not *yet* died with Him, then we cannot possibly be living with Him as one of His disciples. The natural question would be, "*When* was Paul 'crucified with Christ'—that is, *when* did he 'die' with the Lord?" Was it when Paul asked Jesus into his heart to be his personal Savior? No, because no one in the New Testament was saved in that way or instructed to be saved in that way. Was it during some spiritual experience that to which Paul was oblivious and that was imposed upon him? No, because no one in the New Testament was saved in *that* way, either.

The visible, historical, and event-oriented point of reference for Paul's "death" was not a born-again epiphany in his heart. Rather, it was a born-again experience in *water*, which exactly conforms to everything we have examined so far. It is the water of one's baptism into Christ that separates his former life from his new life in Christ. This is also exactly what Paul says. Carefully read the following passage (Romans 6:3-11), focusing on the connection between *baptism* and "newness of life," "united with Him," and "alive to God":

> Or do you not know that all of us who have been baptized into Christ Jesus have been baptized into His death? Therefore we have been buried with Him through baptism into death, so that as Christ was raised from the dead through the glory of the Father, so we too might walk in newness of life. For if we have become united with Him in the likeness of His death, certainly we shall also be in the likeness of His resurrection, knowing this, that our old self was crucified with Him, in order that our body of sin might be done away with, so that we would

no longer be slaves to sin; for he who has died is freed from sin. Now if we have died with Christ, we believe that we shall also live with Him, knowing that Christ, having been raised from the dead, is never to die again; death no longer is master over Him. For the death that He died, He died to sin once for all; but the life that He lives, He lives to God. Even so consider yourselves to be dead to sin, but alive to God in Christ Jesus.

Paul directly and unmistakably links one's baptism in water—the act of being *buried* in a type of watery grave—with his *new life* with God. This is not an optional ceremony after the fact; this is not merely "an outward sign of an inward grace." Quite the contrary, this is the *point in time* and *the event in one's life* when he is separated from his old allegiance to sin and his new allegiance to Christ. If this event has not yet happened, then neither has this change of allegiance been made. If this *death* has not yet happened, then he remains alive to the world but dead to God (cf. Ephesians 2:1). The one who has come through the water can forever point back to that experience and say, "*That* is when I gave my life to God—when I *died* in the water and was *raised* to newness of life."

The death, burial, and resurrection experience of the believer is *symbolic* in nature, to be sure. When God provides a symbol that must be *obeyed* in order to conform to His instruction, then that obedience is required and not optional, expendable, or to be delayed until a more convenient time. In going through the motions of one's own death, the *action* is symbolic, but the *death* that he goes through is real and effective. In being buried in the water, the believer's heart dies to his former allegiance to the world, his conscience is cleansed through the sprinkling of Christ's blood, and his soul is

# Being Born of God

sanctified by the Holy Spirit. (We do not bury what is alive, but what is indeed dead; likewise, what is resurrected is no longer dead, but has been made alive again.) Even though these actions are carried out in the spiritual realm, they are real and are necessary for one's salvation.

Once again, we cannot interchange what *God* does and what the *believer* is expected to do (in order to remain a believer). If one hears the gospel of Christ and learns that he must be baptized to be born of God, then he must do whatever it takes on *his* part to cooperate with this. In the passage just cited, Paul makes it clear that baptism is what the believer does to separate himself from the world and be identified with Christ. "For if we have become united with Him [Christ] in the likeness of His death" (6:5) indicates a conditional situation: If we have done this, then we enjoy the results—we "walk in newness of life." But if we have not done this, then we cannot claim to walk in "newness of life," since we have not yet died to the old life. Being united with Christ involves dying with Him, just as Paul said in Galatians 2:20 and 2 Timothy 2:11 (cited above). We *unite* with Him by going through the same process that the Lord did. He did this *literally*—that is, He *physically* died, was buried, and was raised from His grave—whereas we do this *symbolically*. Nonetheless, this is not something you can do in your head or in your heart; it must be carried out *in the water* of your baptism.

### Dying to Bear Fruit for God

While a person remains a sinner, he cannot rely upon his own merit for salvation, since God's law condemns him as a law-*breaker* rather than a law-*keeper*. (The presence of *sin* necessarily demands the presence of *law*, since "where there is no law, there also is no violation"—Romans 4:15.) The *intent* of the law will not be satisfied with anything except the lawbreaker's execution. In the case of one's conversion, however, the one who "dies" to law does not literally die, but he does undergo a *type* of death. It is Christ who has literally died *for* us, on our behalf, as though carrying out the due penalty of the law in Himself: His execution satisfies law's demand of us. Through His death, we are freed, and "there is now no condemnation for those who are in Christ Jesus" (Romans 8:1). Thus, while Christ's literal death was carried out on the cross, the believer's representative "death" is carried out in the watery grave of his own baptism.

Paul explains this further in Romans 7:1-6. He begins with an analogy (7:1-3): a wife is legally bound to her husband as long as he lives; if he dies, she is released from that commitment. Their covenant-binding relationship—which is the foundation of their marriage—is ended upon his death to that covenant. She is not the one who died in this case, but he did; regardless, there is no such thing as a one-person marriage, since marriage cannot function without both a man *and* a woman.

This is not a perfect analogy to the "death" one undergoes in baptism, but it does illustrate this critical point: death ends one's allegiance to any pledge to which he was once bound. "Therefore, my brethren, you also were made to die to the law through the body of Christ, so that you might be joined to another, to Him who was raised from the dead, in order that we might bear fruit for God" (Romans 7:4). It is not (the) law that dies, but the one who is condemned by it; likewise, it is not sin that dies, but the one who is being mastered by it. It is the *person* who "dies" to law and sin, not law and sin that dies to that person. "For one who has died has been set free from sin" (Romans 6:7)—this does not mean he is free from ever *sinning*

*Being Born of God*

again, but that sin is no longer to be his master (see 6:16-19).

The occasion of this person's "death" is his baptism. Remember what Paul said in Romans 6:4: "We were buried therefore with Him by baptism into death...." Remember, too, that no one can be "born again" who does not die first, since one cannot serve his old life of sin *and* his new life with God at the same time. He cannot walk in "newness of life" unless (or until) the old "body of sin" is put to death. Christ literally died on the cross; we symbolically "die" in immersion in water. Christ was literally resurrected from His tomb; we symbolically are raised from our watery tomb. The believer's "death" is *through* the body of Christ, which is to say that His death fulfills what our "death" only symbolizes. Once we have died *to* law and *with* Christ, then we can be "joined to another"—that is, we can be joined to the resurrected Christ who lives forever. (The implication of this union is twofold: we are "raised" to live "in Christ" in this life, but also look forward to being raised from our literal grave in the future resurrection just as He was raised from His grave—see 1 Thessalonians 4:13-17.)

A person who remains alive to sin but dead to God cannot bear "fruit" for God. This does not mean that he is incapable of doing anything morally good, since even wicked people can perform good deeds when they want to. When Paul (or other New Testament writers) talks about "bearing fruit for God," he refers to performing deeds consistent with one's regenerated life *and* his allegiance to Christ (Ephesians 5:9, Philippians 1:11, Colossians 1:9-12, Revelation 14:13, et al). Prior to his conversion, the sinner has no life with Christ, and he has no salvation; no matter what "fruit" he performs, he is still "dead" to God. Thus, he is only able to perform "dead works" (Hebrews 9:14) and "fruit for death" (Romans 7:4).

Having died to law and been raised to "newness of life" with God, everything changes. Now he is able to "bear fruit for God"—not because he is a morally superior person, but because he is now being led by the Holy Spirit and is able to produce Spirit-filled works (Galatians 5:22-23). He also has *recourse* for his sins: instead of simply remaining in condemnation for those sins that he commits, he can appeal to God for forgiveness through Jesus Christ, his Advocate (1 John 2:1-2). After this symbolic death-burial-resurrection process, he also: is made a member of Christ's spiritual body (His church); is blessed with every spiritual blessing (Ephesians 1:3); looks forward to his eternal inheritance in the kingdom; etc. In other words, many good and positive things are provided for him *after* he becomes a Christian, which is *after* he "dies" to the world and begins life anew with God. One writer says of this: "The specific point [of our union with Christ] is that our relationship with Christ is so close that all the power and life that spring from His redeeming work belong to us and flow into our lives."[57]

### Summary Thoughts

In this chapter, we have highlighted the need for *separation* and *identification* with regard to one's salvation. When we are born of God, then—and only then—can we truly be called "Christians," since it is no longer we who live for ourselves but Christ lives in us. Yet, no one can claim identification with Christ who has not first severed his allegiance to the world. God has chosen *water* to be the agent of this separation: in the case of Israel's passing through the Red Sea, Jesus' baptism, and the believer's baptism into Christ, water separated the two lives (so to speak) of those involved, and allowed for a new life to take the place of the old life. We are made "sons of God through faith" (Galatians 3:26), but this

*Being Born of God*

faith must *at least* be demonstrated in baptism if we are to be clothed with Christ (3:27).

Paul's discourse in Romans 6:3-11 powerfully and irrefutably explains the need—not just the symbolism of, but the *need*—for baptism. Paul further underscores this need in Romans 7:1-6, where he explains that when we die *to* law, we are freed from the condemnation *of* law. This makes that death not just important but also essential to one's salvation. Since that death is symbolized in one's baptism into Christ, this makes *baptism* not only important but also essential as well.

## Chapter Six:
# The Sign of the Covenant

> *... And in Him you were also circumcised with a circumcision made without hands, in the removal of the body of the flesh by the circumcision of Christ; having been buried with Him in baptism, in which you were also raised up with Him through faith in the working of God, who raised Him from the dead.*
> Colossians 2:11-12

Throughout the Old Testament, God used *signs* to remind people of a covenant relationship that had been established. The rainbow, for example, was (and continues to be) a sign of God's covenant with the world that He would never again flood the earth with water (Genesis 9:12-13). The sabbath was a sign given exclusively to Israel for this same purpose: "I gave them My sabbaths to be a sign between Me and them, that they might know that I am the LORD who sanctifies them" (Ezekiel 20:12).

Such signs refer to a completed action in history ("This is what God did") as well as anticipate an *ultimate* completion in a spiritual context ("This is what God will do"). The rainbow, for example, looks back upon God's promise not to destroy the world with water again, yet it also anticipates a future life with a God who Himself cannot be destroyed (Ezekiel 1:28, Revelation 4:3). Likewise, the sabbath looks back upon the seventh day of Creation, but it also anticipates a future "rest" for those who are in Christ (Hebrews 4:9).

Signs are not equal to the thing that they represent, since they find their completion in something outside of themselves. The rainbow is not the actual covenant that God made with the world but a sign *of* it. The sabbath is not the actual rest that God enjoyed when His work of creation was completed but a sign *of* that work.[58] Nonetheless, signs are extremely important, and—if God so commands—are required to be observed. In the case of the rainbow, God provided a sign that only needed to be visually seen; nothing else was required in response. In the case of the sabbath, however, Israel was commanded to "keep" that sign in a ritual observance that directly affected their lives. The sign was directly tied to the covenant: in order to honor the *covenant*, the Israelites had to honor its *sign*. Failure to honor the sign was tantamount to failure to honor the covenant—a failure which is always expressed, in some form or another, as idolatry.[59]

## The Importance of Covenant

Our common use of *covenant* refers to a mutual agreement between two or more parties in which *each party* has certain responsibilities and obligations to the other(s). While some covenants can indeed be informal and even unspoken (such as friendships), formal or binding covenants are verbalized, written out, and/or legally notarized (such as marriages or business arrangements). The covenant has stipulations for entering into it as well as maintaining it once it has been established. It offers a reward for compliance (in the form of benefits or compensation), as well as consequences for failing to comply.

It is the covenant agreement that makes relationships both functional and durable. Marriage, for example, is a type of solemn covenant between a man and a woman; wedding rings serve as signs of that marriage covenant. It is the covenant that allows them to function as husband and wife, and to provide a relationship of trust, commitment, fidelity, and sexual fulfillment. Without this covenant, they are just two people living together in an unholy union (cf. 1 Corinthians 6:16). Whatever benefits they enjoy from that union are temporary and artificial, since the union itself is not approved by God. In a wedding, "two individuals enter as single people and emerge as a married couple. A wedding is not just symbolic of an already existing union but itself creates a new form of union."[60]

In Scripture, we see a consistent association between the *fallen human condition* and the need for that condition to be restored through a *covenant relationship*. Fellowship with God cannot be based upon perfect human performance once a person has fallen from God's "glory" (cf. Romans 3:23); a new relationship must be established upon new conditions. Thus, whenever God provides a *covenant* to men for salvation, it is in some way necessitated by human sin. The rainbow, as a visible sign of God's covenant with the earth, is directly related to the great wickedness of mankind that required the Flood in the first place.[61] The sabbath was given to Israel as a reprieve for the great curse that God had placed upon the world as a result of Adam and Eve's sin (Genesis 3:17-19). Even the marriage covenant has been provided in order to *avoid* sexual immorality between a man and a woman (1 Corinthians 7:1-3).

It is through a *covenant* relationship that God provides mercy and grace for the human condition. The only way that God can have a relationship with us after we have sinned against Him is through covenant: law-*keeping* will not justify us, since it is through law-*breaking* that we became sinners. God cannot enter into a holy union with law-breakers, but He *can* enter into a holy union with those who seek His forgiveness through some means *outside* of law itself. Since law cannot justify the one who has sinned against it, another method of justification must be used. This other method—a covenant agreement for salvation—has terms and conditions which both parties must uphold. Through this covenant, the sinner finds his justification in the blood of Christ rather than in his law-keeping. (This is what Paul means when he says that we are "justified by faith apart from works of the law"—Romans 3:23-28.)

There are some who teach that we are all born into a covenant relationship with God, and that the fact of our very existence makes us covenant-bound people. But this is not true and does not make sense. We are all born under the *law* of God, and we are expected to keep that law—and law and covenant are not the same things. Adam and Eve were not given a *covenant* to uphold when they were first put into the Garden of Eden, but a *law* to keep. Once they broke that law, a covenant was necessary in order for them to continue in a relationship with God. Likewise, a child is not born into a covenant relationship with God, but is expected to keep His law upon reaching an age of accountability to Him. At some point, however, he will break that law and will no longer be a law-*keeper* but a law-*breaker*.[62] One who is not guilty of any wrongdoing does not need mercy and grace; he is justified on the basis of his own innocence. A sinner, however, stands condemned by God and can only be justified thereafter through mercy and grace. Such gifts—mercy, grace, forgiveness, propitiation, etc.—are not found *outside* of a covenant relationship with God, but only *within* it. The sinner who remains outside of God's covenant of salvation is "dead" to Him (Ephesians 2:1); only the one who is within that covenant *and* remains faithful to it will be saved by Him.

Our relationship with God is not established upon or maintained by our feelings, emotions, church attendance, or personal stipulations. It is based upon *God's* terms of *His* covenant, since He alone has what we need, and we are not in a position to negotiate or offer a counter-proposal. These terms are what we call "the gospel of Christ"; obedience to the gospel is equal to entering into a covenant with God through Christ. God invites each person to enter into a covenant agreement with Him when He "calls" him with His gospel (2 Thessalonians 2:13-14). God does not "call" those who are completely unable to respond, but calls those who most certainly *can* respond, and in whose best interest it is *to* respond. A sinner can either accept God's covenant of salvation or reject it altogether. There is no third alternative.

It is only *by* God's covenant that we can come into contact with the blood of Christ, which is the atonement for our sin. Every life-giving covenant that God makes with men requires *blood* in order for the covenant itself to be made alive. Christ's blood is what gives life to God's covenant of salvation (Matthew 26:27-28, Hebrews 9:15-25). If Christ's body had not been a perfect specimen for sacrifice, His blood would have been corrupted and could not have given life to our covenant with God. If His blood had not been shed for the very purpose *of* this covenant, we could not have all the life-giving provisions that the covenant provides; "without shedding of blood there is no forgiveness" (Hebrews 9:22). It is the body and blood of Christ that makes our covenant with God both *possible* and then *functional*.

This is why Christians are to honor this sacrifice in the observance of the Lord's Supper, which is a sign of our covenant *with* God *through* Christ.[63] Without a proper observance of this sign, we show contempt for what it represents. And, as we observed earlier, the sign of the Lord's Supper looks back to what God *did* for us (i.e., Christ's sacrificial death) as well as anticipates a future event that fulfills the sign in every way (i.e., Christ's return) (1 Corinthians 11:23-27, Hebrews 9:28).

## The Sign of Circumcision

The above explanation serves only to explain the importance of our covenant with God *and* its signs. Despite all that we have said, we have still only scratched the surface of the discussion; yet, we have laid the groundwork for the subject at hand—the link between a sign of the first covenant (with Abraham) and the "better" covenant (through Christ).

In Genesis 12:1-3, God made a covenant with Abraham by which ultimately all the families of the earth would be blessed. God also promised him that he would be the father of many descendants, and would inherit the land of Canaan as his own possession. "Then he believed in the LORD; and He reckoned it to him as righteousness" (15:6). God made this covenant real to Abraham when He passed between the sacrificial animals (15:7-21).

In Genesis 17, God commanded Abraham—and any male in his household—to be circumcised. This act provided a sign of God's covenant with him. "And you shall be circumcised in the flesh of your foreskin, and it shall be the sign of the covenant between Me and you" (17:11). This circumcision was *not* the covenant itself, but a sign of it. Abraham's willingness to accept this sign indicated his faith in God's covenant with him. If he had refused to accept the sign, then this would have shown his unbelief in or contempt for God's covenant. In fact, God put a curse on any man of Abraham's household that *did* refuse the sign, since this implied a rejection of the covenant: "An uncircumcised male who is not circumcised in the flesh of his foreskin, that person shall be cut off from his people; he has broken My covenant" (17:14).⁶⁴ These people were not *born* into the covenant, but were made participants in it *when* they were circumcised. Likewise, all future males born into Abraham's household were to be circumcised on the eighth day of their lives (17:12). Even then, the covenant was made with Abraham's entire family, and ultimately with the nation (of Israel) that descended from that family. It came to be understood as a national sign (carried only by the males of that nation) and not merely an individual one. Circumcision identified a man as belonging to a covenant-bound people, and this made him a recipient of all the blessings and privileges of that covenant.⁶⁵

Of course, circumcision *by itself* meant nothing. Likewise, a non-Israelite who was not *physically* circumcised but was circumcised in his heart, so to speak, could also walk in fellowship with God *if* he lived by faith in Him (Habakkuk 2:4, Romans 1:17). A faithful heart is what God wanted even from Israel, just as Moses told them: "So circumcise your heart, and stiffen your neck no longer" (Deuteronomy 10:16; see also 30:6 and Jeremiah 4:4). Paul later argued that an Israelite's physical circumcision was rendered useless if he did not keep God's Law: "For he is not a Jew who is one outwardly, nor is circumcision that which is outward in the flesh" (see Romans 2:25-29). In other words, circumcision was never meant to be a replacement for one's faithfulness to God, but instead an emblem *of* it.

The emphasis, then, was not limited to the sign itself, as many Jews mistakenly believed, but what the sign represented: faith in God's ability to perform, even against all hope of human effort (as what Abraham manifested—Romans 4:18). This did not make circumcision optional for the Israelite, however, since he was *commanded* to receive it (Leviticus 12:3). The "circumcision" of the Gentile [non-Jewish] believer of the pre-gospel era was manifested in the disposition of his heart, but the Israelite had to be circumcised in his flesh *as well as* in his heart. ("In the flesh" is what physically identified him with the nation of Israel; "in the heart" is what identified him with God.) The Israelite could never say, "I know that I am not circumcised in the flesh, but God knows my heart—and what is in my *heart* is more important than any physical act." This kind of reasoning was impossible since indeed God *commanded* the physical act to be accomplished in order for that Israelite to have a covenant relationship with Him. No one can have a right heart with God who deliberately refuses to obey His command—whatever the command may be. And no one can enter into a covenant relationship with God who refuses the sign *of* that covenant—again, whatever that sign may be.

As important as the sign of physical circumcision was, it was still limited to the nation of Israel (and proselytes to the Law of Moses). Also, it could only be given to men, since it was through the males that land inheritance was perpetuated. This did not mean that women were exempted from the *covenant*, but that only the men were allowed to receive the *sign* of the covenant since they served as legal representatives and property holders of the nation itself. Once God's covenant with Israel was fulfilled in Christ, it would be necessary that believers be given a new sign—one that is better than physical circumcision, and one that can be given to all believers regardless of nationality or gender.

## The New (or True) Circumcision

No one today can be bound to Israel's covenant with God, since that relationship—as well as the law that defined it—has been fulfilled in Christ. The change of covenant requires a change of law also.⁶⁶ Likewise, the priesthood has changed (Hebrews 7:12); the temple has changed (Ephesians 2:19-21); and the signs, types, and ritual observances have changed (Colossians 2:16-17). In having fulfilled these things, Christ has also *become* that which He has fulfilled: He is our Sabbath, He is our Passover, He is our Jubilee, etc. He is also our circumcision: in Him, our old body of sin is cut away, and in Him we have newness of life. No longer is this a physical act performed on the physical body by the physical hands of men. This is now a spiritual action performed upon the human heart—an act that Christ alone can perform. No longer is this limited to Israel, or to males, but is available to every person who comes to Him in faith seeking salvation, regardless of nationality or gender.

Just because this is a spiritual act, however, does not mean that it has no physical point of reference. In other words, there is a time and event in one's life *when* this spiritual circumcision actually takes place. Paul spelled this out for us in Colossians 2:11-13:

> In Him you were also circumcised with a circumcision made without hands, in the removal of the body of the flesh by the circumcision of Christ; having been buried with Him in baptism, in which you were also raised up with Him through faith in the working of God, who raised Him from the dead. When you were dead in your transgressions and the uncircumcision of your flesh, He made you alive together with Him, having forgiven us all our transgressions...

In this passage, Paul links together everything that we discussed in the previous chapters *and* adds a new element to the picture: "a circumcision made without hands." This involves the death

## Being Born of God

of one's old body of sin in order for a new creature to be born of God—thus, a born-again experience. This occurs at the time of one's baptism in water for the purpose of calling on the name of the Lord for salvation. In baptism, the sinner is lowered into his death (the watery grave of his baptism), and then is raised to newness of life.[67] When he dies *with* Christ and then is "made alive together with Him," he is forgiven of his sins. A comparison of Romans 6:3-7 and Colossians 2:11-13 helps to magnify these thoughts:

| Romans 6:3-7 | Colossians 2:11-13 |
|---|---|
| "Or do you not know that all of us who have been baptized into Christ Jesus have been baptized into His death? Therefore we have been **buried with Him through baptism into death**, so that as Christ was raised from the dead through the glory of the Father, so we too might walk in newness of life. For if we have become united with Him in the likeness of His death, certainly we shall also be in the likeness of His resurrection, knowing this, that our old self was crucified with Him, in order that **our body of sin might be done away with**, so that we would no longer be slaves to sin; for he who has died is freed from sin." | "…And in Him you were also circumcised with a circumcision made without hands, in the removal of the body of the flesh by the circumcision of Christ; having been **buried with Him in baptism**, in which you were also raised up with Him through faith in the working of God, who raised Him from the dead." |

The spiritual circumcision that Christ performs alludes to the physical circumcision of Israel, but then supersedes it in every way. Physical circumcision served as a sign of the covenant between God and Abraham, which was also incorporated into His covenant with Israel (since they were recipients of the *physical* inheritance of Abraham—namely, the Promised Land). Spiritual circumcision is not of the flesh, yet it is necessary for one's induction into the new covenant with God through Christ.

Baptism is the visible *sign* of that which was done in the spiritual realm. Baptism in water symbolizes the *time* (the "when") that corresponds to the *reality* (the "what") of that action. Calvinists describe baptism as "an outward sign of an inward grace"—but they claim that baptism is done *after the fact* of this spiritual circumcision, rather than simultaneous *with* it. The outward/inward concept is biblically accurate, but their application of its timing is not. Baptism symbolizes outwardly what Christ does inwardly as an act of divine grace, yet *both actions* are done at the same time, as though a singular event. One is not "saved" first and then baptized; rather, baptism marks the *event* of his salvation. He cannot choose to observe the outward sign of God's covenant at his convenience (or not at all) while allegedly inducted into the covenant through a "circumcision made without hands" anyway. Rather, he is inducted into the covenant *when* he submits to the outward, visible, and necessary *sign* of that covenant: his baptism. Again, spiritual circumcision is the "what" that happens; baptism is the "when" that this circumcision happens.[68]

This is *not* to say that "baptism replaces circumcision," for this confuses what Christ does with what the believer does.[69] Christ's "removal" of the "body of the flesh" is not accomplished by immersion in water; likewise, one's immersion in water means nothing without this spiritual "removal" of his sinful state. Nonetheless, the two actions—what Christ does for the believer *and* what the believer does for Christ—are performed at the same time. The one being baptized believes that Christ does for him what he could not do for himself. His baptism serves as a visible demonstration of that belief.

The covenant that God makes with Christians is different than the one He made with Israel. The law is different; the priesthood is different; and the signs and forms are different. Jesus did not just "replace" God's covenant with Israel with God's covenant with Christians; He *fulfilled* the one in order to *establish* the second. Likewise, He did not just replace laws meant for Israel with laws meant for Christians; He *fulfilled* their Law in order to *establish* a new law for us. So it is with the priesthood, and so it is with the signs and forms of the two covenants: He fulfilled the first in order to establish the second.

Those who claim that "baptism replaces circumcision" overlook this most important distinction. This oversight leads to all sorts of errors that are based upon a false premise— i.e., the premise that water baptism is exactly like physical circumcision in every respect. One of these errors is the idea that infant children may be baptized because of their parents' covenantal relationship with God (since Hebrew boys were circumcised because of their Israelite parents' relationship with God). In fact, virtually the entire argument for infant baptism rests upon this one grand assumption. We *can* say that baptism for the believer who comes to Christ *serves as a visible sign* of his identity with Christ just as literal circumcision served to identify Israel as God's people, but this compares similar objectives, not interchangeable actions. No (male) person can presently enter into a covenant with God by being physically circumcised; likewise, no person who is circumcised by Christ needs to be physically altered for any reason in connection with his salvation. The two things have related ideas, to be sure, but they each belong to entirely separate covenants.[70]

"Having been buried with Him [Christ] in baptism," Christ performs upon the human heart the radical surgery, so to speak, that is required in order to save our souls. Without this act, we remain uncircumcised and still dead in our sins; our allegiance is still with the world, since we have not yet died *to* the world and *with* Christ. Baptism is not passively connected with this change of allegiance, but is inseparable from it. If we are not buried with Him in baptism, we fail to comply with *our* part of this great transaction. Thus, we resist altogether the born-again process defined for us in the terms and conditions of our entrance into God's covenant of salvation (i.e., the gospel of Christ). We cannot be become born *of* God if we will not submit to His will, and one who is *not* born of God *cannot* be a Christian. Only those who are of the "true circumcision"—that which *Christ* has performed, not man—have citizenship in heaven (compare Philippians 3:2-3 and 3:20-21).

### Summary Thoughts

Baptism is a physical symbol or sign of what happens in the spiritual context. Nonetheless, if it is necessarily required for one's conversion to God, then it is not an optional symbol or an expendable sign of that invisible action. Just as God told Abraham that any man of his household who refused to be circumcised must be "cut off" from that household, so any person today who *thinks* he is of the household of God but refuses do what the covenant requires of him will not be recognized as belonging to the family of God. "Unless one is born of water and the Spirit" (John 3:5) means that it cannot be any other way. It also means that we cannot teach any other instruction and still be true to the gospel of Christ.

Israel could not refuse to "remember the sabbath" without being disobedient to the covenant to which the sabbath belonged. Similarly, by refusing to be baptized in water, one also refuses to comply with the covenant to which this baptism belongs. One who says, for example, "I have entered into a covenant of salvation with God, but I just haven't been baptized yet," does not yet understand that the two things—the covenant itself and the visible expressions *of* covenant—either exist together or not at all. It is correct to say, "I entered into a covenant of salvation with God *when* I was baptized." Only when a person is obedient *to* the covenant can he enter into it. Yet, that person is also bound to act in obedience to the terms and conditions of that covenant from his baptism forward.

Just as the Israelite could not ignore his physical circumcision, so the Christian's sign of his covenant with God is to remain ever before him. Every day he should remember the day of his new birth by the love for Christ that is in his heart. He ought to constantly remember that he does not belong to himself, but now is the possession of the One who gave him newness of life. Then, on the first day of every week, he renews his covenant with God through another sign, the Lord's Supper. Indeed, the memorial for Christ's death for the believer ought to bring to mind the believer's "death" (in baptism) for Christ. These are not two unrelated signs, but are inseparably connected. One is personal, the other is communal; both are required.

# Chapter Seven:
# The One Baptism

*There is one body and one Spirit, just as also you were called in one hope of your calling; one Lord, one faith, one baptism, one God and Father of all who is over all and through all and in all.*
Ephesians 4:4-6

When talking about the subject of baptism, not everyone is immediately on the same page. For one thing, "baptism" is used in more than one context in the New Testament. For example, the baptisms that John the Baptist performed had nothing to do with making people Christians. John also referred to a baptism of the Holy Spirit and a separate baptism of "fire" or judgment (Matthew 3:11). Jesus spoke of His suffering on the cross as a kind of "baptism" (Mark 10:38, Luke 12:50). Then, of course, there is the baptism that is directly associated with one's conversion to Christ, which has been the focus of our present study.

Additionally, there are varieties of baptism that have arisen from denominational doctrines. For example, someone might say, "Your church has its baptism, but our church has a different one." Such usage indicates a liturgical or ritual baptism that has nothing to do with salvation. At least one denomination that I know of uses baptism as a requirement for membership in its churches, and not for anything else. That is "a" baptism, to be sure, but it does not accomplish what is described in Galatians 3:26-27. The baptism Paul speaks of is "through faith"; this other one is for congregational membership. Another denomination practices a literal

## Being Born of God

baptism for the dead—a doctrine predicated entirely upon an assumed interpretation of 1 Corinthians 15:29. A number of groups baptize infants and/or young children, but this actually accomplishes nothing *for* the child himself. As we have consistently seen in our study, baptism follows faith, and faith is predicated upon New Testament doctrine. Thus, the baptism of children does not make those children Christians, but serves some other purpose.

In Ephesians 4:1-6, Paul provided seven doctrinal statements that believers must maintain in order to preserve the unity of the Spirit. Not surprisingly, baptism is included in these requirements. But not just any baptism will do; instead, there is only "one baptism" that the Holy Spirit recognizes as being authentic. Whatever *this* baptism is, it must be as important to the believer as are the body of Christ, the Spirit of God, one's calling from God, etc. The question is: to *what* baptism does he refer? Directly connected to *that* question is this one: what are the right *reasons* for which a person must be baptized?

### The Unity of the Spirit

The "one baptism" must be that which God requires, especially since He is the possessor of the salvation sought *through* baptism. This immediately removes from consideration any baptism that comes solely from man-made religion and denominational teaching. No doctrine that has originated from men, however pious or spiritual it appears to be, can be imposed upon all of humanity for the purpose of salvation. Paul's stress on the seven things mentioned (in Ephesians 4:4-6) is to underscore the *unity* of the Spirit's teachings as well as the *authority* of those teachings. "One body, one Spirit, one calling, etc." are unified teachings that are given from heaven for *all* men to believe and obey. They comprise the doctrine of Christ, upon which one's faith in Christ is predicated. No man or group of men has the authority to add to, subtract from, or amend such teachings. Simply put, we cannot re-define God's terms and conditions for salvation, and then teach these changes as though they are acceptable to Him.

The "one baptism" must also be that which would be an established and consistent part of gospel teaching. Paul did not have to explain this baptism to the Ephesians because they knew exactly what he was talking about: they had all participated in it themselves. The "message of truth, the gospel of your salvation" (Ephesians 1:13-14) had to include this baptism, just as the gospel of Christ always does. In another example, when Philip "preached Jesus" to the Ethiopian traveler in Acts 8:26-39, the man clearly understood that he needed to be baptized in water in *response* to that teaching, since baptism was itself a *part* of that teaching. Today, if we "preach Jesus" accurately, it will lead to this same conclusion.

The "one baptism" is directly related to one's salvation in Christ. Paul's words (in Ephesians 4:1-6) define the basis by which the Ephesian Christians were called into fellowship with God. In essence, Paul says, "Remember the *foundational teachings* by which you were called into Christ, which came to you by the authority of the Holy Spirit of God, and *preserve* these in your own teachings to others." Thus, one is saved upon his having been admitted into the "one body"—not one congregation or denomination, but Christ's spiritual body of believers (Colossians 1:18)—and no other. He is saved by the authority of "one Spirit"—the Spirit of God who has provided, authenticated, and testified to that person's obedience to the gospel terms and conditions (Romans 8:16, 1 Corinthians 12:12-13). The believer has been called by "one calling"—that

# Being Born of God

which came from God, through the message of His gospel (2 Thessalonians 2:13-14). There is "one Lord"—the Lord Jesus Christ—to whom he must give his allegiance, for he cannot be saved by any other lord or authority. He must adhere to "one faith"—not his personal faith, but "the faith" that is specifically defined by the gospel. This is the only faith that God recognizes as being legitimate, and that is common to the salvation of every believer (Jude 3). Likewise, he must believe in and practice only "one baptism"—that which admits him into Christ's body, in which he receives the forgiveness of sins (Ephesians 1:7, Colossians 1:13-14). Finally, he must believe that there is "one God and Father" over all of Creation who is the Giver of life and salvation.

### What the "One Baptism" Cannot Be

The "one baptism" cannot be that which John the Baptist conducted during his ministry. That baptism was specifically intended for Israelites who had strayed from their *already-existing* covenantal commitment to God, not an entrance into a *new* covenant. John's mission was to restore the hearts of the Jews in preparation for their coming Messiah: "It is he [John] who will go as a forerunner before Him in the spirit and power of Elijah, to turn the hearts of the fathers back to the children, and the disobedient to the attitude of the righteous, so as to make ready a people prepared for the Lord" (Luke 1:17). Thus, his baptism was to symbolize one's genuine repentance in order that God could forgive him under the terms and conditions of the *old covenant* (Luke 3:3-6).

John was not a Christian; he was a faithful Jew who served as God's prophet. John's baptism never made people Christians; those who were baptized by him remained what they were—Jews under the old covenant. It is true that Jesus' disciples also baptized for the same reason as John (John 4:1-2), but the results were the same. John's baptism served an important purpose, but it was not performed for the purpose of salvation in Christ under the new covenant. In fact, those who were baptized according to John were later—after the church had been established and not before—commanded to be baptized into Christ (Acts 2:37-38, 19:1-5).

Some have argued that the "one baptism" is that of the Holy Spirit—often dubbed "Holy Spirit baptism." Any link between the Holy Spirit and *His* baptism is rare in the New Testament, and is always in a very specific context. John the Baptist promised the Jews that Jesus would come and baptize them in this manner: "I baptized you with water; but He will baptize you with the Holy Spirit" (Mark 1:8). Jesus reminded His apostles of this just prior to His ascension: "Gathering them together, He commanded them not to leave Jerusalem, but to wait for what the Father had promised, 'Which,' He said, 'you heard of from Me; for John baptized with water, but you will be baptized with the Holy Spirit not many days from now'" (Acts 1:4-5). The *manifestation* of this baptism was through the miracles, signs, and wonders performed by those who received power to do so (Hebrews 2:3-4). The *purpose* for this baptism was to confirm the presence and activity of the Holy Spirit in Christ's church—a presence not limited to those early converts, but for all Christians. In a very real sense, the entire spiritual body of Christ was *immersed* in the Holy Spirit—the Jews first (Acts 2) and then the Gentiles (Acts 10). In this way, both groups were brought together by one Spirit and made into "one new man" which has its access to the Father *through* the Spirit (Ephesians 2:13-18). Even so, it is necessary to distinguish between the authoritative *power* given exclusively to the apostles as Christ's spokesmen (Acts 1:7-8) and the *general manifestation* of the Spirit which was given only to those upon whom the apostles' laid their hands (Acts 8:14-17). Sadly, a great deal of confusion concerning the Spirit and His gifts today exists because of a failure to keep what we read in the New Testament in its proper biblical and historical context.[71]

The visible *manifestation* of baptism with the Spirit was not something done repeatedly, or for each new member.[72] Only two times in Acts did the Holy Spirit *on His own initiative* manifest His approval to each group—first Jews, then Gentiles (Acts 2, 10). This action was accompanied each time with miracles specific to those two events. This was not a baptism that could be performed by men, but was only performed by God Himself. It was not a baptism *required* by men in obedience to any gospel command, because there is no command to *be* baptized in this way. (Do not confuse *receiving the power to perform miracles* by the Spirit [as in Acts 8:14-17] with *baptism with* the Spirit [Acts 1:4-5], for these are two completely different contexts. Christ's entire church has been immersed in the Holy Spirit, but not every believer has been given the ability to perform miracles.) The baptism with the Spirit was never intended for any individual believer.

In contrast, the "one baptism" (in Ephesians 4:5) does *not* refer to what has been done for the entire church, but what each *person* is required to believe and obey in order to become a Christian. It is illogical for God to demand something of one who calls upon Him for salvation that He alone can perform. Furthermore, one who insists that the "one baptism" *is* "Holy Spirit baptism" must explain why every believer who heard the gospel message preached (in Acts and otherwise) was baptized in *water* in response to it. We have already examined in detail the pattern by which men and women became Christians in Acts, and it was not through a "Holy Spirit baptism."

The "one baptism" cannot be a "baptism for the dead." As mentioned above, at least one denomination teaches that a living person can be baptized *on behalf of* a dead person. Thus, a person who died as an unbeliever can allegedly be saved anyway by the living person's baptism. Yet, such a practice is completely foreign to the gospel. There is no teaching or example in the New Testament of anyone being baptized on behalf of someone else. Paul wrote in 1 Corinthians 15:29, "Otherwise, what will those do who are baptized for the dead? If the dead are not raised at all, why then are they baptized for them?" But this is spoken in the midst of a discourse on the resurrection, which establishes the proper *context* for what he said. Paul refers to those who are being baptized in anticipation of being raised from the dead—i.e., their actual bodily resurrection—just as those who died in faith before them hoped to be raised (cf. Philippians 3:10-11, 1 Thessalonians 4:13-17). It is a rhetorical point, not a new doctrine; it is meant to emphasize the reality of resurrection, not create an entirely new practice for the church. This is evident in the fact that nowhere in the New Testament is anyone actually baptized "for" or on behalf of a dead person. Baptism is a personal act of faith; it cannot be done for *you* anymore than you can have faith for someone *else*.

### What the "One Baptism" Must Be

Given its direct connection with salvation in Christ, the "one baptism" can only have one meaning: immersion in water for the distinct purpose of becoming a Christian. "One" indicates its unique usage and special importance. It does not speak to the time, place, ethnicity, or gender of the person being

## Being Born of God

baptized; rather, it speaks to the propriety—the rightness and properness—of the thing being done. To designate something as the "one" thing puts it above all others that may appear to be similar in nature. This is true for each of the "one" things that Paul mentions in Ephesians 4:4-6:

- ❏ There are many "bodies" of men, but only "one body" into which the saved are added (Ephesians 1:22-23).
- ❏ There are many "spirits" in the world, but only "one Spirit" who has revealed the Father's will concerning salvation (1 John 4:1-3).
- ❏ There are many "callings" to which men will give their attention, but there is only "one calling" by which God invites men into fellowship with Him (1 Corinthians 1:9).
- ❏ There are many "lords" in the world, but only "one Lord" (Jesus Christ) to whom men are to give allegiance for the purpose of salvation (Acts 4:12).
- ❏ There are many "faiths" in the world, but only "one faith" that defines God's expectations for those who wish to be saved by Him (Romans 1:17).
- ❏ There are many "baptisms" that are performed for various reasons, but there is only "one baptism" which the Spirit commands of those who wish to be born of God.
- ❏ There are many "gods" in the world, but only one God who holds the power of life and salvation (1 Corinthians 8:5-6).

In other words, there is a consistency between what Paul said in Ephesians 4:5 and what is taught elsewhere in the New Testament *and* practiced among those who call upon the name of the Lord for salvation. Two or more baptisms would create a division among those who are called by God—a division not only of doctrine, but also of method.  Furthermore, if there is only "one baptism," then this forbids creating a "new" or "alternate" baptism method (such as sprinkling or pouring rather than immersing) for special circumstances.  Christ has established the terms for admission into His church, and no one has the authority to alter or amend those terms.

## What Are the Right Reasons?

Water baptism is the "one baptism" that Christ requires for admission into His church.  But even with this understanding, people may be baptized for reasons other than what would be appropriate for those seeking salvation in Christ.  Just because the method is correct does not mean that the intention is automatically correct.  For example, some of the Pharisees and Sadducees came to John the Baptist to be baptized by him, but he would not permit this.  Their attitude was entirely inappropriate; they were seeking baptism for the wrong reason.  John's baptism was meant to accompany one's genuine repentance, but these men refused to repent (Matthew 3:5-9).[73] For them, baptism was for a different purpose than what God intended it to be.  The outward response was correct; the inward response was lacking altogether.

So it is today with respect to one's baptism as a response to apostolic teaching.  A person may pursue the right instruction but with an insufficient or incomplete reason.  It is also possible to seek baptism with the wrong heart, just as men might preach the right gospel with the wrong intention (Philippians 1:15-17).  For example, a person may want to be baptized only because:

- ❑ **He feels guilty for his sins.**  It is true that baptism is the visible process which symbolizes one's sins being "washed away" (Acts 22:16).  However, it is not true that baptism is to be reduced to a mere salve for one's guilty conscience and nothing more. When people feel overwhelmed with guilt, they may do whatever it takes to make the guilt go away—but not necessarily what needs to be done out of *love for the Lord*. For such people, God is merely a Divine Warden who hands out instructions; He is not a God to be loved, but only an Authority to be obeyed. To "believe in the Lord" means more than just finding relief from personal guilt; it means to surrender one's heart to Him as is expected of all those who desire to "come after" Christ (cf. Matthew 16:24).

- **He is afraid of God's punishment for his sins.** This certainly is *part* of the reason for seeking salvation in God—after all, we want to be "saved" from *something very bad*. Yet, baptism cannot be *only* for escaping punishment; there must be something more than this involved. Nearly every mention of "the wrath of God" in the New Testament is countered with a reference to God's love for man and man's reciprocating love for God. In other words, God *will* destroy those who are disobedient, but He will also destroy those who fail to love Him, regardless of their technical obedience to specific commands. God's wrath should motivate us to move away from our present situation; God's love should motivate us to obey and draw near to Him.

- **He feels pressure from peers, family members, or parents who have already been baptized.** In this case, "baptism" is intended to be equivalent to salvation, but it is instead a mere desire to conform to other people's will rather than God's. Someone may be baptized simply to escape other people's constant hounding ("When are you going to be baptized?" or "Why haven't you been baptized yet?"), which translates to, "What is your *problem*? There must be something wrong with you for taking this long." People may mean well, but this does not always lead to appropriate encouragement. Or, the person being baptized may not be hounded at all, but is simply overcome with the guilt of non-conformity (as he sees it). One is active pressure from others ("You must do this!"); the other is passive pressure from within ("I can't let these people down"). In either case, his baptism is not necessarily out of love for God or obedience to His Word, but an avoidance of shame or further harassment from others.

- ❑ **He is "of age."** This (often) refers to a young person who has "grown up in the church"—a phrase that is entirely misleading—and is expected to be baptized when he reaches a certain age. That child's parents are usually the one's pushing for their son or daughter's baptism, but it may be that other members of the church can be just as vocal, insistent, or outright intimidating. Usually, the fear is that if a teenager is not baptized, he stands in jeopardy of losing his soul. If he *is* of age—that is, if he is capable of making an adult decision to serve the Lord for the rest of his life—then this jeopardy may be very real. However, being baptized just because he feels pressured by family or church members does not change his status before God: he may believe in Him in a general sense, but he is not yet the *kind* of believer that He seeks. Thus, his baptism will be one of formality or conformity, not an expression of faith in God and His love. Instead, he needs to be baptized because of his own faith in God's ability to save him, not because everyone else thinks it is a good idea. Being "of age" can never be a replacement for one's genuine faith in the Lord.

❑ **He wants to get everyone off of his back.** This is essentially a restatement of several of the above scenarios, but cuts to the chase. Those who are being unduly pressured to conform will either leave altogether or will bow to that pressure and do whatever it takes to alleviate it. This is hardly the kind of heart that Christ wants. In this particular case, however, serving Christ is not even this person's objective.

❑ **He wants some form of attention or financial assistance.** I have seen this happen on a number of occasions. A person "comes forward" during the invitation, offers a tearful plea for prayers, and requests to be baptized. Yet, he is hardly dried off from his immersion before asking for "benevolence" for rent, to pay his electric bill, or other mundane concerns. Whether or not he receives this money, it is extremely unlikely that we will ever see him again—he is already on his way to find another bunch of patsies like ourselves. We will withhold comment on what we think of someone using God's church for that person's own con games. We can say, however, that one's baptism under those circumstances is entirely useless.

Frauds and scammers aside, it is safe to say that no one has a perfect understanding of baptism when he *is* baptized. Yet, if there are right reasons to be baptized, there must be wrong reasons as well. Hopefully the comments above have adequately defined some of these wrong (or insufficient) reasons. Now we want to focus on the *right* reasons for the "one baptism" that God seeks of believers. This list is short and simple, since one's conversion to God is itself not meant to be a complex matter.

The right reasons for a person to be baptized are because:
- ❑ He wants to obey God, and God has *commanded* that he be baptized as a necessary demonstration of this obedience.
- ❑ He wants to become a disciple of Christ—a Christian— and Christ's own instruction requires that he (for his part) be baptized in order to accomplish this.
- ❑ He wants to be "in Christ"—that is, in Christ's spiritual church—and baptism is the act that indicates his new membership in the body of Christ.
- ❑ He wants to be "born of God," and his part in this process is his own baptism.
- ❑ He wants his sins to be forgiven ("washed away"), and baptism is the necessary means by which this is done.
- ❑ He wants to be saved, and baptism is an established doctrine for and an essential part of the salvation process. "In reality, all reasons given in the New Testament for the design of baptism boil down to the **same point**: baptism is the dividing line between being lost and being saved. If the recipient of baptism does not **understand** that, he has not been baptized in a manner that pleases God."[74]

These points provide a sufficient case for why a person should be baptized. A person does not have to take a special class, endure a three-month probation period, learn a catechism, seek the approval of a church board, or go through any formal counseling. He simply has to understand the seriousness of his decision to follow Christ, and the means by which this commitment is historically and publicly declared.

While the baptism candidate's knowledge will certainly be limited (for now), he is not acting blindly or out of ignorance. He knows enough in order to make an intelligent and sincere

# Being Born of God

decision to obey the Lord, and he does so. This is likely the situation with many of the cases of conversion in Acts—and millions of other situations since then. Our present study is a deep investigation into the subject of baptism, but not every person has this opportunity when the Word of God convicts his heart and compels him to act. What he really needs is sincerity, humility, love for God, a desire to obey Him no matter what, and an understanding of his decision to become a Christian.

## Summary Thoughts

The "one baptism" is not something that any of us can define apart from or in contradiction to Scripture. Whatever *we* determine is the "one baptism" must be what God has *already* determined in His Word. This conclusion cannot be something so difficult or mysterious, either, that only someone with a seminary degree can figure it out. The New Testament was not written for seminary students or clerics; it was written so that every person could "read and understand" its message and respond rightly to it.

Just because God recognizes only *one* baptism does not mean that others do not exist. Instead, it means that regardless of their existences, participating in them does not change a person's spiritual status with God. Submitting to a baptism that He does not require may make a person *feel* clean, righteous, pious, or saved, but this does not mean that he has actually *become* any of these. God is the One who imparts salvation, and thus He is the One who determines the conditions—as well as who is sincere in meeting those conditions—for salvation. If a person will not submit to the "one baptism" that God requires, then he is not acting in obedience but is seeking something else.

What God seeks above all is a heart that yearns to worship Him "in spirit and truth" (cf. John 4:23-24).[75] He longs for each of us to set aside our pride, personal agendas, emotional baggage, adherence to man-made religion—even our primary devotion to those whom we love—and serve Him above all else. This is an attitude that must be present in our heart when we come to Him, but admittedly it takes a lifetime to fully appreciate and master. Given all that we have studied so far, it is clear that the person who genuinely seeks God in open and honest faith will not hesitate to comply with the "one baptism" in order to enter into a covenant relationship with Him.

# Part Two:
## Challenges to Baptism

# Chapter Eight:
# The Thief on the Cross

If there is one scenario that is brought up more than any other as "proof" that baptism is not required for salvation, it is that of "the thief on the cross." Despite all of the passages that defend the necessity of baptism in the New Testament, this one citation—and those that appear similar to it—allegedly overrides or nullifies all of them. With a single sweep of the hand, so to speak, this one argument is thought to reduce baptism to a mere symbolic gesture and nothing more.

This citation refers to Jesus' ordeal on the cross in which He forgave a dying man of his sins and promised that his soul would be saved that very day (Luke 23:39-43). This man had been a thief and was crucified alongside Jesus as a direct result of this crime (Matthew 27:38). Yet, he had a change of heart toward his criminal life and a sincere conviction about Jesus as he underwent his own slow and torturous execution. He rebuked a fellow thief who was being crucified on the other side of Jesus and had been sneering at Jesus' claim to be the Christ. Then he said, "Jesus, remember me when You come in Your kingdom!" And Jesus responded, "Truly I say to you, today you shall be with Me in Paradise." And thus, we have a man who became a Christian and was added to Christ's church *without being baptized*—an action sanctioned by the Son of God Himself! And since this is true, then no one *needs* to be baptized for salvation—end of story. Right?

Wrong. There is nothing incorrect with Luke's account—that is not the problem. We should have no doubt that Jesus really did grant forgiveness to this man, who was a Jew being executed by the Romans just like Jesus was. We should also have no doubt that this man truly was saved that very day and upon his death was ushered into glory in the hereafter—the Paradise of God's world (cf. 2 Corinthians 12:2-4). Yet, it is a huge and unfounded leap to conclude that this man became a *Christian* in the process, and was added to Christ's *church*. The evidence for this is altogether missing, and such a conclusion contradicts all the evidence that we *do* have. It is yet another huge and unfounded leap to presume that, since this man was allegedly saved in this way, therefore it nullifies everything that Christ's own apostles later commanded by inspiration of the Holy Spirit. Something is very wrong with this argument, if indeed it can be called an argument at all. But you should not take my word for this. Instead, let the Scriptures speak for themselves.

## Consistency, Not Contradiction

One of the persistent errors of modern evangelicalism (for example) is that Jesus had the authority to speak and act *above* the Law of Moses. For example, when Jesus gave His so-called "sermon on the mount" (Matthew 5 – 7) and used His "You have heard it said…but I say to you" formula, some believe He was re-writing the Law to accommodate the Christian religion. This is simply not true. In fact, at the *beginning* of that "sermon," Jesus declared that His intention was to *uphold* the Law, not redefine or abolish it. It was the Law of Moses—the Jewish Law to which all Israelites were bound *by covenant* to keep—under which Jesus Himself was born, lived, and died (Galatians 4:4). It was the Law of Moses that justified Jesus as a perfect man: when the Scripture says that He did not sin (1 Peter 2:22), it was *this Law* that He did not sin against. He lived and died as a perfect, law-abiding Jew. He could not be found worthy or obedient in any other way. If He had broken the Law in any way—and teaching *against* the Law would be breaking it—then this would have undermined His ability to be our Savior. It would have also contradicted His own declaration that He would *not* teach against it.

With this thought in mind, we cannot impose a different scenario upon the circumstances of His death and assume that He created a *new* condition for salvation other than what was already required of every Jew. In other words, we cannot assume that He could unilaterally and arbitrarily *violate* the Law of Moses in order to save anyone. His pronouncement of salvation to this Jewish criminal on the cross, then, was not in conflict with the Law, but was—and had to be—in full agreement with it. This criminal also lived and died under the Law, and thus he could not be saved by some other means unless or until that Law was fulfilled and a new law was established. He was, after all, under Israel's covenant with God; he could not break *that* covenant and enter into a *new* covenant at the same time. This not only is illogical, but it is unbiblical.

What all this means is: the thief on the cross was not saved as a *Christian* under a "new covenant" made alive by the blood of Christ, but as a *Jew* under the Law of Moses.[76] Jesus, with the authority He possessed *as* Christ (i.e., the Jews' Messiah), certainly had the authority to impart forgiveness to those who sought it in faith, but He did so as a perfect and infallible *keeper* of the Law, not as a *usurper* of it. As the Son of God, He had the right to judge a man's heart accurately because He knew the hearts of all men (John 2:24-25). He knew, then, that this thief's heart was genuine and his faith sincere, and so He forgave Him according to the terms and conditions of his covenant relationship with God.

## False Premises Lead to False Conclusions

John MacArthur is one of the best-known evangelical ministers in America. He is a prolific author and speaker, and his messages reach millions of people every week. MacArthur is also strongly opposed to baptism having anything to do with the actual salvation of someone's soul (or so he says). On his "Grace to You" website, he writes:

> Perhaps the most convincing refutation of the view that baptism is necessary for salvation are those who were saved apart from baptism. The penitent woman (Luke 7:37-50), the paralytic man (Matthew 9:2), the publican (Luke 18:13-14), and the thief on the cross (Luke 23:39-43) all experienced forgiveness of sins apart from baptism. For that matter, we have no record of the apostles' being baptized, yet Jesus pronounced them clean of their sins (John 15:3—note that the Word of God, not baptism, is what cleansed them).[77]

Not only does MacArthur employ the "thief on the cross" argument, but he also extrapolates the erroneous premises of that argument to include *everyone* whose sins Jesus forgave. Since all such people were forgiven of their sins without baptism, therefore baptism is unnecessary for salvation. Yet, the reasons that make the thief on the cross' situation incomparable to ours are the same that make all these other situations incomparable. The people that MacArthur mentions were all under a different covenant, different law, and different expectations than any person could possibly be under today. This would be like trying to naturalize a foreigner to a nation that did not (yet) exist—it is not only illogical, but it simply cannot be done.

Furthermore, MacArthur confuses the act of forgiveness itself with that of becoming a Christian. He either assumes that those people whose sins Jesus forgave became Christians, or that those whose sins He forgives today become something *other* than Christians. If all that is needed to become a Christian is to have one's sins forgiven, then all the ancient Israelites back to the time of Moses became Christians when God forgave their sins according to the Law (Leviticus 4:20, 26, 31, 5:10, 13, et al). According to this line of reasoning, Christians existed some 1,500 years before Christ was born, died on the cross, or established His church! Of course, this is impossible, but it is exactly what MacArthur (and many others) proposes when he makes forgiveness of sins the only criterion necessary for becoming a Christian. And if these people that he mentions—the penitent woman, the paralytic, the publican, etc.—did *not* become Christians, then his entire premise is completely undermined. What is the point of bringing up such examples if they have nothing to do with what *is* required to become a Christian?

It is absolutely true that God's forgiveness is necessary in order for one to become a Christian (Acts 2:38). It is absolutely *not* true that every person in the Bible whose sins were forgiven automatically became a Christian. No one could have become a Christian until Jesus had fulfilled Israel's covenant with God, kept the Law of Moses perfectly, and given Himself as a ransom for all who would call upon Him for salvation (Mark 10:45). With His authority as Messiah, He was thus able to pronounce people "forgiven" or "clean" in anticipation of that sacrifice, just as God did with the ancient Israelites in Moses' day.

Becoming a Christian—one who has been purchased with the blood of Christ (1 Corinthians 6:19-20) and lives by the name of Christ (Galatians 2:20)—necessarily requires that Christ's church actually exists. One cannot be added to the body of Christ (His church) if there is not yet any "body," and if Christ has not yet been made its "head" (Ephesians 1:22-23). Thus, arguments that maintain that the thief on the cross became a Christian must overlook or purposely ignore these important points.

Incidentally, the declaration that baptism is not necessary for salvation because the apostles were pronounced "clean" by Jesus is completely unfounded. We do not have a record of the twelve apostles being baptized; yet, we do have a record of what it takes to become a Christian, which necessarily includes baptism.[78] Since it is the apostles themselves that provided that information, it would be hypocritical and unwarranted for them to be excused from the very same instruction that applied to everyone else, especially when *they* were to teach everything that was first commanded to *them* (Matthew 28:20). The apostles were just as in need of being added to Christ's church as all other sinners-turned-believers. There is no good reason to assume that they had not conformed to the same requirements as did the thousands of other believers in Acts. The silence of Scripture in one particular instance does not constitute an authority to create doctrine *out* of that silence, especially when God *has* spoken definitively on the matter elsewhere.

## Summary Thoughts

The "thief on the cross" argument has been used for quite some time now, and yet it remains just as weak and misapplied as ever. It is rather presumptuous to think that we can absolve ourselves of all of God's instructions in the New Testament concerning salvation based upon the desperate appeal to one remote example taken completely out of context. Certainly there are some who have used this argument because they did not (yet) know the facts, but the facts have not been hidden, either. In other cases, we see those who are forced into accepting unfounded conclusions simply to accommodate their predetermined religious agenda. In some cases, these conclusions only work if you buy into the premise upon which their religion was founded; in other cases, they simply do not work at all.

If you have appealed to the "thief on the cross" premise to justify *your* salvation apart from baptism, know this: your argument does not work and will never work. It does not matter how many people—despite their popularity or credentials—insist otherwise: it still does not work. If you have tried to become a Christian through *any* manner other than what the revealed Word of God *does* teach, then you are not yet a Christian. Thinking that you are a Christian does not make you one; conforming to man-made or denominational expectations for becoming a Christian does not remove your responsibility to the Word. No one is saved apart from God's forgiveness of his sins, yet no one today receives this forgiveness apart from baptism.

On the other hand, if you have been immersed in water, this *by itself* does not make you a Christian, either. Baptism is one critical factor in the conversion process; it is not the only one. Those who equate baptism with salvation are just as much in error as those who think the thief on the cross became a Christian. Baptism is rendered useless (as a demonstration of obedience) if indeed it has not been offered *in* obedience, but only as an empty ritual or a response to peer pressure. In other words, "baptism now saves you" (1 Peter 3:21), but only the baptism that submits entirely to God's Word.

Thankfully, the thief on the cross *was indeed* saved, but you cannot be saved exactly like he was. There is something different being asked of you than was ever required of him. His situation is not your situation—and it never will be. You know far *more* and far *better* than he ever knew, and with knowledge and privilege come more responsibility, not less. His and your situation will never be an apples-to-apples comparison, since so much has changed since that man was put upon his cross. He died as an Israelite under a covenant that no longer exists; you must choose to *live* under a "new covenant" that has been made alive by the blood of Christ (cf. Matthew 26:27-28). The only way to enter into this covenant is to be born of God, and the only way to be born of God is through *water* and the *Spirit* (cf. John 3:5). It cannot be any other way.

# Chapter Nine:
# Hypothetical Arguments

A "hypothetical" is basically a made-up scenario that intends to test the strength or logic of a given argument. For example, imagine that you say, "It is wrong to violate traffic laws under any condition." In response to this, I might say, "Suppose a man is in desperate need of life-saving medical attention, and you are the only one able to drive him to the hospital. Will you place obedience to traffic laws and speed limits as being more important than this man's life? Will you not exceed the speed limit, for example, in order to get him to the hospital as soon as possible?" Of course, there is no such situation pending, but I am simply intending to test the validity of your argument.

This is the crucial characteristic of hypotheticals: they are *imaginary* and *artificially-constructed* scenarios. (Even if a hypothetical argument is based upon an actual past incident, that incident is still being introduced as a *new* possibility, not a present-day, real-time scenario.) What I did was produce—out of my own imagination—a scenario that puts your belief to the test. The fact is, you and I are not faced with a man requiring life-saving medical attention, and you are not driving anyone to a hospital. I constructed this scenario, however, in order to test the integrity of your argument. We know that laws are not to be violated—that is why they are called "laws." But your (alleged) modifier of "under any condition" compelled me to see whether or not this is really the case in every context.

In itself, a hypothetical can be a useful tool. It can show the strengths or weaknesses of a given argument up front. Or, it can force the one making the argument to revise his premise in order to produce a much stronger one than before—or abandon it altogether. In the above scenario, having heard my hypothetical argument, you might say, "Well, except in the case of *extreme emergencies*, it is wrong to violate traffic laws." You modified your argument because of the weakness that I exposed within it. In other words, you were on the right track—and you meant well—but you created a limitation that does not appear logical or defensible. It is far more logical to argue that saving a human life is superior to obeying man-made laws. (You might debate that, and then I might debate the definition of "extreme emergencies," but at least we are getting closer to a better argument than when we began.)

The point is that hypotheticals have their place in sharpening our arguments (or beliefs) about one thing or another. They can be helpful, but they are also limited in what they can accomplish. For example, while a hypothetical may test whether or not a personal theory is legitimate, it cannot become the new standard by which all other things are measured. In the above scenario, you argued that it *is* wrong to violate traffic laws, which is generally true. My exception to the rule, contrived as it was, does not take the place of that general truth. If I argue, "It is permissible to violate traffic laws in order to save a human life," that must never translate to, "Since a condition *does exist* for which traffic laws can be justifiably violated, therefore they do not have to be obeyed *at all*." I cannot make laws out of hypotheticals; furthermore, I cannot use a hypothetical situation that has no bearing on me *personally* in order to determine *my* personal future course of action. Likewise, I cannot impose a hypothetical situation that *does* bear upon me personally ("This is what *I* would do") upon a universal audience ("Therefore, this is what *everyone* should do from now on"). In other words, unless I am confronted with having to drive over the speed limit, etc., to race a dying man to the hospital, I am going to obey all traffic laws. Or, even if I *am* confronted with that situation, this does not justify a *universal* non-conformity to traffic laws because of what I did under that extreme situation.

The reason why I am bringing up hypotheticals in a discussion about biblical doctrine is because people use these in a manner that is not always appropriate. If you or I make an argument about something, someone else may expose its weaknesses or fallacies in order to refine our point (or force us to abandon it altogether). After all, we are only human; we make errors in reasoning; we misjudge one thing or another; etc. But when the Holy Spirit makes an argument, it is entirely improper for you or me to put Him to the test to see whether or not He makes sense, or whether His initial point needs to be refined. God's Holy Spirit has no human weaknesses; He does not err in His reasoning; He does not consult with us to see how we might improve His arguments. To create a hypothetical, then, to test the legitimacy of what He has revealed to us (i.e., the Word of God) is tantamount to disbelief in His authority, which is blasphemous. If God says, "Do this thing," and then I say, "That's a good idea, but suppose there is this one situation that appears to make your command unnecessary or inappropriate," I have not humbled myself before Him but have made myself a judge of Him instead.

It is true that there will be situations that we cannot answer, and that are not specifically defined by the letter of the law, so to speak. For example, God told the Israelites not to honor the sabbath and (thus) not do any unnecessary labor on it. Then Moses was confronted with a man who was caught gathering sticks on the sabbath, and he [Moses] brought the matter to God for clarification. God's answer was clear: the man was to be executed by stoning. Until then, no one knew what the punishment would be for violating the sabbath; God's answer provided the necessary instruction (Numbers 15:32-36). In another case, Moses was confronted with a question about inheritance through marriage that was not specifically covered in God's earlier commandments on this subject. He brought the matter before God, and the Lord answered him with specific reference to the ones who had the question (Numbers 36).

In such cases, God could be directly consulted through one of His genuine prophets. In our present case, however, the Word has been "once for all delivered" to mankind (Jude 3), and there are no legitimate prophets who can mediate for us with questions on one thing or another. This means that what we have is *all-sufficient* for what needs to be done; otherwise, God would have provided some other recourse or appeals process in order for us to resolve our dilemmas (real or imagined).

It is necessary to understand, however, that not all questions *need* to be answered, and not all questions are even legitimate to begin with. For example, suppose I say, "I will not believe in Christ's divine conception until God explains to me how the Holy Spirit can make a woman pregnant apart from the natural method of procreation." That is a question that does not *have* to be answered, since I can believe in Christ's divine conception without knowing all the details of it. After all, "faith" believes in God's ability to perform without Him having to explain everything He does (see Romans 4:16-21). If I put a condition upon *my* belief that God did not require of me—"You must answer this question first!"—I am attempting to add to His gospel, not obey it.

There are other questions that we *think* need to be answered, but do not. For example, suppose someone asks, "If God's gospel never reached China (or some other country distant from Palestine) for hundreds of years after it was first revealed, how will He deal with those ancient Chinese people who died having never heard of salvation in Christ?" While this may seem an intriguing question, none of us have to answer it—and it does not change His instruction to those who *have* heard His gospel.[79] What God does with these other people is His business, but we know that He will be merciful, balanced, and infallible in His judgment. There are other questions that we could cite that remain unanswerable, but this does not change what *has* been revealed, or what we *have* been told to do. Similarly, Moses told Israel, "The secret things belong to the LORD our God, but the things revealed belong to us and to our sons forever, that we may observe all the words of this law" (Deuteronomy 29:29). In other words, there are some things that God did not reveal, but we are not to concern ourselves with them. Instead, we are to pay attention to—and obey—those things which He has told us to do.

Yet, suppose someone says, "Because you cannot answer what happened to all those ancient Chinese people who [allegedly] never heard the gospel, therefore I am absolved from having to respond to it myself. After all, I cannot be expected to obey something that others are *not* expected to obey—that isn't fair." This person has put a legally-binding stipulation on the gospel that was not there before and that God is not obligated to honor. This is not an innocent question being asked of God but insinuates that God is being "unfair" to him (and many others).

Furthermore, this person wants you (or God Himself) to prove him wrong based upon a situation that he himself has plucked out of thin air. He (essentially) fabricates a scenario in order to nullify a command, and then dares anyone to question his position. Interestingly, he appeals to what is "fair"—a transcendent standard based on God's righteousness—yet refuses to obey God's command. In a real sense, he implies, "Since God is not being 'fair' with me, I don't have to listen to everything He says—but I still want what He offers." Thus, he absolves himself of all responsibility to the command, yet assumes that God will accept his reasoning and welcome him into heaven anyway.

## Dangerous Methods of Reasoning

We have now laid the groundwork for discussing the application of hypothetical arguments to water baptism. If there is a religious subject that people have tried to re-define, re-invent, or evade altogether through hypothetical reasoning rather than appealing to the teaching of Scripture, this is it. One of the classic examples of this is the alleged "man in the desert" scenario: "Suppose a man is wandering through the desert, hears the Word of God. He believes in the Lord and wants to become a Christian, but there is no water around in order for him to be baptized. Then suddenly the man dies while still in the desert. Are you saying that this man will be lost just because he was not baptized?" To date, I have never heard of a man in this situation, and especially one that would mysteriously learn of the gospel while wandering in the desert (was he carrying a Bible?). This is a contrived, artificially-constructed, completely fabricated situation that is intended to defeat all of "my" arguments (as if I came up with them) concerning the necessity of baptism for salvation. So then, despite all the biblical evidence, instruction, and examples of people being baptized in Scripture in order to be saved, all of this must be scrapped for the sake of this one situation that no one can prove has ever existed.

Not only does this *not* make sense, but it is an extremely dangerous method of reasoning. The one who cites a human-crafted hypothetical in order to counter the authority of Scripture certainly puts himself in a perilous situation. Someone might call this a hypothetical *argument*, but really it is not an argument at all. Technically-speaking, an argument is made up of three major parts: relevant evidence, sound reasoning, and a logical (or inescapable) conclusion based upon proper application of that evidence and reasoning. In the case of the "man in the desert," there is no evidence that this has ever happened, there is nothing sound (or legitimate) about its reasoning, and the conclusion (i.e., baptism is not necessary) is one that is desirable to some, but remains entirely unproved. After all that the New Testament has to say on the subject of water baptism for salvation, there cannot be any sound argument against it. To take what God says and respond with a "Yes, but…" or "Suppose a man in the desert…" scenario does not manifest obedience, but evasion—or sheer defiance.

Yet, to be fair, let's grant the premise of this desert scenario: let's assume that there really *could* be such a man in such a situation. He reads the gospel and believes it; he wants to respond to it—which, the hypothesis implies, actually *does* require baptism!—but there is no water. Then, unexpectedly, he dies before he can obey the command. My first response to this is: Why do I need to address this man's situation, much less bring about a final conclusion concerning his eternal destiny? That is not my business; I do not have any such authority. This situation, if indeed it could ever exist, is one that God alone can answer. If God saves this man without his having been baptized (in his extreme circumstances), then that is His decision. If God does not save this man because he did not show moral responsibility toward Him earlier in his life when he had opportunity to obey Him, then that is His decision. In either case, this is not a situation for which *any* of us can provide a conclusive and binding judgment.

Someone might see this as ducking the question. In reality, I am being more genuine than the person who posed it in the first place. I am admitting that I do not know the answer; I am not pretending otherwise. Yet, it is very likely that the one who posed the question has done so with the idea that *since* I cannot answer the question, *therefore* he has an "argument" that defeats my appeals to Scripture for baptism. Think of what is happening here. Since *I* cannot answer *his* contrived question, therefore *God's* teaching is invalidated. The method of salvation for all men is thus determined by *my* ability (or lack thereof) to answer a certain question!

Where is this person's appeal to Scripture to support his own scenario? Where does it *ever* say in the New Testament that a person ought to be baptized if he can, but if he can't, then it's okay—God will save him anyway? When Jesus said, "UNLESS one is born of water and the Spirit he CANNOT ENTER into the kingdom of God" (emphasis added), how can one reply, "Yes, but if he is *not* born of water because of his special circumstances, he can still enter"? This is brazenly stepping into an area where angels fear to tread.

Remember what we said earlier: we cannot use hypotheticals to nullify or re-write laws—especially *God's* laws. If Jesus commanded people to be baptized in order to become His disciples (Matthew 28:19), then our theoretical situations cannot undermine that instruction. If Peter commanded people to repent and be baptized in order to receive God's forgiveness (Acts 2:38), then clever hypothetical arguments cannot change that command. If Paul had to be baptized to wash away his sins and call upon the name of the Lord (Acts 22:16), then artificially-created stories about people that do not even exist cannot trump that instruction and become the "new" law instead. Yet, this is exactly what the "man in the desert" scenario is meant to do: it attempts to overlook these (and other) appeals to Scripture *and* create a new method of salvation instead. How many cases are there in the New Testament that support this "new" model of salvation—one in which baptism is *not* required because of one's circumstances? The person offering the hypothetical will not find one.

Appeals to hypothetical situations like the one discussed above are almost always based upon an emotional premise, not a logical one. In other words, the person offering the hypothetical is saying, in essence, "How can you be so cold and uncompassionate so as to deny this man's salvation just because he doesn't do what *you* teach?!" This is not an appeal to sound reasoning; it is instead an attempt to make me out to be a heartless monster who imposes his personal convictions on the eternal destinies of other people. This is not only an emotional vent against my alleged character, but it completely misrepresents the situation in order to *make* me this heartless monster. The reason for this is because it is far easier to disagree with a heartless monster than it is the commands of God. If what I believe is disagreeable to a person, then all he has to do is "prove" that I do not care about people's souls, and he feels justified in condemning my beliefs (and allegedly vindicating his own). If what I believe is consistent with what God has taught, however, then his complaint is really not with me at all, but is with God Himself. Thus, the hypothetical is meant to show how uncompassionate and absurd "my" beliefs are in order to distract attention from the reality of the situation, which is what God has commanded in His Word. The fact is that even if I did not believe in baptism for salvation, God still teaches this to be so. My agreement or disagreement changes nothing. Truth can be ignored, suppressed, and misrepresented, but it cannot be killed—and it simply will not go away.

### More Stories

There are other hypothetical situations that I have heard over the years. These all have the same premise: they are purposely posed in order to stump me (as if that meant anything in itself) or lure me into making a statement that reveals me to be a cold, heartless monster (which, even if it were true, does not change the need for baptism). Here is a sampling of these:

- ❏ "Suppose a man believes in the gospel, and wants to be baptized in obedience to it. On the way to his baptism, he is killed in a car accident. Are you saying that he will be eternally lost because he never got dunked in water? (You heartless monster!)"
- ❏ "Suppose a man hits his head on the baptistery and is killed immediately on his way down into the water. Are you saying that, since he was not technically baptized while he was alive, therefore his soul is forever lost?"
- ❏ "Suppose a man lives in a country where Christianity is illegal. After hearing the gospel and wanting to obey it in baptism, a group of Christians try to take him secretly to a place to be baptized. Along the way, they are all captured and sentenced to life in prison. The prison will not allow the man to be baptized. Are you saying that he is not a Christian, even though he was prevented

from being baptized due to circumstances beyond his control?"[80]

- ❑ "Suppose there is a primitive tribe of people living in the Amazon who have never heard the gospel of Christ, and therefore could not have learned about baptism. Are you saying that they will all be lost because they were never baptized for the remission of sins?"
- ❑ "Suppose an Eskimo learns of the gospel in the middle of winter, but all the accessible water is frozen, and he has to wait for the summer thaws to be immersed. Are you saying he cannot become a Christian until then?"
- ❑ "Suppose a man is on his deathbed, and someone teaches him the gospel and he believes in the Lord Jesus. However, he is too physically weak to be baptized in water. Are you saying that he will be eternally lost anyway? God would never be so cruel—but apparently *you* are, you heartless monster!"

What is interesting about all of these scenarios—including the "man in the desert" one—is that they all *acknowledge* that baptism is essential for salvation. The problem, then, is *not* that these people fail to understand the connection between baptism and salvation. Rather, they *do* see it, but they also *resist* it because they believe there will be exceptions to the rule. Thus, these people wish to abdicate their responsibility to be baptized because of some extreme and contrived situation that (maybe) happened to someone else. Even if I *did* say, "Yes, in all of those cases, the individuals you mentioned *will* be eternally lost," this does not consign those people to their doom. My decision cannot compare to or supersede God's decision. My decision—even if I am correct—cannot take the place of God's final say regarding a person's soul.

## What Is That to You?

My question to the one posing the hypothetical is: What does this fictitious person's situation have to do with *you*? If you have access to the Word of God *and* opportunity to obey it, then it is your moral responsibility to respond to that Word in obedience *regardless* of what anyone else says or does. A person cannot escape his responsibility to God by deferring to someone else, or to someone else's situation. Whatever God's Holy Spirit says to *you* in His Word is what you are expected to obey—and it is the same thing He says to *me*. For example, Jesus told Peter to "Follow Me," but Peter turned and pointed to John and asked, "Lord, and what about this man?" To this, Jesus replied, "If I want him to remain until I come, what is that to you? You follow Me!" (John 21:18-21).

This same scenario applies in principle to all of us: what does it matter what Jesus will do to those whose situations are rare, exceptional, and seemingly problematic? The *rest* of us are told to listen and obey Him regardless. The instruction is clear: "Baptism now saves you" (1 Peter 3:21), therefore *you* will not be saved otherwise. Someone says, "Yes, but what about this other guy...?"—*what is that to you?* You have been told what to do. You now have the opportunity either to obey the instruction or reject it. You do *not* have the opportunity to change the instruction without serious consequence (cf. Galatians 1:8).

## Summary Thoughts

As we have discussed, there is a time for hypothetical situations to be used. Defining (or amending) God's Scripture is not one of those times, however. God alone possesses the authority to establish the requirements for salvation; this cannot be changed or undermined by any human authority, and especially not by an appeal to human fiction. If there really are exceptions to what God has instructed, then it is God who will decide what those exceptions are. It is not our place to impose our exceptions on His instructions. We cannot define "special circumstances," whether ours or anyone else's, by our own criteria. Or, if there will be no exceptions to these instructions *regardless* of one's circumstances, then that is His to uphold. No amount of emotionally-driven appeals can overcome His will.

    Biblical doctrine bears upon all of us equally. There are not some people who are to be *more* obedient than others, but we are *all* to be obedient to the best of our given ability. Likewise, there are not some people who are allowed to be *disobedient* while the rest of us have to be obedient. God makes no provision for disobedience, and His grace will not be given to those who refuse to demonstrate their faith in Him and His Word. In other words, we cannot create artificial scenarios of people whose situations seem impossible to answer in order to excuse our own obedient response to Scripture. We are all in need of the same salvation; we are all given the same message; we will all answer to the same God. Baptism is not something separated from that message of salvation, but is an integral part of it. Even if a "man in the desert" scenario did exist, it does not change the message that you and I are expected to read and understand. We know too much to claim ignorance.

# Chapter Ten:
# Infant Baptism

The practice of baptizing infants for the purpose of salvation has been around for a very long time. There are mentions of this even in the writings of early church "fathers" from the 2nd century AD onward.[81] The Roman (Catholic) Church has always maintained that infants need to be baptized. Even many of the Reformers, though they strongly protested the teachings and policies of the Roman Church, still clung to infant baptism. Most of the denominations that came out of the Reformation (16th century) also continue the practice of baptizing babies and young children even to this day.

Obviously, those churches that practice infant baptism allegedly do not seem to have a problem with associating baptism with salvation.[82] The reason why this subject is in this section of the book—a section that deals with challenges to baptism—is because infant baptism oversteps the purpose *and* application of what the gospel actually teaches on baptism. Simply put, there is not a single instance in the New Testament of babies *or* young children being baptized in order to become Christians. Not only this, but there is nothing in apostolic teaching that supports this practice. Amazingly, proponents of infant baptism are usually willing to concede these points, yet go on to provide conjectural "reasons" why this should be done anyway.[83] While we cannot determine whether or not those people's motives are genuine, in the end, this does not matter. Their *reasoning* is seriously flawed, even if their intentions are good (and we will give them all benefit of doubt that their intentions *are* good).

Keep in mind that dealing with salvation is neither a minor nor subjective concern. In discussing how souls must be saved, we are also necessarily implying how souls (that are *not* saved) will be lost. People who *think* they are saved but are not (because they chose to base their salvation upon human opinions rather than God's truth) will be lost, unless they listen to God rather than men. If this were not true, then we really never needed God to tell us anything—we could obtain our salvation on whatever we choose to believe. This is clearly not the case. Thus, the claim that an infant is "saved" because he has been baptized is a most serious one, and this must be supported with God-given evidence, not personal feelings, conjecture, or church policy. Leading a young child to believe that he is already "saved" when there is no biblical proof of this puts a stumbling block in his path—and Jesus has strong words for those who do this (Matthew 18:4-6).

Such warnings have not stopped untold generations of parents, church leaders, and religious zealots everywhere from supporting this doctrine, however. If a practice cannot be intelligently defended from the New Testament, then it should be abandoned altogether. One would think that those familiar with the Bible, of all people, would understand this. Yet, man-made teachings posing as the "doctrine of God" continue to persist in many churches, and sadly, relatively few people seem very concerned about this.

Arguments that are provided in defense of infant baptism range from the highly questionable to the absolutely absurd. Most of them descend into sheer emotionalism, as though refusing to baptize a child is tantamount to barbaric and heartless cruelty ("How can you *possibly* deny this child his salvation!" or "We dare not imperil this child's faith by delaying his baptism until he is older!"). Nonetheless, it seemed inappropriate for me to ignore this doctrine in light of our present study. Furthermore, there is nothing barbaric or heartless about teaching only what God actually *says* about salvation rather than what people *want* God to say. In fact, this is what teaching "sound words" is all about (cf. 1 Timothy 6:3-5).

### Attempts to Defend Infant Baptism

The best place to start our investigation into the subject of infant baptism is in the New Testament. If Christ wanted us to baptize babies, then He would have said so—or, we would have the record of His apostles teaching this. We should also see actual examples of this being done as an implementation of the instruction (like we do with adult baptism). Nothing of the sort exists, however, so there is nothing to cite in the form of teaching or example. Instead, supporters of this doctrine usually argue from what they claim is "necessary" inference: first, there are a few cases where entire "households" were baptized (Acts 11:14, 16:15, 16:31-33, 18:8, and 1 Corinthians 1:16); second, Jesus blessed children [lit., babes in arms], and this allegedly constitutes an authority in itself; and third, Jesus includes infants when He commanded that "all nations" be baptized (Matthew 28:19). We will examine each of these positions in the order in which they were just given.

Appealing to the use of "household" as a doctrinal authority for the salvation of infants and young children is weak and subjective at best. People today often think of their own "households," in which they include their children, and then impose this present-day perspective upon scenarios mentioned in Scripture. Therefore, infants and children were baptized as part of every "household" that obeyed the gospel—or so the argument goes. Yet, while the ancient concept of "household" by itself *could* include infants and children in its most general sense, this is not its natural usage in Scripture. Instead, it often referred to the immediate and extended family that lived under one roof, and often included anyone else that put himself or herself under the authority of the *head* of the house (slaves, servants, boarders, friends, etc.). The "members of a man's household" (cf. Matthew 10:36) was understood to mean the *adult* members, not little children, and *never* infants. Beasley-Murray writes, "Luke, in writing these narratives [in Acts], does not have in view infant members of the families. His language cannot be pressed to extend to them. He has in mind ordinary believers and uses language applicable only to them. Abuse of it leads to the degradation of the Scripture."[84]

In 1 Timothy 3:4-5, 12, when Paul speaks of candidates for elders or deacons, he mentions that they must be good managers of their households, then mentions children separately. "Household" comes from *oikos*, which has a variety of meanings ranging from the literal house to a general familial relationship, including the church itself (1 Timothy 3:15). The manager (or "ruler") of a household has charge over all the business of that house—lit., its "economy" (from *oikonomos*, "the law of the house")—as well as his own children.[85] Ruling one's house requires managerial and leadership abilities; overseeing one's children requires skills of teaching and compassion (Ephesians 6:4); being an elder or deacon requires both sets of skills.

The point here is that we cannot be dogmatic on who is or is not included in "household" as the word is used in the New Testament. This means we cannot create a *doctrine of salvation* out of a word whose actual meaning and application remain inconclusive. In order to mandate the baptism of infants

*Being Born of God*

or young children, we must *know for certain* that this was the teaching *and* practice of the early church under the personal direction of Christ-appointed apostles. Given what we have to work with, however, this is an impossible argument to defend. We cannot teach assumptions as though they were facts, and we certainly cannot base salvation on human assumption rather than the direct teaching of God.

We turn our attention now to Jesus' having blessed little children. There is no question that Jesus had compassion for these "little ones." People brought children to Him to bless, and He did so—even to the chagrin of His own disciples (Mark 10:13-16). Yet, turning an occasion of His having blessed little children into a doctrinal authority for infant *baptism for salvation in Christ* is completely unwarranted and indefensible. The two things have nothing in common with each other, except for the literal involvement of both Jesus and children. Jesus conferred blessings upon these little ones; He did not make disciples out of them. Jesus showed regard for and compassion upon these children; He did not "save" them. If anyone wishes to argue that these children whom Jesus blessed became *Christians*, he does not understand that this would have been impossible. (Remember our earlier chapter on the "thief on the cross": no one could become a Christian until the church had been established, which could not happen until Jesus ascended into heaven [Acts 2:33]. Even so, we have no actual instance in Scripture of an infant or child becoming a Christian *after* Jesus' church began.)

Jesus blessed these Jewish children in His role as the Jewish Messiah (Christ) of the Jewish nation. He had the authority and responsibility to do so. Jesus did not make these children disciples (Christians), and we cannot cite His example of blessing these children as an authority for infant baptism. To do so demonstrates a great and unfounded leap of logic as well as a misunderstanding of biblical interpretation. This does not stop people from committing both errors, however. One Catholic blogger, for example, says:

> There is a strong case that this practice goes back to the New Testament and that even Jesus himself baptized infants. When He said in John 3 that it is necessary to be born again of water and the Holy Spirit to enter the Kingdom of God, he surely meant to include infants for in Matthew 19:14 he says "the kingdom of heaven is for such." That he meant infants here is clear because the parallel passage in Luke says "they brought to him also the infants, that he might touch them." The Greek words *brephe* and *prospheron*, used in these passages, both refer to babes in arms. St. Paul tells us in Colossians that baptism is to take the place of circumcision. Since circumcision was applied to infants, so is baptism.[86]

First of all, the presumption that Jesus baptized children has been plucked out of thin air. This is sheer human imagination at work, not Bible study.[87] Secondly, the writer assumes that since circumcision applied to infants, then so must baptism, since Paul used one to talk about the other (in Colossians 2:11-12). If we are going to follow that logic to its natural end, then this would mean that we can only baptize *male Israelite children on the eighth day of their lives*, since this is what Paul literally alluded to (Leviticus 12:3). According to this manner of interpretation, female children, male children younger or older than eight days old, or Gentile children, are all ineligible for baptism. With all due respect to the blogger, his proposed argument really is not

## Being Born of God

an argument at all, but is a futile attempt to support his church's doctrine, not an attempt to let Scripture speak for itself. Yet, his manner of reasoning is, unfortunately, typical. In fact, it is likely that many people will not even question the logic or conclusions of this man because they have already bought into his *emotional position*.

The kingdom of heaven does indeed belong to those who are child-like in their faith and humility (cf. Matthew 18:1-3), but this will never mean that literal children need to be baptized in order to become Christians. These two concepts are incompatible with each other; they cannot be forced together without legitimate supporting evidence, and the New Testament does not provide a shred of such evidence. If there is an area in which we must be very careful to be both clear and accurate, it is in the matter of salvation. So far, the case for infant baptism is neither clear nor accurate; on the contrary, it is entirely lacking in substance.

With regard to children being included in the "all nations" of Matthew 28:19, one must ask the question: since when does "nations" include a separation of ages and gender? This is not how it is used in the Bible, and it is not even how the word is used today. "Nation" is consistently used in Scripture to describe a collective people of a given regional or ethnic identity (Israelites, Edomites, Assyrians, Babylonians, etc.), not people of different ages or gender (see Mark 13:8, Luke 7:5, 23:2, John 11:50-52, et al). Yet, below is a good example of the "nations" argument in defense of infant baptism:

> Many raise the objection: "There is not a single example of infant baptism in the New Testament, nor is there any command to do so. Therefore Christians should not baptize babies."

> But Jesus has commanded infant baptism. In Matthew 28:19 He says, "Go, therefore, and make disciples of all nations, baptizing them in the name of the Father, and of the Son, and of the Holy Spirit..." Before He ascended, the Lord of the Church commanded us to baptize "all nations," a phrase the Church has always understood to mean "everyone." Matthew 25:31-32 also uses the phrase "all nations" in this way. All nations are to be baptized, regardless of race, color, sex, age, class, or education. Jesus makes no exceptions. He doesn't say, "Baptize all nations except..." Everyone is to be baptized, including infants. If we say that babies are not to be included in Christ's Great Commission, then where will it stop? What other people will we exclude?
>
> It is true that there is no example in Scripture of a baby being baptized. However, to conclude from this that babies are not to be baptized is absurd. Neither are there any specific examples of the elderly being baptized, or teenagers, or little children. Instead we read about men (Acts 2:41; 8:35) women (Acts 16:14-15), and entire households being baptized (Acts 10:24, 47-48; 16:14-15; 16:30-33; 1 Cor. 1:16). The authors of the New Testament documents didn't feel compelled to give examples of every age group or category being baptized. Why should they have? Certainly they understood that "all nations" is all-inclusive.[88]

This kind of reasoning is amazing—and not in a good way. The author of this article admits more than once that he does not have a leg to stand on, yet then boldly contradicts himself and says, "Jesus has commanded infant baptism." This is entirely based upon this person's (and his church's) interpretation of

# Being Born of God

"nations" and absolutely nothing else. He and his church are entitled to their own opinions about this, but God's terms and conditions of salvation have never been left to anyone's opinion. You cannot be saved because of another person's opinion, even your own. Your child cannot become a Christian because of anyone's opinion, including your own. The above quote is not sound doctrine; it is a passionately-held *opinion*, and opinions are not arguments or doctrine.

What Jesus meant is exactly what Peter and Paul both expressed later (Acts 2:5-11, 10:34-35, and Galatians 3:8, for example). "Nations" means the ethnic families of men, or the collective population of various groups of people known by a distinct name. In Acts 2, for example, we have a list of several "nations" all identified by their *national distinction*, not their age groups or gender. Conspicuously absent from Scripture is any definition to support this latter sentiment. Furthermore, think of the reasoning process being offered: "It is true that there is no example in Scripture of a baby being baptized. However, to conclude from this that babies are not to be baptized is absurd." Why is this absurd? If, for example, there is zero evidence for the literal existence of unicorns throughout all of human history, would it be "absurd" to think that unicorns are imaginary animals? This is not an absurdity, but is a clear and inescapable deduction based on relevant evidence and sound reasoning. Likewise, if there is zero evidence for infant baptism in the New Testament, then it is not "absurd" to conclude that the church is not in the business of baptizing babies. Rather, it is an intelligent conclusion.

## Faith Must Be a Personal Decision

The practice of infant baptism not only implies that Christians are *supposed* to be baptizing infants, but that the infants themselves are inherently qualified to *be* baptized. In Acts, there is not a single example of anyone being baptized into Christ against his will or without his knowledge. The conversion process of becoming a Christian is a *voluntary* one, not one that is coerced upon a person. In other words, people *choose* to become Christians—or they choose to reject the opportunity. Thus, people *choose* to be baptized—or they reject baptism, repentance, and all the entrance requirements for a covenant relationship with God altogether. In Acts 2, three thousand people chose to be baptized; perhaps there were just as many who chose *not* to be baptized. Those who were baptized were identified as disciples (of Christ) or Christians; those who did not were identified otherwise. Both groups made a conscious and deliberate choice in the matter.

Biblical teaching is clear: anyone who desires to become a Christian must hear the Word of God and obey it (see 1 Corinthians 15:1-2, Ephesians 1:13, and Colossians 1:5-6, for example). Obviously, an infant cannot fulfill this most basic requirement for salvation. (Even a young child, while he can literally "hear" it, will not be able to fulfill the responsibility that it requires of him.[89]) To get around this, some religions practice a "sponsorship" program in which an adult believer can "sponsor" a given child until he (or she) becomes old enough to accept this responsibility on his own.[90] Yet, this is a teaching that has been plucked out of thin air to accommodate another teaching (infant baptism) that itself has yet to be proved. This practice has zero biblical support or precedent. There are no examples in the New Testament of *anyone* vouching for or taking responsibility for someone else's salvation. Furthermore, the idea of sponsorship undermines the very thing that it claims to uphold: if an infant literally becomes a Christian upon its baptism, then that child must "answer" to God directly, not through a third party. Nonetheless, this practice attempts to address the glaring problem that infant baptism supporters cannot resolve otherwise—i.e., that infant baptism literally sidesteps the need for human faith in conversion.

The point is: if we are going to decide for infants—or children of *any* age—that they should be baptized, then we impose *our* will upon them, and do not allow them to voluntarily put themselves into submission to God's will. In ancient Israel, baby boys were circumcised on the eighth day because their parents already belonged to the nation of God (Israel), not because those children had an understanding of what it meant to live in a covenant relationship with God. Israel's relationship with God was on a *national* level, not an individual one (as far as circumcision was concerned). With regard to one's relationship with Christ, however, the situation is considerably different. Baptism, unlike the circumcision of an infant, is a deeply personal, private, and individual decision. In making this decision, some members of a family will give allegiance to Christ, while others will give allegiance to someone else, thus actually dividing families (cf. Matthew 10:34-36). Relationship with God is no longer a *national* experience as it was with Israel under its exclusive covenant with Him, but a person-by-person choice. By forcing our children to believe what *we* believe or conform to a religion that *we* have chosen, we contradict the free will that each person has to believe or not believe. (Those who believe in Calvinism also contradict their own belief: the *parents* and *church officials* decide who belong to the "elect" on their own, with zero knowledge of what God has "decreed" for those children. Why should anyone baptize a baby that God has destined—I am citing their own belief system here, not mine—for eternal damnation? Doesn't *that* question God's sovereign will?)

The gospel has "been written so that you may believe that Jesus is the Christ, the Son of God; and that believing you may have life in His name" (John 20:31). But if one never has the opportunity to choose salvation for himself, then he is allegedly "saved" without the need to believe. This is not an accurate representation of the gospel, but skews it entirely. Imagine strong-arming a fully-grown man into a baptistery and immersing him, then claiming that he is "saved," regardless of his own will.[91] Such is the case when parents and church leaders baptize a child that has no say, cannot understand, and is overwhelmed by those who may have good intentions but have no right to act in this way.

This begs another question: How can an infant "believe" anything? Or, how can a young child understand what is required of him to become Jesus' disciple? If "faith comes by hearing" the word of Christ (Romans 10:17), then how can a person *have* faith (much less demonstrate it) if he is not even capable of learning words or instructions?[92] Jesus Himself said, "If anyone wishes to come after Me, he must deny himself, and take up his cross and follow Me" (Matthew 16:24). Can a six-year-old child have any concept of what self-denial, self-sacrifice, and lifelong devotion really means? I realize that even an adult may struggle with this to some extent, but an adult has far better knowledge, perspective, and maturity than does a young child, and especially an infant. People often confuse a child's ability to regurgitate Bible verses with the maturity to make an adult-like decision. Just because an eight-year-old child can cite a number of verses does not make him prepared to take on adult responsibility. Even if he could cite the entire Washington State

Driver's Manual, for example, he still has to wait until he is old enough to get his license to drive. The retention of facts, by itself, does not translate to and is not a replacement for wisdom, experience, and maturity. Even if a seven-year-old "feels" like he can become a Christian, the fact is that he is still only *seven years old*. And if a seven-year-old remains too immature to be a Christian, then there can be no case made for an infant who does not have a clue what is happening to him.

### The Imposition of Parents (and Others)

Often, the driving force behind infants and young children getting baptized has far more to do with the parents (and possibly church leaders) than it does the children themselves. The parents do not *want* their children to leave their [the parent's] religion, so they indoctrinate them into that religion from the earliest of ages. (Or, the *church* indoctrinates the child through its rituals, sacraments, and catechisms.) F. LaGard Smith calls infant baptism "evangelism by procreation," which seems to describe accurately this situation.[93] The expectation that is put upon a young child may naturally compel him to conform to his parent's wishes regardless of whether or not he really believes or understands anything. His parent's approval is interpreted by the child as his own personal "readiness." Failure to comply incites the lack of approval or attention—something children do not wish to experience ("Since my daddy thinks I'm ready to be baptized, I don't want to disappoint him").

Parents are supposed to *lead* their children to Christ, not shove them into His presence. It is a parent's *God-given responsibility* to say "not yet" or "you're not ready" to a child who really does not have the capacity to understand what is required of him. All the examples we have in Acts of those being baptized are "men and women" (Acts 5:14, 8:3, 12, 9:2, and 22:4). Putting children into a scenario that is designed for "men and women" not only does them a great injustice, but it also deceives those children into thinking that they are far more ready, prepared, mature, capable, etc. than they really are. It is an even greater injustice and deception to force *infant* children to conform to what is clearly an *adult* responsibility. Again, much of what drives this is the parent's fear that their child will be lost, and/or the church leadership's fear that the child might not choose the religion over which it presides. This sidesteps the child's own decision (later on) to make his own choice to serve the Lord, and attempts in vain to do it for him.

But the deception goes further than this. If we teach that salvation really *is* imparted to infants upon their baptism, then we necessarily imply that they do not have to *obey* in order to be saved. If they do not have to obey while they are infants, then why should they be required to obey when they become adults? No one really believes this, of course—that is, no one really believes that an adult does not have to *believe* and *obey* in order to be saved. But if we communicate this message of salvation-without-believing to children when they are young, and then demand that they be morally-responsible teenagers and adults, we preach out of both sides of our mouths. Kids are not oblivious to this hypocrisy, either. It is this very kind of duplicity that sours children on continuing in their parent's religion when they reach adulthood. Can we really support such a contradictory message and call it the gospel of Christ?

Unfortunately, it is not uncommon for parents to forego a reasonable or intelligent dialogue when it comes to children, and especially *their own* children. Anyone who has ever observed parents during a Little League baseball game or a children's soccer match knows this. When people argue with emotions rather than reason, then this leads to all sorts of misunderstandings and misapplications. When people say, "I know the Scripture does not teach this doctrine, but I want it to be doctrine anyway," they admit that their belief system is guided by what they *feel* rather than what is true. In this case, any teaching that appears to be *against* children (by denying them something which they or their parents feel is entitled to them) will be viewed as unacceptable, and the one who proposes such a teaching is considered to be "down" on children ("You heartless monster!").

Along this line, people will say things like, "How *dare* you deny a child his (or her) right to believe in the Lord!" when someone like myself challenges that child's right to become a *Christian*. Yet, believing in the Lord and becoming a Christian are two different things. I would never stand in the way of a child of *any* age to believe in Christ! Yet, becoming a *Christian* implies something far beyond acknowledging and having a great respect for Jesus as the Son of God. Even though children can learn about the rigors and responsibilities of discipleship to Christ, these responsibilities are not intended for them.

### "Children of the Covenant"

Some church denominations teach that children of Christians are permitted to be baptized because they are children of the covenant. This is a teaching of what is often called "covenant theology." The basis for this teaching rests heavily upon Peter's words in Acts 2:39: "For the promise [for forgiveness and the Holy Spirit, based on 2:38—MY WORDS] is for you and your children and for all who are far off ..." This also follows the practice of the ancient Israelites: since they circumcised their males at eight days old in order to become children of the covenant, therefore this justifies Christians today baptizing their children for the same reason.[94] This fails to address all those children (like myself) whose parents were *not* Christians when they came to Christ, but that is another matter.

This position assumes that the promise to Abraham is fulfilled, in essence, in Christian believers rather than in Christ. Since physical circumcision was given to Abraham, and Christians are heirs of Abraham, therefore Christians are "circumcised" by baptism into Christ—or so it is taught. But we have already shown in a previous chapter ("The Sign of the Covenant") that baptism does *not* replace physical circumcision, and that whatever circumcision is performed upon the believer is performed spiritually by Christ, not by water. More importantly, Christ is the One—and not His church—who has fulfilled in Himself the covenant given to Abraham (Galatians 3:15-16). Christians are "heirs" of this promise—recipients of its blessings, as the result of what Christ has done (Galatians 3:29)—but we do not perpetuate this promise in the act of our baptism. The greater emphasis is on Christ and what He did, not upon us and what we do.

Parents' entrance into a covenant relationship with God does not grant special favor to their children, other than providing them with a Christian home environment. Peter's words to the Jews (in Acts 2:39) can easily be understood as, "This promise is *available* to this generation of Jews and every generation of Jews thereafter," just as it will be available (at the time he spoke those words) to those who are *not* Jews.[95] This is supported by the rest of the New Testament. Yet, except for a very subjective reading of this passage, nothing else in the New Testament supports covenant theology. "The idea of baptizing 'children of the covenant' is for many a comforting theological theory. But is only a theory. There is neither biblical nor historical support for such a practice."[96]

## The Doctrine of Original Sin

We have yet to deal with the real question of *why* people baptize infants in the first place. Yes, there is the parent's angst over their child's spiritual welfare. Yes, there is often the church leadership's own pressure—upon parents *and* young children—to conform to its own beliefs. But what lies at the root of all of this is the idea that babies are born sinful creatures, and are already condemned by God even on the first day of their lives here on earth. If this is true, then it explains why there would be a driving need to "save" young children as soon as possible. (Even so, this would not legitimate infant baptism, for the reasons already stated.) If this is not true, however, then the entire premise for infant baptism is hopelessly destroyed, and there literally is no justifiable reason for it.

The doctrine that teaches that babies are born in sin is known as "hereditary depravity," or more familiarly, the Doctrine of Original Sin. This idea has been around since at least the time of Augustine (died AD 430) and is the backbone of Catholic and many Protestant doctrines, and especially Calvinism. "Original sin" refers to the sin of Adam (not Eve) in the Garden of Eden, specifically, his eating of the forbidden fruit (Genesis 3:6, 17). Not only was the human race infected by Adam's sin, but it was also infected with Adam's guilt.[97] This is allegedly underscored by David's comment in Psalm 51:5: "Behold, I was brought forth in iniquity, and in sin my mother conceived me."[98] But the doctrine is almost completely founded upon Romans 5:12-19, and its sister passage, 1 Corinthians 15:22:

> Therefore, just as through one man [Adam] sin entered into the world, and death through sin, and so death spread to all men, because all sinned... So then as through one transgression there resulted condemnation to all men, even so through one act of righteousness there resulted justification of life to all men. For as through the one man's disobedience the many were made sinners, even so through the obedience of the One the many will be made righteous. (Romans 5:12, 18-19)[99]
>
> For as in Adam all die, so also in Christ all will be made alive. (1 Corinthians 15:22)

The context of Romans 5:12-19 is not meant to expound upon "original sin," and especially not infant baptism. The purpose of Paul's remarks is to magnify the contrast between the first Adam (a morally-fallen physical man) and the second "Adam" (Jesus Christ, a morally-perfect physical man *who also is* a Divine Being). While Adam did introduce sin into the world, Christ introduced *salvation* from that sin. Thus, there is no question that Adam brought sin into "the family," so to speak, and that we have been reeling from the effects of this ever since. But to put the responsibility for the eternal damnation of every soul that is born into the world upon Adam far, far exceeds what Paul actually said, what Paul even meant, or what Adam was even capable of doing.

Adam opened the door to human rebellion against God. But opening the door and entering through that door are two different things. Likewise, Christ opens the door to salvation, but only those who *enter through* that door (or "gate"; see Matthew 7:13-14) will receive it. Just because the opportunity exists—whether to sin or to be saved from sin—does not mean the opportune thing is literally imposed upon anyone. If I am

# Being Born of God

floundering in the ocean and someone throws me a lifeline, I do not *have* to take hold of it. The opportunity exists, and I can either accept or reject it. Jim McGuiggan's comment on Romans 5:12 says it well:

> We have all followed Adam's ways; we all made the kind of choice he made. He is our father not only in the sense that he was the physical ancestor of all of us; he's our "father" in that he led us into sin and we willingly followed him. His fall was our fall in the respect that our own fall followed his pattern. He is used here to represent all who followed in his footsteps. He, for example, doesn't represent Christ because Christ didn't follow him in his sinful ways. But he well-represents the rest of us.[100]

The potential *to* sin is within the family of man, but the responsibility *for* sin lies with each person that commits this act. This is clear in Paul's own words: "so death spread to all men, *because all sinned*" (emphasis added), not simply because all were born. "Death"—or, God's condemnation of the human soul—"spread" to those who committed the act of sin. Prior to this act being committed, a person was not "dead" to God, but very much alive. This fact is made evident later in Romans 7. There, Paul says he was not *born* "dead" to God, but that he "died" when he himself came to a knowledge of the Law and then broke it; "I was once alive apart from the Law; but when the commandment came, sin became alive and I died" (7:9). In other words, Paul *was* "alive," but he "died" *when he sinned*, which is exactly what he says in 5:12. This is also exactly what is meant in Ephesians 2:1-5: "And *you* were dead in *your* trespasses and sins, in which *you* formerly walked according to the course of this world...." Paul goes on to say that "when *we* were dead in *our* transgressions," Christ saved those who became Christians (all emphases are added). Paul is clear and consistent: the responsibility for one's guilt comes from that person's *own* disobedience to God, not Adam's disobedience.

Thus, Paul himself—the author of Romans 5:12-19, the passage that allegedly is the foundation for teaching "original sin" *and* infant baptism—says later that we are specifically *not* born sinful, but we are born *alive* to God. This means that Paul's words in Romans 5:12-19 are meant to be applied to the whole of humanity (as a family), not each individual person. It also means that each person is responsible for his *own* sin, and not the sins of someone else. This is exactly what God already stated in Scripture over 500 years before Paul ever wrote Romans: "Behold, all souls are Mine; the soul of the father as well as the soul of the son is Mine. The soul who sins will die" (Ezekiel 18:4; see also Deuteronomy 24:16). If you read the entirety of Ezekiel 18, it is inescapably clear that God places responsibility for sin upon each individual person, not on someone else, and never on Adam. It is impossible to find any support for "original sin" in that passage—or in any passage of Scripture, for that matter. R. L. Whiteside says on Romans 5:19: "It is pure assumption to argue that the disobedience of Adam is imputed to his offspring, or that the obedience of Christ is imputed to anybody. Neither guilt nor personal righteousness can be transferred from one person to another, but the consequences of either may, to some extent, fall upon others."[101] Consequences *for* sin are not to be confused with one's guiltiness *of* sin.

To get around this obvious conclusion, supporters of the "original sin" doctrine utilize a clever but unconvincing line of reasoning. "Original sin is called 'sin' only in an analogical sense; it is a sin 'contracted' and not 'committed'—a state and not an act."[102] This is a teaching invented out of thin air. It means nothing, and it certainly is not consistent with the teachings of Scripture. The New Testament never refers to sin as a "state," but always an "act." Paul (and others) clearly defines the moment of spiritual "death" as being when a person sins against God's law. Prior to this, a person did not live in a "state" of sin in which he was already guilty of someone else's transgression.

The Doctrine of Original Sin is entirely without biblical support, is contradicted by the Bible, and remains an incorrect attempt to explain human sin *and* divine grace. Yet, despite the great preponderance of evidence against it, this doctrine remains the primary reason why anyone even considers infant baptism in the first place. In other words, since people choose to believe that "original sin" is real, therefore infant baptism is necessary. This is perhaps most plainly expressed in the Catholic Catechism:

> Born with a fallen human nature and tainted by original sin, children also have need of the new birth in Baptism to be freed from the power of darkness and brought into the realm of the freedom of the children of God, to which all men are called [cites: Council of Trent (1546)]. The sheer gratuitousness of the grace of salvation is particularly manifested in infant Baptism. The Church and the parents would deny a child the priceless grace of becoming a child of God were they not to confer Baptism shortly after birth.[103]

This assumes that children are born into sin, and thus are born guilty and damnable. When pressed, however, few of those who teach this will actually admit that God sends those who die as infants or young children to hell because of Adam's sin.[104] This not only smacks of inconsistency but also insincerity to one's own beliefs.

There is no reason to believe that children are born into sin, or that they are inherently guilty of anything. First, there is simply no evidence for it in Scripture. God does not impart guilt to human beings that are completely unable to understand the nature or scope of their own actions.[105] A person does not need to be forgiven who is not guilty. If children are not born guilty then they cannot become guilty except by their own decision *and* only at a time when they are mature enough to make that decision. Jesus would never cite a child's purity and innocence as something to imitate if indeed that child was just as condemned and lost as any adult (Matthew 18:1-3). Thus, baptizing infants or young children is like trying to heal someone who is not sick, putting a cast on someone whose bones are not broken, or giving life-saving medical attention to someone who is not in any danger. It is completely unwarranted, unnecessary, and illogical. "Forgiveness of infants, even in baptism, is a notion exegetically unjustifiable and theologically indefensible."[106]

Second, there is sufficient evidence to the contrary, as was discussed above. These two reasons alone ought to silence any serious pursuit of this subject. Any pursuit of "hereditary depravity" beyond this will be based on sheer human conjecture, not the revealed doctrine of God.[107] As James Coffman says (on Romans 5:19), "The salvation of infants who die before attaining an age when they might either believe or obey the Lord does not come within the purview of Paul's teaching here, nor for that matter, of anything in the NT. The Lord did not see fit to enlighten men on how those dying in infancy are saved.

*Being Born of God*

Why? It was absolutely unnecessary."[108]

## Summary Thoughts

Those who believe in infant baptism also believe in water baptism as being necessary for salvation. If they did not, then the entire subject *of* infant baptism becomes pointless. (We have not even touched on the method that is used *for* this "baptism," however, which is often pouring of water and not actual immersion. Such a method is itself completely foreign to the Scriptures, as is the practice of infant baptism itself.) The glaring and conspicuous absence of any biblical support for this practice ought to be persuasive enough that it cannot be a *doctrine of God*, and thus not a *doctrine of salvation*. If it had been necessary for salvation, we can be certain that God would have been clear and specific on this in His revealed Word. We cannot create divine doctrine where God has not provided it. We have no authority to change the terms and conditions of God's covenant of salvation—not for ourselves, our children, or anyone else.

In this section, we have learned:

- There is no teaching or example in Scripture supporting infant baptism or even the baptism of children into Christ's church. All arguments in support of this practice appeal to unwarranted assumptions, human emotions, personal convictions, or "evidence" plucked out of thin air.
- Just because church "fathers" may have endorsed infant baptism does not prove anything. We are not to follow men but only the revealed Word of God ("sound doctrine").[109]
- You cannot create a binding and universal *doctrine of salvation* based upon the assumed implications of a single

word ("household").
- ❏ Jesus' blessing of infants or young children does not constitute a *doctrine of salvation* to be taught or practiced by His church.
- ❏ "Nations" does not mean "people of all ages"; thus, the commandment to teach and baptize "all nations" does not mean "baptize people of every age, including infants."
- ❏ It takes a mature person to have the kind of faith required to make a life-long and self-sacrificing commitment to become a Christian. An infant or child cannot produce this kind of maturity, faith, or commitment. Thus, God does not require children to become Christians—and neither should we.
- ❏ One person cannot "sponsor" the faith, commitment, or baptism of another person.
- ❏ Parents and church members do great harm by imposing their convictions upon an infant or young child, or by convincing a child that he is prepared to obey the Lord when in fact he really is not.
- ❏ Parents (and others) often default to emotional pleas rather than logic or Scripture to support the baptism of infants or children.
- ❏ "Children of the covenant" is an idea lifted out of the Old Testament covenant system and erroneously applied to New Testament theology.
- ❏ The Doctrine of Original Sin does not come from Scripture but is a desperate and hopeless attempt to justify the baptism of infants and young children.
- ❏ Children are not born with Adam's guilt; instead, they are born pure and innocent.

- ❏ Since children are innocent before God, baptizing them for their "sins" is illogical, unbiblical, and completely unnecessary.
- ❏ Only after children reach adulthood are they capable of being responsible to God's laws and therefore accountable for their own moral conduct.

The alleged "proofs" for infant baptism are in fact subjective interpretations at best and completely unfounded suppositions at worst. Baptism for salvation is a teaching that comes from God; He alone is able to tell us whatever we need to know about it. We do not need church officials, synods, a magisterium, or a new revelation to point us in a different direction than that which the Spirit leads us through the once-for-all revealed Word. The New Testament pattern for salvation is extremely important to God; it must also be extremely important to those who wish to come to Him.

Infant baptism is from men, not from God. Nonetheless, people will continue to support this practice until they choose to respect the authority of Scripture rather than the authority of men or man-made religions. Remember what we said earlier: salvation is not a subject that should be given emotional or superficial consideration. Instead, it should be given our most serious attention and intelligent examination. When it comes to whatever is required *for* salvation, including baptism, we would do well to look to God and God alone for our instruction.

# Chapter Eleven:
# The Doctrine of Calvinism

Many people's understanding of salvation—and, consequently, of baptism—is pre-conditioned by a religious doctrine known as Calvinism. In a nutshell, Calvinism leaves everything having to do with one's salvation in God's hands; the person being saved (the "elect") is not responsible for anything—in fact, he is *unable* to do anything—for his own salvation. The basis for this is the idea that the sovereign will of God cannot be changed or denied; thus, if God wills a person to be saved (or lost), then that person has no choice in the matter. No one can usurp God's own sovereign decisions.

Proponents of Calvinism naturally believe that they are sincerely and accurately representing God's Word, just as I believe I am doing. But sincerity by itself does not guarantee accuracy or objectivity for me or anyone else, and even the most sincere person in the world can still be wrong. The real test of one's belief system is to compare it with the only authoritative standard that God approves of: His revealed Word. Thus, the purpose of this chapter is to examine Calvinism as yet another challenge to what the New Testament actually teaches, and especially with respect to the subject of baptism.

## The Doctrine Defined

Calvinism (a.k.a. Reformed Theology, The Doctrine of Predestination, or The Doctrine of Election and Reprobation) is a particular interpretation of Scripture and salvation in which God's sovereignty determines the salvation (election) or condemnation (reprobation) of every single human soul. This view was popularized by Augustine (died AD 430) and formally

# Being Born of God

codified by John Calvin (1509 – 1564) during the Reformation Era.[110] Calvinism is the theological backbone of the Presbyterian and Baptist denominations, but borrows its teaching on "original sin" from Catholicism.

Calvinists are fond of appealing to church history as justification for their beliefs. Thus, they regularly cite the various religious councils (or synods) in which landmark decisions have been rendered by a high court of church officials. In some of these councils, Calvinism has been exonerated; those who oppose it have been summarily condemned as heretics. Two of these so-called heretics—Pelagius (354 – 420?) and James Arminius (1560 – 1609)—are prominently described as "founders" of modern anti-Calvinistic teachings. Thus, non-Calvinists who call themselves Christians are referred to as "Pelagians," "semi-Pelagians," or "Arminians." This, of course, assumes that all such non-Calvinists are in full agreement with all that these two men taught—a point which is neither true nor relevant.

In bold response to James Arminius' remonstrance (or formal grievance) against Calvinism, Calvinists convened a historic council in the city of Dordrecht, Netherlands—commonly referred to as Dort (or Dordt)—from 1618 to 1619. In this council, Calvinists outlined a five-point statement of their beliefs, mnemonically referred to as "TULIP":[111]

- ❏ *Total Hereditary Depravity:* Since man's heart, emotions, will, mind, and body are completely affected by Adam's sin, he is born *sinful*, wholly depraved, and thus condemned. He is "dead" in his sins, and thus unable to respond to God's gospel.
    - This must mean, then, that Jesus was also born sinful, since He is the Son of Man ("born of a

woman"—Galatians 4:4) as well as the Son of God. This must also mean that all babies are born sinful, and will suffer punishment for actions for which they cannot possibly be held responsible. (Calvinists explain that those who die as infants or children may be "called" by God without us knowing it, so that their souls are actually saved. They offer zero proof or citations for this theory.)

- Calvinists take Paul's "dead" reference (in Ephesians 2:1) quite literally, but never really explain *what*, exactly, is "dead." If it is a man's soul, then how can he function as a living being? If it is a man's spiritual awareness, then how can he have *any* consciousness of God? If it is a man's relationship (or fellowship) with God, *this makes sense*—but the Calvinist wants it to mean so much more than this. The New Testament teaches: an unconverted man *is* dead (or "fallen"—Romans 3:23), but this refers to his inability to walk in fellowship with God. Yet, he is not *unable to respond* to God's gospel, for God has made it available to him for this very purpose (Romans 10:5-13). If a man is *expected* to "call upon the name of the Lord," then he most certainly has the ability to *take the initiative* with regard to his salvation (Acts 2:21, 22:16).

- If men cannot respond *to* the gospel, then this undermines the entire need *for* the gospel or its proclamation. Why do we need to hear a message that changes nothing—a message that is pointless to share with anyone? Jesus said, "For the Son of

Man has come to seek and to save that which was lost" (Luke 19:10), but this is a useless statement if the *lost* cannot be saved and the *saved* cannot be lost! Or, it is useless if the lost will become those who *will* be saved (whether they like it or not), and the rest of humanity is doomed without any hope of salvation. And if *this* is true, then there is no one to "seek" *or* "save," since each person's destiny has already been decreed. In that case, Jesus did not come with a message of hope for those facing eternal ruin, since the "elect" never really faced eternal ruin at all. He came *pretending* to care about all people, but offers nothing for those who are destined for destruction through no decision of their own.

- ❏ *Unconditional Election:* God does not base His "election" upon anything He sees in an individual person. He is unconcerned with what men do or do not do. He saves (or does not save) based solely upon His sovereign decision.
  - This is a complete distortion of the meaning of "sovereignty of God." There is no question that it is God who regenerates the human soul, or that His grace—the atonement of Christ and the power of His Spirit—is the means of that regeneration (John 1:12-13, Titus 3:4-7, 1 Peter 1:2, et al). But to place the *full responsibility* upon God for whether or not this regeneration takes place (and thus to deny man's free will) makes God a "respecter of persons" and a God of partiality— exactly the opposite of what the Bible teaches

(Acts 10:34-35, Romans 2:11, Ephesians 6:9, and Colossians 3:25). If God justifies a man based upon his faith in Him, then He would be unjust to *deny him that opportunity* for which Christ has died (John 12:32, 20:31).[112]

- To allow man his free, independent will to *choose* this opportunity or *refuse* it is not questioning God's decision. His gospel stands intact, whether or not one chooses to obey it; His sovereignty remains unchallenged, whether or not one chooses to acknowledge it. Furthermore, in every case of conversion in Acts, people believed *and* were baptized after hearing the message of truth. In other words, they made a conscious decision *to obey* based entirely upon the good news preached to them. It was God's sovereign will to provide this good news; it is man's human will to obey or reject it.

- It is conspicuous, too, that every person who supports Calvinism is conveniently part of the "elect," and thus has no problem upholding God's decision to save *him (or her)*. This strongly indicates religious bias and conflict of interest. One loses all objectivity in interpreting Scripture when he believes that he cannot be wrong *in* his interpretation—and cannot be lost no matter what.

❏ **Limited Atonement:** "Jesus died only for the elect. Though Jesus' sacrifice was sufficient for all, it was not efficacious for all. Jesus only bore the sins of the elect."[113]

- This is based upon statements like Isaiah 53:12

and Matthew 26:28, where it says Jesus died for "many," but not for "all." It is also based upon John 17:9, where Jesus prayed only for His disciples, but not for "the world." It is clear to any objective Bible student that when one uses passages like these in such a restrictive manner, this method works only for the one who so interprets them but it makes sense to no one else.

- Jesus was *sent* to die for the entire world (John 3:16, 1 John 2:2); He appeared for the benefit of all "mankind" (Titus 3:4). Just because the entire world does not rightly respond to His death does not mean that He did not *die* for all people. Passages that assert that Jesus died "for many" and not "all" cannot be construed to mean that Jesus' death was ineffectual for those not included in the "many," but that only those ("many") who *do* call upon His name for salvation will be atoned by His blood. This limited number does not restrict His work on the cross, but only proves that *not all* will appreciate that work.

❑ *Irresistible Grace:* "When God calls His elect into salvation, they cannot resist. God offers to all people the gospel message. This is called the external call. But to the elect, God extends an internal call and it cannot be resisted."[114] Being born again is just like physical birth: the one being born has no part in the decision to be born.

- This line of reasoning misunderstands and misapplies what *is* taught in Scripture. In Philippians 2:12-13, for example, it says "God...is at work in you," which is straightforward enough.

It does *not* mean, "God chooses salvation for you," but that God does things *for* the believer that he cannot do for himself. This is called *grace*, but it is not irresistible. People can receive grace "in vain" (2 Corinthians 6:1-2); they can turn away from the Spirit of grace (Hebrews 10:26-29); and Paul warned the Galatians that they were in danger of *falling* from grace (Galatians 5:4). One cannot "fall" from something he never had in the first place.

- The truth is: people *can* and *do* resist God's grace. This does not undermine God's sovereignty, but is a refusal of what His sovereign decisions have offered them. God's commandment is eternal life (John 12:30), but not everyone chooses to obey this command (Hebrews 4:2). This does not make Him any less "God," but only makes those who refuse Him foolish people (Romans 1:21-22).
- "Born again" in the spiritual sense is an *analogy*, not a literal *replication* of one's physical birth. While it is true that I did not choose to be physically born, it is not true that my spiritual rebirth is held to this same condition. One is biological, the other is spiritual; one is natural, the other is supernatural; one regards my human (earthly) existence, the other regards my spiritual (eternal) existence. The two births may share some common features, but they are not identical or interchangeable. Calvinists often conspicuously avoid John 3:5: "Unless one is born of water and the Spirit...." Being born of the *Spirit* is what God

*Being Born of God*

does for the believer; being born of *water* is what the believer does for God, in faithful obedience to what He has commanded. It is not only necessary that the believer participate in his born-again experience, but he is expected to initiate it through his baptism.

- **Perseverance of the Saints:** "You cannot lose your salvation. Because the Father has elected, the Son has redeemed, and the Holy Spirit has applied salvation, those thus saved are eternally secure." Jesus said in John 10:27-28 that His "sheep" cannot perish; Paul said in Romans 8:1 that the believer has passed out of condemnation; see also 1 Corinthians 10:13 and Philippians 1:6.
  - It is clear that this point disregards the *conditional premise* of each passage being considered. God promises that He will never leave us (Hebrews 13:5), but this does not mean we cannot leave Him (Hebrews 6:4-8). Jesus will present every believer before the Father, but only *if* each person will "continue in the faith firmly established and steadfast, and not moved away from the hope of the gospel that you have heard" (Colossians 1:21-23).
  - Calvinists also wrestle with passages like Romans 11:22 which necessitate this conditional situation: "Behold then the kindness and severity of God; to those who fell, severity, but to you, God's kindness, if you continue in His kindness; otherwise you also will be cut off." Calvinists like to make *God's decree* the "condition," but Paul

clearly teaches that *man's faith* is the variable. Paul (in Romans 11:22) did not write to Gentiles who were guaranteed to be lost, but to those who had been saved: he warned them not to *forfeit* their salvation through unbelief. Thus, the burden is placed upon the believer to continue *in* his belief, not upon God to save someone *regardless* of his belief. God simply finalizes man's decision concerning his salvation; He does not unilaterally make that decision for him.

- When someone *does* "fall away" from the faith, the Calvinist claims that that person was "never really saved at all," but only experienced "worldly sorrow" or a "dimension of enlightenment."[115] This theology is convenient, but not biblical; it has simply been plucked out of thin air. The New Testament teaches that not only *can* men fall away from the faith (1 Corinthians 10:12), but that some *will* (Acts 20:28-30, 1 Timothy 4:1, 2 Peter 2:20-22, et al).

## A Theology in Reverse

The preeminent teaching of Calvinism is that no one can resist God's saving grace because no one can overrule His sovereign authority.[116] If God has predetermined to save you, then you *must* be saved. Likewise, if God has predetermined to condemn you, then you *must* be condemned. There is nothing you can do about your situation one way or another, since you are not able to change God's "decree." Calvinism also maintains that man is not just blinded by his sin (as stated in 2 Corinthians 4:3-4), but is literally *dead* and therefore entirely *unresponsive* to God's gospel call. Since man is dead and it is impossible for him to respond to anything spiritual, it is up to God to bring him back to life. This leaves the decision to be *saved* or *left for dead* to God and God alone. Thus, no one can have faith in the gospel of Christ who has not first been "made alive" (or regenerated) by God *first*.

This view turns Paul's argument concerning faith on its head: instead of a man being credited with righteousness *because* of his faith (Romans 1:17, 4:3), Calvinism teaches that a man cannot even *have* faith until he has first been regenerated by God. Instead of God's grace being a response to man's faith, the Calvinist believes that man's faith is a compelled response to God's grace. Furthermore, he believes that man is not born again *after* hearing the Word of God (because he is "dead"), but God must make him born again *first*. Once "made alive," a person can then respond rightly to God's commands for repentance, holy living, and good works. Calvinism necessarily implies that one who is born again retains all of his sins and guilt, since that person is taught to take the necessary steps of repentance and seek God's forgiveness.[117] He is not born again *pure* and *uncorrupted*, but is apparently reborn *in* his impurity and corruption.

Calvinists do support baptism, but not in the way the New Testament teaches it. In their understanding, it is God who makes one born again—the person being reborn has no say in the matter. Thus, Calvinists do believe that baptism is an act of faith, but it is an act of faith *after* salvation, and not an act of faith *for* salvation. Baptism is merely an "outward sign" of an already-present "inward grace," not a necessary act of obedience for salvation. In fact, Calvinism teaches that anyone who dares to think that he can actually decide for himself whether or not he wants to be saved stands in defiance of God's sovereign will.[118] John said, "These have been written so that you may believe that Jesus is the Christ, the Son of God; and that believing you may have life in His name" (John 20:31), which leaves each person to *choose* to believe (or not) based upon what he *reads*. This is consistent with the rest of New Testament teaching; it is not, however, consistent with Calvinism.

According to Calvinism, a person is "dead" as the result of Adam's sin (a.k.a., the Doctrine of Original Sin). When Adam sinned, he "killed" the entire family of man, and destroyed each person's ability to willfully obey God's truth. In this condition, one is given *permission* to come to God, but he *cannot* come because he is "dead." "…All people are conceived in sin and born children of wrath, unfit for any saving good, inclined to evil, dead in their sins, and slaves to sin; [and] without the grace of the regenerating Holy Spirit they are neither willing nor able to return to God, to reform their distorted nature, or even to dispose themselves to such reform."[119] Thus, it is as if Christ is preaching salvation to a sea of corpses, knowing full well that none of them can actually respond to His message.

Those who are not called by God's grace will be punished for being in this condition (even though it is not their fault); those who *are* called by God's grace will escape all condemnation (even though this is not their decision). Calvinists commonly cite the following passages for support of their doctrine. (The brief summaries after each citation are their own interpretations.)

- ❏ John 6:44, no one can come to God unless He first regenerates that man.
- ❏ Acts 13:48, no one can have eternal life whom God did not "appoint" beforehand.

## Being Born of God

- Romans 3:10-18, no man does any "good" without God's having first regenerated him.
- Romans 8:29-30, God "predestines" whomever He will; those whom He has not predestined are eternally lost. No one can dispute God's having *not* called him, since His sovereign authority is not to be questioned.
- Romans 9:10-18, God "calls" whomever He wishes, and does *not* "call" whomever He rejects. Thus, God called Jacob, but "hated" Esau; God called the Israelites, but did not call Pharaoh. These callings or rejections refer to these people's eternal destinies. So with Pharaoh: God "hardened" his heart to be *lost*, but He shows mercy to others so that they will be *saved*.
- Ephesians 1:3-11 (and every passage which speaks of God's "choosing" His people, His "choice," or the "elect"), God has "predestined" those who are saved; He has also predestined who will be lost. The entire matter rests in God's own decision; man can only accept whatever sovereign decree He has made concerning him.
- Ephesians 2:1-2, man is "dead" in sin, and thus is unable to respond to God's gospel until God makes him "alive" in Christ (2:4-5).
- Ephesians 2:8-9, man's "works" play no part in his salvation, but he is saved by divine grace *alone*. "Faith" is what a person gives to God *after* he is thus saved.

The above citations do not *prove* Calvinism, but instead are interpreted *in light* of it. This is like an evolutionist "proving" evolution with carefully-arranged bones and fossils that he claims are the result of evolution! The *context* of each passage, and of the New Testament as a whole, does not support the interpretations that the Calvinist has assigned to it.

When Paul speaks of "predestination" (as in Romans 8:29-30 or Ephesians 1:5ff), he does so in reference of the entire *body* of believers, not of individual people. In other words, Christ's *church* is predestined for salvation and glory, but it is left up to each individual person to determine whether or not he will be *part* of that church, based upon his own response to the gospel (Romans 2:4-11). In the case of Jacob and Esau, it is clear in the context—as well as throughout the Old Testament—that God's reference was to the *descendants* (or nations) of Jacob and Esau, not to the two men themselves (Romans 9:13). Neither Paul nor God speak of the *spiritual destiny* of each man, but how their posterity will play out in history. God did not say, "Jacob's soul I will *save*, but Esau's soul will be *lost*." To turn Paul's example into a doctrine concerning each man's eternal destiny is to misrepresent his point entirely. Paul's point in Romans 9 is that God's decisions concerning what people He chooses to carry out His work in history are His, not men's. If God wishes to use Israel to bring Christ into the world, that is His choice; if He now chooses to allow Gentiles to benefit from this Messiah, that is also His choice. But He *never* says that He will decide who will be eternally saved or lost; that decision rests with whoever chooses to *believe* in God or not (cf. John 8:24).

### Riddled with Contradiction

Calvinism is a convoluted doctrine filled with double-speak. Calvinists "pray as if everything depended on God; and yet they preach and work as if everything depended on man."[120] Indeed, prayer, evangelism, good works, and benevolence are rendered pointless if indeed God is going to do what He does and save whom He saves regardless of what men—believers and unbelievers alike—do or fail to do. (The Calvinist will respond: first, the non-elect are *permitted* to come to God, just not *able*; second, since we do not *know* who the "elect" are, we are supposed to discover them through prayer and evangelism. Yet, this is an unwarranted assumption, smacks of elitism, and is nothing more than a desperate attempt to justify one's position.)

Ashley Johnson, over a hundred years ago, exposed the pointlessness of, say, a Baptist revival in which the preacher invites people to come forward and give their lives to the Lord. If those who respond are the "elect," then they are *already* saved—nothing on their part will change this. (And, if one must "come forward" and give his life to God, aren't those works of *human effort*? According to Calvinism, he should be saved *regardless* of whether or not he came forward or did anything at all.) If those who respond are "reprobates," then they are already doomed—and they always have been—and no one can change their state of being. In either case, these people have *no choice*. Yet, preachers "cry to God to save the elect, which He cannot and will not do until the time comes [for that salvation], and they cry to Him to save the non-elect, which He cannot and will not do unless their doctrine is false."[121] (And how do we know that the preachers themselves are among the elect?) If God's will forces men to be saved against their own will, then they will be saved even without evangelism or prayer. And if we are *forced* to evangelize or pray or believe, then we are no longer intelligent human beings capable of choosing our own destiny, but are merely robots without free will.

Calvinism is not an objective interpretation of Scripture; it is an imposing and damaging one. It misrepresents both God and His plan of salvation. Even though its supporters claim to honor God's sovereign will, they handcuff the *application* of His will to their own interpretations of it. Listening to their arguments, they place high confidence in their champions of biblical interpretation—chiefly, Augustine and John Calvin—but do not allow the Bible to speak for itself as a *whole* rather than in its dissected pieces. They rely heavily on the conclusions of historic councils rather than on an objective study of Scripture. (Remember, too, that it was just such a religious council that condemned Jesus—Matthew 26:57-68.) The apostle Paul was not a Calvinist, nor was Christ. Paul was a Christian and nothing more—and so will everyone be who abides by the same gospel that Paul preached. Calvinism appeared long after the fact; it was not a part of what was taught to the early church. Any doctrine that challenges what Paul actually preached deserves to be exposed for what it is: a "different gospel" (Galatians 1:6-8).

### Salvation Is One's Personal Responsibility

If Calvinism was an authentic teaching of Scripture, then we would not need to call it "Calvinism" at all, but simply "the gospel of Christ." Likewise, if it accurately represented the purpose of baptism in the New Testament, then we would not need John Calvin's *Institutes of the Christian Religion* (1536) to learn why or how to be baptized; we would simply refer to the New Testament itself. If a person needed John Calvin (or anyone else) to tell him how to be saved, or how he *is* saved, then certainly God would have referred us to him and his teachings. Obviously, He did not do this because we do not need Calvin, Augustine, or anyone else but Christ and His Word to be saved.

Each person makes a personal *decision* to be saved. The New Testament evidence for this is plentiful and compelling. And no one is usurping God's authority by choosing the very thing He put in front of us *for* that purpose. Jesus told the Jews, "Unless you believe that I am {He} [the ever-existent Son of

## Being Born of God

God—MY WORDS], you will die in your sins" (John 8:24). These Jews were under covenant to God, yet a necessary expectation *of* that covenant was that they would believe in the One of whom Moses himself prophesied (see Deuteronomy 18:15-19, John 5:45-47, and Acts 3:19-23). Jesus did not force the issue; He left it to each Jew to make up his own mind. He did not say, "Some of you *will* believe because you have no choice—it is irresistible!—but others of you are predestined *not* to believe." Instead, He put the invitation to enter the kingdom of God before them, and some *chose* to believe while many others chose *not* to believe.

So it is today: the gospel is proclaimed throughout the world, and some *choose* to believe while many others choose *not* to believe. God has already made His choice: He desires that *all* men be saved (1 Timothy 2:3-6). If God claims publicly that He desires all men to be *saved*, yet knows secretly that He has decreed that many men be *lost*, what does that say about the genuineness, compassion, and love of our God? Such a position questions His integrity, and misrepresents His message to us completely.

To illustrate our personal choice in the matter, consider the parable of the so-called prodigal son (Luke 15:11-32). Jesus showed us a portrayal of God's relationship with two different men: one, a self-serving man of the world who sought happiness through indulging in sin; the other, a self-righteous man who felt entitled to God's favors because of his personal justification. One man left his father's house and wasted all of his father's money. The *result* of this act of rebellion made him "dead" to his father—in other words, he was not dead because of Adam's sin, but because of his *own* sins. Yet, when he came to his senses and penitently returned home, his father rejoiced because he "was dead and has begun to live, and was lost and has been found" (15:32). The *decision* to become "dead" *or* to "live" was not the father's, but the prodigal son's. It is true that the son had to come back to the father and have his relationship with him re-established; it is also true that the father never wanted the son to leave in the first place. Yet, it is entirely *untrue* that the son was destined to be saved against his own will. Unless he had come to himself, abandoned his rebellious heart, and put himself entirely at the mercy of his father, he never would have "begun to live."

Consider yet another account: the parable of the unforgiving servant (Matthew 18:21-35). This parable does not have a happy ending like the first, but follows the same thought process. Jesus showed us a man who owed his lord a ridiculously huge sum of money—an amount that simply could not be repaid even in several lifetimes. The servant pleaded with the lord to "be patient," yet the lord had great compassion upon him and forgave him of the entire debt. This illustrates the person who comes to God with his huge debt of sin, and God—because of his mercy and grace—forgives him. So far, so good. Unfortunately, this servant was unaffected by such a demonstration of kindness, and sought out a man who owed *him* money—a paltry amount by comparison to what *he* had owed his lord—and demanded repayment. This servant's actions were reported to the lord. In anger, the lord recalled the servant and *reinstated* the debt that he had forgiven because the servant violated the terms and conditions *of* that forgiveness (see Matthew 6:14-15). "My heavenly Father will also do the same to you, if each of you does not forgive his brother from your heart" (Matthew 18:35). This is the chilling conclusion of the parable: God will *not* forgive those who *choose* to withhold forgiveness from their fellow man. Forgiveness from God is equal to salvation, since one who is forgiven by God is also saved by Him.

The point here is this: forgiveness is not predicated on a predestined decision of God, but the self-determined heart of the one who seeks it. This fact alone does not support Calvinism, but undermines it completely. No amount of explanation on the Calvinist's part will avoid the inescapable conclusion that Jesus Himself established through this parable. Even though Jesus spoke to Jews, the principle of divine forgiveness is universally applied. Everyone who comes to God seeking His forgiveness must abide by whatever terms and conditions He requires *for* that forgiveness. No one can usurp God's authority by abiding by the very terms *He* offered in order to receive what *He* wants to give.

## Summary Thoughts

We do not need Calvinism to explain the process of becoming a Christian. We do not need to become Calvinists in order to be saved. The TULIP doctrine of Calvinism is a huge misrepresentation of Scripture, not an objective exposition of it. We need only to "read and understand" the written Word of God, believe it, and obey it. This written word clearly teaches what is required for this obedience; we are not left to wonder about something so critical to our spiritual survival.

The apostle John wrote, "Beloved, if our heart does not condemn us, we have confidence before God; and whatever we ask we receive from Him, because we keep His commandments and do the things that are pleasing in His sight" (1 John 3:21-22). Commandment-keeping is a necessary expression of one's obedience to God; without it, no one should expect to receive anything from God, including salvation itself. Jesus said, "If you love Me, you will keep My commandments" (John 14:15). Whether these commandments have to do with *becoming* a Christian or *walking* in a manner worthy of the gospel, they are just as important. If God commands us to be baptized, then we demonstrate our love to Him when we comply with this—and so with any other divine command.

    Calvinists are not against the act of baptism, but they *are* against the biblical teaching of it. They want people to be baptized, but only because (they believe) such people are already saved (even though they cannot prove it). Christ also wants people to be baptized, but as an act of obedient faith *for* salvation, not after it has already been accomplished. Christ and His apostles taught that every soul is personally responsible to respond to God's invitation for salvation, which has been proclaimed throughout the entire world (Colossians 1:23). God *has* predestined His church to glory—there is no question of this—but this is a far different statement than to think that He has predestined *each person* to glory. The decision to be "in Christ" is an individual one; likewise, the decision to be baptized is an individual one. No one can come to God on his own terms, but if he obeys those terms which God has defined, then He will give to that person what he seeks—*eternal life*.

## Chapter Twelve:
# The Doctrine of "Faith Only"

Many modern evangelicals claim to believe in "faith only" for salvation. ("Evangelical" is, in essence, the modern term for Protestant, but not all Protestants would consider themselves evangelicals. In today's common usage, evangelical often implies Baptist.) In the most general sense, "faith only" means that no human works of any kind can contribute to one's salvation, even though human works are expected of believers *after* one's salvation. This means that a person comes to God only through his belief in Jesus Christ and absolutely nothing more.

Proponents of this doctrine maintain that we are "justified by faith" (Romans 5:1), and not by works (Ephesians 2:8-9). So far, there is no argument: this is a clear teaching of Scripture. However, the concept of justification by faith *alone* or *only* is not found anywhere in Scripture, but it *is* found frequently in the writings of "faith only" supporters. Thus, their actual claim is that a person is "justified by faith *alone*," and thus there is nothing required (up front) to prove that faith.

This latter position is impossible to maintain. First, it is inconsistent with the sum total of God's Word on the subject. Second, even those who try to maintain it quickly contradict themselves when they require *any* action as being necessary for salvation that is not "faith only." Third, there is no such thing in Scripture as faith *only* or faith working *independent* of proof for its existence. "By faith" (cf. Hebrews 11) does not indicate a mere intellectual agreement to God's existence or an abstract confidence in His ability. Rather, it demands that the believer *does something* in order to establish that faith and prove that confidence. This bears directly on baptism, because Scripture teaches that baptism is a *required act of faith* and not an after-the-fact demonstration of piety or a token gesture of religious protocol.

### Faith Demands Works

To say that we are saved *through* faith is accurate and true—except for the "only" or "alone" part that is often attached to this (and what that attachment necessarily implies). We *are* justified by faith, and not by human works. In other words, God credits (or reckons) righteousness to the believer when he puts his full confidence in His power to perform. This is summarized in Romans 1:16-17: salvation comes from God, but the one who comes to Him must live by human faith in His ability to save. What the *Scripture* means by this is that no human works can do what God alone can do. It does *not* mean that God expects nothing of the believer—even in his conversion. What "faith only" proponents want this to say is that *no* works are involved in one's salvation, and especially in the case of one's conversion to God. This is particularly aimed at baptism, since evangelicals do not believe baptism is required in order to become what they call a "born-again Christian"—a redundant if not awkward phrase. This is why they say, "Just ask Jesus into your heart...," because believing in Him *by itself* is all that is required for salvation.[122]

This entire premise is confusing, especially in light of Calvinism, which is the doctrine that underlies many proponents of evangelicalism. Calvinism maintains that everyone's eternal future has already been decided by God's sovereign decree: every person either must be saved no matter what he does *or* he must be condemned no matter what he does. The Philadelphia Confession (of Baptist doctrine), for example, says: "Perseverance of the saints depends not upon their own free will, but upon the immutability of the decree of [divine] election...."[123] In light of that alleged scenario, what is the *purpose* of "faith" at all? As one author points out, "If salvation is wholly of grace and unconditionally wrought by the Holy Spirit directly upon the soul of the sinner when he is unable to make a choice for himself, how can it be conditioned upon faith ["faith only"] or repentance or any other requirement?"[124] Those who maintain such a position talk in circles: on one hand, one's faith is *irrelevant* if indeed God's grace is (in the words of Calvinism) "irresistible." On the other hand, there is all this talk about the need for human "faith" for salvation—a faith that does not require any works to define it.

"Faith only" advocates claim that faith is the sole human condition to one's born-again experience. Thus, baptism is not essential for salvation—it cannot be, they maintain, since baptism is a work, and no one is saved by works. What is implied in the "faith only" doctrine is that we are saved without *obedience*, since "works" necessarily implies obedience. It necessarily follows from this that a person does not need to *obey* to be saved; he only needs to *believe* (as though the very *act* of believing by itself is not a "work"—see John 6:29). Thus, those who *believe* in Jesus without any works to show for that belief are made Christians, but afterward those Christians are expected to *obey* Him in their works. What?

Suppose a foreigner visiting the United States asks an American citizen, "How old must you be to vote in this country?" The American replies, "Eighteen years old." Then the foreigner, being over eighteen years old, attempts to vote in our next election, but is denied. The problem was that he met *one* prerequisite to vote, but not *all* of them. This is analogous to the present subject: a person can have *one* prerequisite for salvation—*belief*—but there is more that is required of him.[125] This one prerequisite *is* mandatory, but this fact does not automatically negate the possibility that *other* prerequisites might also be needed. The only case where this would be otherwise is if God had said, "You *only* need to believe to be saved," but He never said that, and we have a considerable amount of evidence to the contrary.

The "faith only" doctrine continues: Believing is what happens in a person's heart; obedience is what happens in a person's born-again life. Supporters of this will often cite the conversion of the Philippian jailer: "'Sirs, what must I do to be saved?' They [Paul and Silas] said, 'Believe in the Lord Jesus, and you will be saved, you and your household'" (Acts 16:30-31, bracketed words are mine). But they have overlooked the fact that the man could not believe in the Lord Jesus until he was taught of Him. And after Paul taught him of *Jesus*, the man was *baptized*. The man could not "believe" until he was taught, but the teaching required an act of obedience on his part, not merely an agreement to the facts. (See Acts 8:26-39 for a parallel situation.)

Nonetheless, the favorite passage for the "faith only" group is John 3:16: "For God so loved the world, that He gave His only begotten Son, that whoever believes in Him shall not perish, but have eternal life." Does this mean that any *kind* of belief is good enough, as long as we call it "belief"? In other words, is a person saved if he believes *at all*? We have examples to prove that this is not true. Israel claimed to believe in Jehovah, but that people did not obey Him. They were sent into exile *not* because they were unbelievers in the strictest sense

## Being Born of God

of the word, but because of their flagrant disobedience to God's law. As Jeremiah said, "You [Jehovah] are near to their lips but far from their mind" (Jeremiah 12:2). So it is with many so-called "believers" today.

Jesus told those who believed in Him, "If you continue in My word, then you are truly disciples of Mine" (John 8:31). Shortly after this, these same people accused Jesus of being "born of fornication," a Samaritan, and demon-possessed (8:41, 48). And Jesus said of *them* that they really did not believe *the truth*, but chose to listen to Satan (their "father") rather than God (8:44-45). Clearly, these people believed that Jesus *was* a Prophet, but their hearts remained unconvinced of the truth and therefore unconverted. Similarly, many of the Jewish rulers believed that Jesus was a Prophet, but refused to admit this publicly because they loved the approval of men rather than the approval of God (John 12:42-43). Finally, James says that demons believe in God ("and shudder"), but they remain what they are—demonic beings destined for destruction (James 2:19-20).

Does it make sense to you that God justifies you initially by faith ("believe"), but after this He requires obedience, as if these were two separate things?[126] Or is there more to this "faith" or "believing" than merely an inward, intellectual consent to the facts concerning Christ? The question of "What *kind* of faith does God require for salvation?" will ultimately be the death knell for the "faith only" doctrine. When a person understands faith as *God* defines it, he will recognize the need for *obedience* in his salvation and not just a work-less faith. In fact, this is exactly what James wrote: "You see that a man is justified by works and not by faith alone" (James 2:24). You would think that James' words would put an end to the entire "faith only" doctrine. Instead, it shows that people will resist even the clearest of God's instructions.

Evangelicals regularly misrepresent the position (for lack of a better term) of those like myself who believe that baptism is *required* for salvation, and not something done later. When I say "required," the evangelical will respond, "You are saying that baptism actually *saves* you—that salvation is *dependent* upon a human act (or obedience)!" Ironically, Peter himself said, "Baptism now saves you" (1 Peter 3:21), and his authority as an apostle trumps any conclusion of a modern evangelical. Peter means that baptism is a necessary demonstration *of* faith, not a replacement *for* it. This is exactly where I am at. It is wrong to say that we are saved without works, for baptism is a work that God *requires* of the believer as *part* of his salvation. It is also wrong to say that we are saved by faith *and* works, since this is going beyond (or, adding to) what God had said. (This is the error to which many of those who *oppose* "faith only" succumb.) It is biblically correct, however, to say that we are saved *through* faith which can only be expressed *by* works. God is the source of our salvation, but He only saves those who live by faith in Him. If a person will not demonstrate his faith *in* God, then neither should he expect to be saved *by* God.

"Faith without works is dead" (James 2:26)—whether that "faith" is necessary in *calling* upon God for salvation or *after* he has already been born of God. Faith that cannot be identified by specific, active, demonstrable works to *prove* that it exists is really not faith at all. God requires an *obedient* faith (like the Philippian jailor's response to Paul and Silas' words) and not just a spoken faith (like what demons have) or a heartfelt faith (as in the case of those Jews who longed for a

# Being Born of God

hero [Messiah] but remained unconvinced of "the truth"). Faith is not merely a receptacle *of* God's salvation (which is what Martin Luther and other Reformists argued), but is indeed a catalyst *for* it. In other words, faith is not what God gives to *us*, but it is what we give to *Him*. A person who does not have faith is in the same boat as a person who claims to have faith but offers no proof for its existence: both of these people are not yet saved.

### What "Believe" Means (and Does Not Mean)

As mentioned above, part of the issue here also revolves around the meaning of "believe." Christ said that whoever "believes" in Him will be saved (John 3:16). But that word "believe" does not exist in a vacuum, nor can we define it according to our preference or personal understanding of it. In other words, I cannot say, "Well, to *me*, 'believe' means [insert: my "take" on this], and so that is what Jesus meant." It really does not matter what I *think* Jesus meant; it only matters *what* Jesus meant. If I *think* "believe" absolves me of any action of obedience on my part, then that is just my opinion—and no one will be saved because of his opinion. However, if I conform to what Jesus *meant* by "believe," then I will also conform to His expectations for *all* sincere believers. Thus, my salvation is no longer based upon my opinion of a word (or command), but is based upon His gospel of salvation.

Nonetheless, "faith only" proponents insist otherwise. One of their preachers argued it this way: "We believe before baptism, therefore we are not condemned before baptism. ... A man who is not condemned cannot be sent to hell. If he can't get to heaven until he is baptized and he can't go to hell because he is not condemned, where will that man go if he should die without baptism?"[127] This kind of reasoning attempts to create an unsolvable dilemma based entirely upon a subjective understanding of the word "believe." This man's use of the word "believe" *automatically* means "saved," and if we accept this premise, then his argument stands. However, he has jumped to a presumed conclusion without first having defined the most critical term of his argument: what does *Christ* mean when He says "believe"? This involves other related questions as well: What constitutes the substance or requirements of faith in Christ? Is "faith" merely an intellectual assent to Jesus' lordship? Is "believe" merely a mental exercise and nothing more? Is *that* what Jesus meant in the context of John 3:16-21, for example? Furthermore, can one's personal *claim* to "faith" or "belief" contradict God's definition of such requirements and still be acceptable to Him?

To "believe" in Jesus (as in John 3:16) does not mean—and *cannot* mean, given the context of New Testament theology—that a person merely has a desire to follow Him, or a willingness to receive His salvation. People get hung up on that word "believe" because they interpret it in light of man-made or denominational teaching rather than how the New Testament actually uses it (in the context of salvation). In John 3:36—just twenty verses after the infamous John 3:16 statement—John the Baptist said, "He who believes in the Son has eternal life"—which reiterates verse 16—"but he who does not obey the Son will not see life, but the wrath of God abides on him"—which *further expounds upon* verse 16. "He who believes" is presented as the direct opposite of "does not obey"; thus, to "believe" necessarily implies "to obey." In other words, "whoever believes…shall not perish, but have eternal life" actually *means* "whoever <u>obeys</u> Me as an expression of his belief…." This is the "obedience *of* faith" of which Paul spoke

*Being Born of God*

in Romans 1:5 and 16:26 (emphasis added). Jesus also said, "If you love Me, you will keep My commandments" (John 14:15). This is true (and required) in the process of *being* saved as it is in the life of those who are *have already become* saved. If baptism is commanded by God—and most "faith only" proponents acknowledge that it is—then to refuse the command negates the promise *of* the command—"eternal life" (cf. 1 John 2:25). Thus, a person does not have faith *because* he has been saved, but he needs to demonstrate his faith *in order* to be saved.

We cannot prove baptism is *unnecessary* simply by proving that faith *is* necessary. The latter conclusion does not negate the first. Such reasoning assumes "without proof, a proposition that denies every statement in the New Testament about the design of baptism."[128] All the passages on faith that say nothing about baptism prove *nothing* with reference to baptism, just as all the passages on repentance without the mention of faith prove nothing with reference to faith.[129]

### Playing with Words

Baptism *is* a work—it is a work of faith. It is not a meritorious work—i.e., it is not something that saves us *by itself*, or by our own merit or self-righteousness. But if God requires us to be baptized, then He requires us to *do something* in order to receive His salvation. Anything that is required of *you* in order for *you* to be saved is indeed a "work" that *you* produce, not God. God does the saving—there is no argument here—but He does not save a person who refuses to prove his faith in Him. Baptism is the visible, historical, and required work of human effort that is required of the person seeking salvation. It is in fact the defining moment *of* salvation for the believer. In other words, the believer must participate *in* his salvation in a personal, obedient, and appropriate manner.

God does not confer salvation upon people who have a mental consent to His commandments in their heart ("I believe!"); He grants salvation to those who have proved their faith in Him in the manner in which He has commanded ("*Since* I believe, I will obey"). Baptism is at least one of these proofs.

Those who believe in a "faith only" system of salvation are opposed to baptism above all other works. In other words, they manifest a great prejudice against baptism, while other "works" involved in the conversion process are glossed over (including the work of "faith" itself, "believing," confession, or prayer). Singling out baptism, while neglecting other works of human faith, does not constitute an objective Bible study. Every "faith only" proponent will readily argue that repentance, for example, is absolutely required for salvation. Yet, repentance is a work of human effort; God does not repent *for* you, and He will not save you if you refuse to repent (see Luke 24:45-47, Acts 2:38, 3:19, et al). So then, why is repentance not a "work" that is absolutely necessary for salvation, but baptism *is* considered a work? Even if I have to ask Jesus into my heart to be saved—a popular conversion formula of modern-day evangelicals—this "asking" is still a work of human effort. I know this because God does not do it for me, but (allegedly) I must do it for Him. Or, if I am supposed to say a "sinner's prayer" as part of my conversion experience, then this also is a work that I do for God, not something that God does for me. To focus on one particular work (baptism) to the neglect of other necessary works exposes a personal bias against that one work.

To label some things as "works" in order to avoid them is convenient, but is hardly objective or consistent. If repentance, asking Jesus to come into my heart, or saying a "sinner's prayer" are not works of God, then these must be works of human effort. One side says "works"; the other side says "faith"—but we are both talking about the same thing. The "faith only" doctrine claims that "baptism is unnecessary because it is a work," yet requires several different "works" from those seeking salvation, but calls them something else ("faith"). This is just a semantics argument, nothing more.

Those who insist that we are saved by "faith only" (*sola fide*) often confine their usage of this premise to the subject of conversion. But if "faith only" is true during conversion, why is it not true afterward? If anything we do *for* God is an act of faith *in* God, then what about all the visible works of faith during a Christian's life? How can evangelicals expect you to perform works of faith now that you *are* a Christian if they were unnecessary in order to *become* a Christian? Or, should we remain consistent to *sola fide*: "Have faith—and *nothing more*! Do *nothing* at all for the Lord, since you are saved by faith ONLY, and no effort on your part will EVER contribute to your own salvation!" Such a conclusion is necessary to remain true to the original premise, yet no one who teaches the original premise will ever maintain such a conclusion. It is interesting—and, sadly, contradictory—that evangelicals are quick to dismiss baptism as a necessary expression of faith, yet immediately want "born-again Christians" to attend services, participate in evangelism, give offerings to the church, etc.—all considered works of faith. Who has the authority to dismiss one divine command but insist upon another?

Another argument that is meant to reduce the significance of baptism in being born of God focuses on the use of the word "necessary." For example, if I say, "The New Testament teaches that baptism is necessary for salvation," the "faith only" proponent will argue, "No, it is *not* necessary for salvation. But it *is* a good work, and God expects every believer to perform it." What? If God expects every believer to perform it, then doesn't this make baptism *necessary*? One prominent evangelical says this: "Water baptism is certainly important, and required of every believer. However, the New Testament does not teach that baptism is necessary for salvation."[130] What else is not necessary for believers yet required by God? Shall we say the same thing of, say, prayer?—"It is not necessary for salvation, but it is required of all believers"? This doublespeak is extremely common among evangelicals in their dealing with the subject of baptism.

I have had people tell me that they were "saved" when they accepted Jesus Christ as their Savior, but then were later baptized in obedience to God (their words, not mine). My response has been (in so many words): Where in the New Testament did anyone become a Christian in the manner in which you described? Secondly, if you were baptized in obedience to God, then you admit that your refusal to be baptized would be nothing less than *disobedience*.[131] We cannot have it both ways: baptism cannot be "obedience" only when we want it to be obedience, but not at other times. Likewise, "necessary" cannot mean "required" only when we want it to mean this, but not at other times. God does not do this with anything else: repentance must be done *at* one's conversion as well as any time *after* conversion (whenever we have sinned); obedience is required *at* one's conversion as well as any time *after* his conversion; love is required *at* one's conversion as well as any time *after* his conversion; and so on. All of these are important and required; therefore, all of these are necessary. Logically and biblically, it cannot be otherwise.

The Baptist Manual, however, says this: "It is most likely that in the Apostolic age when there was but 'one Lord, one faith, and one baptism,' and no differing denominations existed, the baptism of a convert by that very act constituted him a member of the church, and at once endowed him with all the rights and privileges of full membership. In that sense, 'baptism was the door into the church.' Now, it is different...."[132] Now *what* is different, exactly? The fact that denominationalism has portrayed Christ's beautiful "bride" as a Frankenstein-like creature? Or, the fact that the early church taught that baptism *was* necessary for salvation, but this teaching has since been corrupted? Either way you look at it, the statement is self-condemning.

The Baptist Manual continues: "...Baptism is not essential to salvation, for our churches utterly repudiate the dogma of 'baptismal regeneration'; but it is essential to obedience."[133] This is exactly the argument used by the evangelical minister (above), yet it does not make any more sense now than it did earlier. Edward Hiscox (the author of the Manual) reduces the necessity of salvation to "dogma"—a pejorative expression. This is ironic, since his entire Manual is intended to provide the official dogma for Baptist churches. Since when did biblical teaching become a group's "dogma"? On the other hand, can anyone—including Baptists—find any support for the denominational system in the New Testament?[134]

## Summary Thoughts

"Faith only" proponents are usually conservative in their biblical interpretation. They generally have a logical and sound approach to reasoning the Scriptures. For this reason, I use some of their commentaries in my own studies, and find myself in agreement with them far more often than not. But in the case of baptism, they seem to jettison the sound and conservative approach and their arguments descend into convoluted snippets of doctrine heavily laced with subjective or irrelevant interpretations. They try so hard to defend their (often denominational) belief system that they have to force things into the Bible that simply are not there. Once again, if there is a subject that demands our best efforts and our most serious attention, it is in the matter of how to be born of God—i.e., how to become a Christian. Yet, the "faith only" doctrine does not truly address the matter of salvation; it is for some other purpose than this. Sadly, millions of people think that they are "saved" through this insufficient and incorrect method.

In the end, there is no such biblical teaching as "faith only"—the word *only* being the point of irreconcilable disagreement. We must have faith, to be sure; but this must be a faith that God defines, not what a man-made religion's creeds, catechisms, manuals, or councils have defined. "Faith only" masquerades as a viable and biblical method of salvation, but what it implies is at severe odds with all the instruction and implementation of the New Testament. The person who is serious about his salvation ought to reject any teaching about salvation that provides zero relevant biblical citations or examples to support it. We are *not* saved by faith only, grace only, God only, or Scripture only. We are saved by a necessary cooperation of *all* of these working together toward one singular objective: the salvation of the one who calls upon the Lord for this very purpose.

The "faith only" doctrine claims that Christians are baptized, whereas the New Testament teaches that people are baptized in order to become Christians (or, "sons of God," "saints," "disciples," or any of the other terms used to denote someone who belongs to Christ's church). We cannot teach it both ways: one way is right, and the other way is wrong—or both ways are incorrect. I have presented the argument here as straightforwardly and candidly as I am capable of doing. The final decision, however, will be left to each person to decide. Yet, God will weigh *all* decisions against what He has revealed in His Word, not what people have chosen to believe despite it.

# Chapter Thirteen:
# The "When" Factor

Events in history are, of course, *time*-oriented. Things do not happen apart from some time in which they happen. The greater the event, the more significant the time it happened. When the Wal-Mart store opened in your neighborhood is ... not very important. Nobody really cares what year that was. But when the French Revolution took place—or Hitler's invasion of Poland, the assassination of John F. Kennedy, or the fall of the Berlin Wall—is considerably more important. The years of these events indicate pivotal times in history.

In a more personal context, this "when" determines a significant change in our own status: "When were you born? When did you graduate? When were you married? When did you begin your career?"—and so on. This is especially true with regard to the beginning of your relationship with God. There are *sequences* of events leading up to that relationship—exposure to the Word, realization of your disposition before God, belief in His power to save, repentance, etc.—and then there is the actual commitment itself. This is important to God and therefore it must be important to you. For example, you cannot be clothed with Christ *before* you have been born of God—in other words, you cannot violate the God-given sequence of the conversion process.

Certain *conditions* have to be met in order for your status to actually be changed (in this case, from "sinner" to "Christian"). Unless such conditions are met, then the fellowship you seek with God does not yet exist. For example,

## Being Born of God

Jesus said that a person must love Him more than he loves anyone else, including his own life (Luke 14:26). If a person does not fulfill this condition, then he *cannot be* His disciple: as far as Christ is concerned, that person's status remains unchanged.

This sequence and/or conditions pattern is consistent with how God has always operated in the realm of humankind. In other words, His plans unfold or advance only after certain conditions have been met and/or they happen in an orderly sequence of events. For example, it was not only important *that* Jesus came into the world, but also *when* He came: in "the fullness of time" (Galatians 4:4). This is an example of certain conditions being met before the next phase of God's plan could be initiated. During Jesus' ministry, it was clear that He had a specific time schedule to follow, since He said on several occasions, "My time has not yet come." This is an example of sequential action: first this thing, then this other thing, then another, etc. It was critical that Jesus die for us, but it was also critical *when* He died: "at the right time" (Romans 5:6). This involves both conditions and sequence: things had to fall into place first *and* they had to happen in a certain order.

Your spiritual rebirth in Christ is a significant event *in* your life, and it is also God's plan *for* your life. This means that it cannot be imagined into existence through feelings, good intentions, religious epiphanies, or the power of (someone else's) suggestion. In order for your spiritual rebirth to be valid—in God's sight as well as your own—you must follow an orderly sequence of events as defined within God's Word. Also, you have to fulfill *your* part of whatever conditions are required for you to become a child of God. You cannot just assume your born-again experience happened without any legitimate *and* time-based point of reference. So then, if indeed you believe that you *are* born of God, *when* did this happen?

### Artificial "Whens"

It is true that we cannot impose physical time upon a spiritual context. For example, we cannot assume that the duration of time for the living is experienced the same way—for the same length of "time"—in the realm of the dead. There is no time in God's world, and our soul does not follow the clock or the calendar. On the other hand, your human existence on this earth *is* bound by time, and everything that God does for us while we are *in* our human existence is based upon some measurement of time. Thus, Paul told the Ephesians that they *were* dead to God in their sinful state, but *now* they are alive in Christ (Ephesians 2:1-5). This is how it *was*, but *now* it is different (see Romans 6:20-22 for a similar example). He necessarily uses a sequential, time-based reference, because the Ephesian Christians lived in such a world, as do you and I.

Someone says, "Yes, I know when I was 'born of God': it was on the day that I accepted Jesus into my heart to be my personal Savior." This is the common expression used among evangelicals and other contemporary religious groups. Unfortunately, this person's determination of *when* he was thought to have been born of God (and thus became a Christian) is based upon an action that is not even mentioned in the New Testament, much less commanded. His "when" is arbitrarily decided; it is not based upon facts and evidence, but rests entirely on an emotional experience that he put on par with an actual spiritual transaction between God and the human soul. It is a most dangerous situation for a person to *think* that he is "saved" when in fact he has no biblical proof that he really is. If there is no legitimate "when" to a person's salvation, then he is not yet saved.

Suppose we illustrate this in a context outside of Christianity. Imagine that your friend wants to go back to school and get a bachelor degree in business management. She tells you about this one day, and then the very next day she says, "I am now a graduate!" You say, "How is that possible? It has only been a day, and you haven't fulfilled any of the school's requirements!" She responds, "But I gave my heart to this university, and I accepted it as my personal learning institution. And you cannot convince me otherwise from what I feel in my heart!" Well, the thought is hopeful and intriguing, but it does not change anything: your friend's educational status remains unchanged, and the conditions and prerequisites for her degree remain unfulfilled. Until she does fulfill these, it does not matter how passionately she feels about this university or how convinced she is that she is a graduate. Her "when" for determining her "new" state of being is predicated arbitrarily upon her own terms, not those of the university. Furthermore, no reputable company is going to hire her based upon her personal, emotional, self-determined experience of a degree that she believes with all her heart that she has earned (though in fact she does not have it).

I am not suggesting that we can earn salvation like a person can earn an academic degree. Rather, I am pointing out the *presumption* and *illegitimacy* of jumping to a final conclusion before the conditions are met by which this conclusion is even made possible. In this way, the above illustration parallels a person's claim to have been born of God before or without having done what God required of her. Her claim sounds convincing to some; she herself believes it is real;

she will passionately defend it as being real; but it is inconsistent with what God requires in order for it to *be* real. And *until* God says this new relationship is real (or does exist), it is *not* real, but remains something yet to be formed. (All "until" or "unless" statements necessarily impose a time factor, as did Jesus' statements in Matthew 5:18, 12:29, 16:28, 18:3, et al.) We cannot imagine ourselves into a right relationship with God. We cannot allow well-intentioned people, family members, or church leaders to convince us of something that God alone determines. We cannot speak our fellowship with God into existence by our own authority, and no one is made a Christian through error or self-deceit.

Once again, the time factor is critical in this case: a person had to have *once* been in one state of being, but *now* he or she is in a different state of being. A literal, time-based point of reference is required: "On this date, I was born of God"; "On this date, I became a Christian." The date is established as the time when God's conditions for the believer were fulfilled—whatever was necessary for entering into a new relationship with Him. Think of the implications of Paul's statement: "If anyone is in Christ, he is a new creature; the old things passed away; behold, new things have come" (2 Corinthians 5:17). There has to be a time when someone is "in Christ" and no longer spiritually associated with the world. There has to be a time when *new* things have come and *old* things have passed away. A person cannot be a "new creature" in Christ unless (or until) he or she has done what it takes to stop being an *old* creature of the world.

### Baptism Provides the Acceptable "When"

The connection to baptism here should already be unmistakable, but conversion itself is not limited to baptism.

God requires you to repent of your sins before you can be born of God; until you do this, you are not born of Him. Jesus requires that you deny yourself, take up your cross, and follow Him unconditionally; until you commit to this, you are not His disciple. The apostle John stated unequivocally that you must love the Father and not the world (1 John 2:15-17); until you give your love to God, you cannot abide in Him.

Scripture is very clear on what *needs* to be done in order to enter into a covenant relationship with God. Those who are in this covenant relationship are provided with everything they need to enjoy fellowship with God, both now and into eternity. Those outside of this covenant remain under God's condemnation for their sinful rebellion against Him. Christ wants all men to come to Him and be saved from this condemnation, but He also requires that we do *our* part—however small it may be in comparison to *God's* part—in our own salvation. If you love Him, you will obey His commandments (John 14:15), whether those commandments have to do with establishing fellowship with Him or maintaining it for the rest of your life.

What is unique about baptism, however, is the visible, public, and historical nature of the act itself.[135] As we have already discussed in previous chapters, baptism serves as the dividing line between one's old life and his new life in Christ. Water is the agent of transition—this is God's decision, not mine or yours—and "baptism now saves you" for this very reason. Until one is baptized, he has not yet fulfilled one of the necessary actions required of all of those who call upon the name of the Lord for salvation. After he is baptized—assuming he has been obedient in whatever else is required of him—he is a "new creature" and is "in Christ."

Asking Jesus into your heart is a sentiment *of* the heart; baptism is an actual event. God never told you to ask Jesus into your heart as a method by which you are born of Him; He *commands* you to be "born" of water for this purpose. Doing *nothing* for your soul is spiritual suicide, whereas living in faithful obedience to God contributes to your salvation (Romans 6:16-17, 1 Peter 1:9, et al). There is a singular point in time in which your life of rebellion to God ends and your life of obedience to Him begins. There is no fuzzy logic or gray area here. It is not a fine line that separates the two, but a division as obvious as an eight-lane freeway.

Granted, it may take years or decades for God's Word to prepare your heart to serve Him, but it is at the moment of your *new birth* that you actually become a Christian. (Recall our earlier analogy of earning a degree: it takes time to *become* a graduate, but you are not *actually* a graduate until you have received your diploma.) Coming to the knowledge that you *need* to be born of God is one thing; actually *being* born of Him is quite another. On the day that you follow through with that commitment, you enter into a covenant relationship with God through Christ. You no longer live for yourself, but Christ lives in you (Galatians 2:20). You are no longer under condemnation, but are set free from that awful state of being (Romans 8:1-2).

### Application of the "When" Factor

The subject of salvation—and especially *your* salvation—must be given your utmost and serious attention. If you fail at playing softball, writing a novel, or other mundane endeavors, you can still lead a productive life of service to God. But if you fail at preparing for your presentation before God—especially because you were never really *born* of God—this has

# Being Born of God

catastrophic results. You cannot afford to be wrong on those things that God has made so clear in His Word. He does not expect you to be a theologian, but He does expect you to treat His Word with respect by reading and obeying it. He does not expect you to be flawless in your obedience, but if you know the right thing to do, then you must strive to do that "thing," whatever it is (Luke 13:24, James 4:17).

To further underscore the critical point of *when* a person is born of God, consider some questions with regard to the matter. No matter where you are in your walk with God, or even if you have not yet *begun* your walk with Him, these are most important questions.

**Question #1: WHEN *does the believer—one who is honestly seeking God, but not yet a Christian—demonstrate his faith in Christ for the purpose of his salvation?***

- ❑ This question has already been answered several times in this study. Nonetheless, a direct wording of the question forces us once again to confront the obvious and inescapable conclusion. One who is *not* born of God has also not (yet) entered into fellowship with Him; therefore, that person does not have the *right* to call himself a Christian (John 1:12-13). No one is born of God who has not yet died to the world. The only death-burial-resurrection process identified in the New Testament for those who come to Christ is water baptism.
- ❑ Nonetheless, there are those who try to minimize the importance of baptism in order to satisfy a predetermined doctrine. Thus, they will say things like, "Salvation is by grace through faith and not inextricably tied to the rite of baptism."[136] This position attempts to divorce baptism *from*

faith, as though the act of baptism does not qualify as a legitimate demonstration *of* faith. Salvation *by grace* cannot be accomplished unless it is *through faith*—i.e., through the obedient faith of the believer.

## Question #2: WHEN is God's forgiveness actually received?

❏ We could word this differently: "Is God's forgiveness given to one who will not show his faith in Him?" But to focus on the "when" factor, we will leave it as it is: *when* is a person forgiven by God? Did He *already* forgive everyone, and we simply have to personally acknowledge this? Are there people whom God will *not* forgive—and if so, for what *reason* does He not forgive them? Does God forgive people who are not Christians? If He does, then what is the point of *becoming* a Christian? If He does not, then it is *necessary* that we become Christians in order to be forgiven.[137] And if we *must* become Christians to receive forgiveness, then we must know for certain *how* and *when* we become Christians.

❏ We have gone to great lengths in this study to examine what the gospel *does* teach: forgiveness is "in Him [Christ]" (Ephesians 1:7), and in order to be "in Christ" one must be *born of God*. If one is not born of God, then neither is he "in Christ"—and neither is he forgiven. And why should he be? That person has not yet called upon the name of the Lord for salvation (Acts 22:16). He has not expressed faith in God's ability to save him. He has not yet obeyed God's commandments *for* salvation, as defined in His gospel *of* salvation. One who thinks that he is forgiven by God without having obeyed Him either lives in defiance of His Word or is under a spell of delusion—whether his own or that of someone else. In either case, you can be sure that no

*Being Born of God*

one is saved through defiance or delusion. Thus, if a person wants to be forgiven by God, then he must be born of God.

**Question #3: WHEN** *is a person united with Christ so as to become a Christian?*

- ❑ This personal "uniting" with Christ serves as the dividing line between one's allegiance to this world (as a sinner) and his new allegiance to Christ (as His disciple). It is critical that this event take place, since it is theologically impossible for a person to be reconciled to God who refuses to submit to this change of allegiance. In conforming to Christ's death, burial, and resurrection, the believer symbolizes his *own* death to this world, his burial (to prove this death), and his resurrection to a new life with God. Paul makes it very clear that one's *water baptism* is the occasion of this critical transition (Romans 6:3-7, Colossians 2:11-13). Since Paul has explicitly defined this requirement, then it is pointless to argue otherwise.

- ❑ Given this specific information, we are not left to wonder at *when* we are joined with Christ. We do not *assume* the point in time when we are born of God; we can know it for certain. Paul also said: "It is a trustworthy statement: for if we died with Him, we will also live with Him" (2 Timothy 2:11). But what if someone has not *yet* "died" with Him? Or what if someone *refuses* to "die" with Him? Or what if someone says, "It is important that you die with Christ, but you can do that later at your convenience. In the meantime, just ask Jesus into your heart..."? Such responses simply cannot be reconciled to what is actually written.

**Question #4: WHEN** *does a believer begin to walk "in newness of life"?*

❑ How many people have assumed that they were "saved" upon asking Jesus into their heart and saying a "sinner's prayer" (or something similar)? After conforming to this condition—a "when" of their own making (since it is not in Scripture)—they conclude that they are now walking "in newness of life." Why would a person stake his *eternal future* on an action that God never asked of him, while avoiding the very action that God *does* ask of him? Man-made theology, no matter how good it seems to the human mind or sounds to the human ear, will never equal or replace the authentic gospel of Christ. God's terms and conditions for entering into a covenant of life with Him remain the same today as when the Holy Spirit spelled them out for us in the New Testament.

❑ So then, what does the New Testament say? In the same passage from which we get "newness of life," we also are told what *produces* this new life: one's immersion in water for the purpose of his identifying with Christ from that point forward (Romans 6:3-7). To clarify: the baptism *by itself* does not produce the new life, as though the water could ever take the place of the blood of Christ. Rather, baptism is an act of obedient faith that is necessary for entering into this new state of being.

❑ No one can be "raised" to a new life until his old life—his "body of sin"—has been lowered into the watery grave. "Asking Jesus into your heart" will not accomplish this, nor will a "sinner's prayer." Assuming this new life into existence because you want it so badly will not make it so. You must *do* what God said to do; you must *act* in the way

God requires you to perform. Such action is not the source or power *of* your salvation—God alone possesses such power—but neither will He impart saving grace to those who refuse to demonstrate human faith. (Remember, we are saved by grace *through* faith, and that faith *must* be proved to exist in order to be genuine.)

**Question #5: WHEN *is the believer "clothed" with Christ?***

❑ Being "clothed" with Christ indicates one's intimate and spiritual identity with Him. No doubt every person who thinks he is a Christian will claim that he (or she) has been clothed with Christ. But *when* did this happen? When did Christ impart His identity upon the believer—the one who desires to be saved? Notice what Paul says: "For you are all sons of God through faith in Christ Jesus. For all of you who were baptized into Christ have clothed yourselves with Christ" (Galatians 3:26-27). Paul makes baptism a necessary condition of one's identification with Christ—and there is no reason to believe that this is anything but *water* baptism, like what he himself underwent (Acts 9:18, 22:16). Baptism serves as the *when* for establishing the dividing line between a person's old identity with the world and his new identity with Christ. Thus, one's baptism is the time—the *when*—that a person becomes a Christian.

❑ If someone says to me, "I became a Christian when I asked Jesus into my heart," I respond, "But what did the apostle Paul instruct you to do?" If someone says, "I was baptized as an infant, and *that* is when I became a Christian," I respond, "But Paul says that we must be 'sons of God through faith in Christ Jesus.' An infant cannot have faith; a young child cannot have the *kind* or *level* of faith Christ demands of him. How, then, did you faithfully obey God with neither faith nor obedience?" We have no authority to modify the terms and conditions of salvation to accommodate our church's teaching, personal convictions, children, or anything else. The gospel is what it is and it says what it says. Do you believe this?

## Question #6: WHEN *is the believer's conscience cleansed of its guilt?*

- ❏ The cleansing of one's conscience has to do with God atoning for that person's guilt for his sins. We know that this atonement is accomplished through the blood of Christ (Ephesians 1:7, Hebrews 9:13-14). Yet, *when* is this accomplished for the sinner-turned-believer who seeks fellowship with God? It happens when that person calls upon the name of the Lord for salvation. *How* he "calls" is not through a pre-scripted "sinner's prayer." This does not mean that prayer itself is absent from the conversion process, but no one is saved by prayer alone, whether one or many. Paul's own conversion account defines "calling upon" the Lord for salvation through the act of water baptism: the two are inseparably linked (Acts 22:16). Thus, baptism becomes the time-stamp or historical event by which a person establishes for certain *when* his conscience was cleansed by the blood of Christ. The water is not the agent *of* salvation, but it most certainly is the God-given link *to* salvation.
- ❏ Peter makes this very clear in his inspired words: "Corresponding to that [i.e., Noah's having been saved through water], baptism now saves you—not the removal of dirt from the flesh, but an appeal to God for a good conscience—through the resurrection of Jesus Christ..."

*Being Born of God* 

(1 Peter 3:21, bracketed words are mine). Baptism is *not* an action that depicts a physical cleansing of the body; it is an act that symbolizes the spiritual cleansing of the human conscience. It is an act of faith that God requires of the one who calls upon Him for salvation. By implication, God will not cleanse one's conscience *until* this act is performed. And why should He? If a person will not obey Him in such a small matter as being immersed in water in His name, why should God expect greater things from him, such as a "living and holy sacrifice" (cf. Romans 12:1)?

❑ God—not water, or the church—is the possessor of salvation. He imparts salvation when *His* terms are met and *His* conditions are satisfied. He does not cleanse the guilty conscience with His Son's blood and *then* require that person to demonstrate his obedient faith in Him, but the other way around (i.e., in the right sequence). "Through the resurrection of Jesus Christ" indicates the *power* of the cleansing: since Christ has the authority and ability to raise Himself from the dead, He most certainly has the power to raise the sinner from the deadness of his spiritual state of being. Beasley-Murray has said it well: "Baptism saves, not because water washes dirt from the body, but as the occasion when a man is met by the Risen Christ."[138] No one "meets" Christ through a mere "sinner's prayer" or by asking Him into his heart. He only "meets" Him when he conforms to whatever God requires of that person in order *to* do so.

## Question #7: WHEN *is the believer sealed with the Holy Spirit?*

❑ To be "sealed" with the Holy Spirit is tantamount to being saved: one cannot happen in the absence of the other. To be "sealed" in this case involves both divine protection and identification. In Ephesians 1:13, Paul wrote, "... After listening to the message of truth, the gospel of your salvation—having also believed, you were sealed in Him with the Holy Spirit of promise...." There is no question that God is the One doing the sealing. But *when* does this happen? "After listening to the message of truth"—this is the message Paul preached, the gospel of Christ (Romans 10:17, Colossians 1:5-6). *Before* hearing the message, a person has no reason to obey God; *after* hearing the message, he now has a reason to believe and obey. In this case, "after" indicates conditions being met as well as a proper sequence of events. We have no shred of evidence in the New Testament of anyone becoming a Christian *before* hearing the gospel message. But hearing by itself is not enough: ancient Israel also heard good news [lit., gospel], but did not respond to it with faith (Hebrews 4:2). "Having also believed": *when* the Ephesians married human faith with divine will, *then* God imparted His Spirit to them.

❑ Someone says, "Exactly! No baptism required!" Such a conclusion overlooks entirely what "believing" requires in itself. (The text does not say "repent" either, but we are confident that no one receives God's Spirit who refuses to do this.) We have examined repeatedly that "believing" demands obedience, and this obedience (in conversion) requires specific actions. One of these actions—not the *only* one, but a *necessary* one—is baptism. In fact, Paul elsewhere says that we all "drink of one Spirit" *through* the baptism that that same Spirit defined and commanded for this purpose (1 Corinthians 12:12-13). This answers definitively *when* we receive the Spirit of God: it is at the time of our baptism into Christ. We have no reason to receive Him before this, and we have no reason to doubt this reception after it, as long as our baptism itself is carried out according to the New Testament instruction and example.[139]

❑ We need to clarify even further, because this is a point of common misunderstanding. Baptism is not the "seal" in itself; the Holy Spirit is. Baptism is not the sealing *process* itself, either; whatever God does to seal the human soul with His Spirit is His work, not ours. We cannot duplicate a divine process by being immersed in physical water. However, baptism is the occasion *of* the sealing, and is not something separate from it. Thus, the two things—sealing and baptism—are directly related, but not interchangeable. Both have a direct bearing upon one's conversion to Christ: no one has access to God apart from His Spirit (Ephesians 2:18), and no one can be born of God until he first "dies" in the act of baptism. Once again, "...Unless one is born of water and the Spirit he cannot enter into the kingdom of God" (John 3:5).

### Saved Anyway?

We could continue to examine these "when" scenarios, but they would all reach the same conclusion. No one can call upon God for salvation without submitting to water baptism as a necessary part of that appeal. This does not mean that *nothing* is done prior to baptism; it means that *until* baptism is accomplished, a person is not yet considered a Christian. In other words, a person can be building his faith, praying for understanding, repenting of his sins, and associating himself with Christians, but none of these actions take the place of or nullify the need for his baptism. Baptism is the visible and historical event that definitively separates his old life from his new self.[140] Baptism ends his allegiance to sin and begins his allegiance to Christ. Baptism forever changes his status from a man (or woman) of the world to a child of God.

Until the conditions and sequences necessary for entering into a covenant relationship with God are met, that relationship has not yet been established. Put another way: if a person shows no regard for the manner in which God wants things done, then God will not save that person. And why should He? Such a person shows impudence and irreverence toward the One to whom he appeals to save his soul. This is not faith, it is foolishness; this is not obedience, it is rebellion. God will save neither fools nor rebels. "But," He says, "to this one I will look, to him who is humble and contrite of spirit, and who trembles at My word" (Isaiah 66:2). To "tremble" at God's Word is to obey it, not to try to re-invent it or cram it into a pre-ordained doctrine of one's own choice.

Once again, the "when" factor is critical in the context of one's conversion to Christ. People do not just gradually or imperceptibly morph into becoming a disciple of Christ, nor can they elect to observe conditions or sequences that appeal to *them* but did not originate with *God*.

## Summary Thoughts

It is highly unpopular today to hear about "conditions" placed upon one's relationship with God. Instead, people have grown fond of *un*-conditional Christianity in which God's love for everyone translates to God's salvation for everyone. Yet, this is not the gospel we read about in the Bible. Whatever we know factually of the gospel of salvation through Christ comes to us from the New Testament. In other words, the same source material that shows us the greatness of God's unconditional love also reveals the conditions of God's saving grace. We cannot

## Being Born of God

have it both ways. If one will not fulfill his part in pursuing his own salvation, God does not save him "anyway."

Some will say, "Conversion is a process, not an event." This is true, but it can also easily distort the *conditions* of one's conversion. It is more accurate to say, "Conversion is a process of conscious actions, and *culminates* in a specific, visible, and historical event." One's conversion is not complete until *all* of these actions have been fulfilled by the believer. Baptism is just one of those actions, but it is a necessary one all the same. We would be wrong to single out baptism as the only requirement—or even the most important requirement—for becoming a Christian. Yet, we would be just as wrong to assume that people are converted to Christ before or apart from being baptized.

The "when" factor is critical in conversion. Even those who do not believe in baptism for salvation recognize a point in time—a *when*—in which a person did *something* to become a Christian. These people will call this "when" a "sinner's prayer," an asking-Jesus-into-the-heart experience, a "confirmation" ceremony, a spiritual epiphany, or some other time-based, historical event that indicates a person's changed allegiance. Such conclusions, however, defy biblical teaching; they are additions *to* it—or reinventions *of* it—rather than being in compliance *with* it. In contrast, baptism is exactly the event *God* requires of those who seek Him in faithful obedience.

Any controversy on this subject does not lie with God, His apostles, or the early church; it lies with modern *resistance* to what God, His apostles, and the early church actually taught.[141] Modern religion has attempted to reduce the importance of water baptism, re-define it in light of contemporary thinking, or remove the practice altogether. But this does not mean for a moment that anything has changed in God's world. His expectations of believers—if they wish to *remain* believers—are the same today as they were in the Paul's day. Baptism is just as necessary and relevant today as it was then. Whether or not you believe this does not change God's teaching, but it has significant effect on how He regards you.

## Chapter Fourteen:
# Common Questions about Baptism

"I was doing just fine in my understanding of conversion. Now I am questioning everything I've done and everything that I had believed. Why did you have to do that?"

- ❑ Despite the popular tongue-in-cheek saying, ignorance really is *not* bliss. Nonetheless, many people hear a version of the gospel of Christ and think that, having followed that version, they have become Christians. Sadly, many of these look no further, ask no more questions, and accept the conclusions of others as their own. Such ignorance does not excuse anyone, especially when we have everything we need pertaining to "life and godliness" in God's revealed Word (cf. 2 Peter 1:3). One of my primary objectives in this book is to force you to re-examine your beliefs—whatever they are—in light of what God says. God wants you to be saved; I also want you to be saved. God does not desire for anyone to be lost; I also do not desire for anyone to be lost, no matter how horrible they might be presently. But neither you nor I can be saved by clinging to convictions that are irrelevant to salvation or that defy what God has revealed concerning it.
- ❑ We would all love to live in the comfort zone of what each of us has come to know as "my personal faith in Christ." I would also. And yet, my own faith in Christ has been strongly challenged over the last number of years, and I have come to a better understanding of what "faith" really means as a result of this. I truly believe that your faith—if you allow yourself to be confronted *with* "the truth" rather than what you *perceive* to be true—will also grow and mature

over time. I also believe that you can have a budding faith in God and still not (yet) be a Christian. Cornelius is a case in point (Acts 10): he was a devout man, God heard his prayers because of his devotion, and He invited him—with His own Holy Spirit—to join in fellowship with Him. This culminated in his baptism into Christ. We can confidently conclude that if Cornelius had refused to be baptized, he would have ceased to be devout and would not have become a Christian.

❑ Given the New Testament, I have no reason to believe that your conversion to Christ—or *anyone's* conversion—can supersede Cornelius' own. In other words, no matter how devout to God you are (or *think* you are), you still have to respond in the same way Cornelius did. God has given you His apostles—not a personal visit like what Cornelius received, but their *teaching* (2 Peter 3:1-2)—so that you also can know what he heard. If you have not been born of God, then God is calling you—not with miracles and tongue-speaking, but with His gospel (2 Thessalonians 2:13-14)—and He expects you to respond rightly. What Peter said to Cornelius is just as true today as it was then: "I most certainly understand now that God is not one to show partiality, but in every nation the man who fears Him and does what is right is welcome to Him" (Acts 10:34). If baptism is part of "what is right" in God's sight, then it is necessary that you do this in order to be born of Him. If you know the right thing to do but refuse to do it, how can you stand in His favor (cf. James 4:17)? But if you do what He says, all will be well.

## Being Born of God

> "Your views appear to be the same as those of Alexander Campbell, the 'father' of the 19th-century Restoration Movement. So then, are you a Campbellite?"

- ❏ Alexander Campbell (1788 – 1866) was indeed directly affiliated with and largely responsible for the so-called Restoration Movement early in American history. Campbell and others came out of denominationalism and sought an earnest return to the Bible as the sole authority for everything having to do with salvation and fellowship with God. It is true that my understanding of baptism concurs largely with his. But what is the point of that distinction? When my views on Scripture concur with the Pope's, this does not make me a Catholic, does it? When I agree with John Calvin (and I do on numerous points), do I become a Calvinist? I was not baptized into Campbell; Campbell did not die to save my soul (see 1 Corinthians 1:12-13). My teaching *must* be consistent with Paul, since he was an apostle of Christ, but Campbell was just another man seeking the truth (and making some mistakes along the way), and whether or not my views reflect his is irrelevant. I am not here to defend or indict him; rather, I am here to uphold the teaching of Scripture.

- ❏ Bob Ross (a Baptist) says this of Alexander Campbell: he is "a religious sham, counterfeit, farce, fake, fraud, impostor, humbug, charlatan, and mountebank."[142] I get the impression that Ross does not like Campbell (and I had to look up "mountebank"). He spends a large part of his book (*Campbellism: Its History and Heresies*) denouncing him and his views on baptism. But what is that to me? I believe Ross is terribly mistaken in his mean-spirited portrayal of

Campbell, but what does that have to do with the teaching of Scripture on being "born of God"? The biblical case for the necessity of baptism is more than compelling, whoever argues it—and regardless of whoever argues *against* it. If a person thinks he can negate biblical teaching based upon discrediting those who hold to that teaching, he is sorely mistaken. Instead, a person should seek to uphold the truth no matter who else does or does not believe it, no matter what consequences, severing of ties, or criticism results from this.

- Let me be clear: I am not a Campbellite—nor should you be one. I am a Christian, and only a Christian. I refuse any other name but Christ's; I am earnestly trying to teach no other teachings than His; I will be saved by no other Savior but Him. If you wish to brand me in some other way, I cannot stop you, but you will be purposely misrepresenting who I really am—and then what would that make *you*? My plea for you, whoever you are, is to abandon all allegiances to one teacher, mentor, historical figure, family member, or religious tradition, and follow only Christ and His Word. This will lead you to become a Christian—nothing more or less. If this puts you in company with those who are frowned upon by others, this must be irrelevant to you. Christ Himself is disparaged by most of the world; many will hate you because they hate Him (John 15:18-19). "For am I now seeking the favor of men, or of God? Or am I striving to please men? If I were still trying to please men, I would not be a bond-servant of Christ" (Galatians 1:10).

## Being Born of God

"What about those who are sincere about their faith in God, but haven't been baptized? Are you saying they will be lost just because they did not accept your 'entrance terms'"?

- ❏ When someone asks a question this way, there often is an underlying scorn or contempt for me personally, as if I stood in the middle of another person's salvation to God. In other words, such a person wants to put the responsibility for salvation on *me*—and then find fault with my answer—rather than listening to all the biblical *evidence* I have provided on the subject of baptism. Let me be clear: I cannot, will not, and am unworthy to stand between *any* person and his or her God. Whoever is saved or *not* saved bears the responsibility for his own actions regardless of what I say or do not say. This does not invalidate the *conclusions* I have drawn, however, if indeed they are true and accurately represented.
- ❏ I have no private "entrance terms" into the spiritual body of Christ, but you can be certain that God *does*. The fact that I agree with these terms and promote them does not make someone accountable to me, but to the God who revealed them. When someone tells me that they are a Christian, it is not uncommon for me to ask, "How did you *become* a Christian?" I do not ask this to compare *their* faith with *mine*, or their conversion experience with my own, but to see if they have done what God actually requires of them. I have no authority to admit anyone into heaven or keep them from being admitted, but God does. What crime have I committed in seeking the spiritual welfare of another?
- ❏ I have gone to great lengths in this book to demonstrate that no one can remain sincere in his faith in God who refuses

to do what He commands. This is as true for refusing the command to be baptized as it is for refusing to repent, pray, or forgive others. The question above implies that a person can maintain a sincere faith in light of known disobedience to what God has instructed for all who wish to enjoy His salvation. This is impossible, and this false premise destroys the integrity of that person's question to me before it is even out of his mouth. "We walk by faith, not by sight" (2 Corinthians 5:7), and no one can "walk" with God who will not *by faith* follow His prescription for becoming a Christian.

❑ F. LaGard Smith wrote, "I'm worried less about how God may judge those who haven't been baptized than I am about the disregard of Scripture that permits such shallow thinking about baptism."[143] Actually, I am concerned for *both* groups, but I understand what he is saying. Given the profoundly important subject of salvation, it is amazing to see so many religious people dismiss the need for baptism with such indifference. And if it is not outright indifference ("Whatever—you see it your way, I see it mine"), then it is often unwarranted resistance ("Baptism is *not* essential, no matter what you say!"). I wonder how many of these people have made an honest investigation into the subject—like *you* just did, in reading this book!—rather than simply shrug it off as one of those things over which theologians like to argue. One man, a denominational preacher, told me that my insistence on baptism was "nitpicking." Hmmm. After all the biblical evidence that we have covered so far, what do you think?

## Being Born of God

"How do you account for those who have been baptized according to the biblical instruction but lead shallow and ineffective spiritual lives? Likewise, how do you explain those who are *not* baptized (and not part of an organized religion) yet exhibit a deep and meaningful relationship with God?"

❑ What is interesting about this question—and people really have asked this question—is that it does not deny the biblical instruction. Instead, it assumes that since some are insincere to their profession of faith, the instruction is rendered null and void for everyone else. Thus, the first part of the question boils down to this: "Since there are hypocrites in the Christian religion, I don't want any part of it," or, "…I don't have to conform to what they believe." The second part of the question boils down to this: "Since good and loving people do exist outside of the Christian religion, this renders that religion as being unnecessary, and even oppressive." This seems to imply that *the Christian religion*—and "church" especially—is the source for all hypocrisy in the world. "And that's why I won't obey God!"—what?!

❑ Here is the huge problem with this kind of (above) reasoning: it is self-refuting. Those who point fingers at all the hypocrites are themselves hypocrites, since they know the right thing to do but refuse to do it (on account of other people's hypocrisy, of all things). Or, those who point to the alleged righteousness of non-Christians confess by their *own* beliefs that such people are still disobedient to God, regardless of their incidental goodness. Either way you look at it, this kind of thinking fails to negate the instruction for obedience to God, or for baptism in particular. All it attempts to do is distract attention away from what *needs* to be done and focuses it on those who are not *doing* this.

❑ So then, I would ask this person: "What is your point?" Are there hypocrites in the church? Of course! I have met them, I have counseled them *not* to be hypocrites—I have even *been* one of them. (In fact, I could be one of them *right now*!) But what does this prove? How does this bear upon the person making the observation—or you yourself? For example, we do not abandon the practice of marriage just because bad marriages exist, or because people choose to live together instead. A sinful relationship does not invalidate a legitimate one, no matter how many people practice the sinful one. In another example, there are many bad drivers "out there"—and I think most of them live in my city!—but this does not negate the need for driver's licenses or driver's training. Obviously, there are many hypocrites on the road—those who *say* they are law-abiding citizens, but *drive* like psychopathic maniacs—but this does not mean anything by itself. There are many excellent drivers as well. One does not invalidate the other; one does not prevent the other from existing.

❑ The reality is: there are hypocrites *everywhere*. It is not a church problem or a religious problem; it is a blight of the human condition. Hypocrisy is found in the most pious Christian congregation, and it is found among atheists, Jews, Muslims, Buddhists, Wiccans, Native Americans, homosexuals, the Ku Klux Klan, and every other specific group of people. Again, *what is the point* of fingering a certain negative characteristic of human behavior as a "reason" why a person does not need to be baptized or have anything to do with Christianity? This is fallacious

# Being Born of God

reasoning. It excuses no one, but simply avoids the truth. The truth is: Christianity, *as it was revealed to us*, provides for the best life on earth, and prepares a person for the eternity to come. We need the grace of God to compensate for our failures, but no one will receive saving grace by refusing to do what He has asked.

❑ Finally, regarding those who are not baptized but appear to have a "deep and meaningful relationship" with God, we are compelled to ask: based upon *what*, exactly? If one is not born *of* God until he obeys Him, how can he have a "deep and meaningful relationship" with Him otherwise? No one can assume he has a relationship with God that does not have any legitimate reason to exist, no matter how sincere or passionate that person is (or appears to be). Entering into a covenant relationship with God requires agreeing to *and* obeying the terms and conditions of that covenant. If one will not do this, then God is not just going to save him "anyway." Nothing in Scripture will lead to such a conclusion.

## "Who is allowed to perform a baptism?"

❑ This is a thorny question in the sense that there is no specific or direct instruction in the New Testament to answer it. Here is what we know for certain from the New Testament record: First, only Christians baptized those who also became Christians (with the exception of the very *first* baptism—see discussion below). Second, no one baptized himself or herself; the action was always carried out with one *performing* the baptism and another one *being* immersed. Third, only men baptized both men and women; we have no instance (or even a plausible implication) of a woman baptizing anyone under any circumstance.

- ❏ Obviously, we can imagine an unwritten exception to the "only Christians can baptize" scenario: anytime there are two or more believers who wish to become Christians at the same time (and no Christians are available at all), *someone* has to baptize the other, and that "someone" will not yet be a Christian until he himself is baptized. This is not an insurmountable problem, however, but is simply a matter of practical logistics. (Similarly, the Law of Moses did not allow a man to marry his sister [Leviticus 18:6, 9], yet in the beginning of human history, this was absolutely necessary if humankind was going to continue.) It is likely that these situations are rare, if they happen at all anymore (with the prolific number of Christians in the world today), but we will concede the possibility.

- ❏ The *primary emphasis* in baptism is clearly on the one being baptized, and only secondarily on the one performing it.[144] This means that, in the end, a person's *baptism (immersion) into Christ* is more important than all other factors surrounding that baptism. It does *not* mean, however, that there is nothing required of the one performing this baptism. In other words, we cannot focus on one thing to the exclusion of all others; rather, we should focus on *all* factors involved, but recognize that some may be more important than others. It is entirely inappropriate—and, outside of extraordinary circumstances (discussed below), *unthinkable*—for a non-believer to baptize a believer, or for someone who *thinks* he is a Christian (but has not been baptized!) to immerse one who desires to *become* a Christian. The New Testament record, and the Book of Acts in particular, have established the precedent for all believers to follow. Extraordinary circumstances that are not defined or explained by this record cannot modify or permanently alter that record. The record stands as it is; we dare not *willfully* or *carelessly* violate it. To do so is not obedience; it is rebellion.

- ❑ Having said this, we must confess that extraordinary circumstances are possible, and people are going to have to deal with these to the best of their ability. If I was not a Christian but learned the gospel and needed to be baptized, I have to believe that I would do everything in my power to find a Christian to baptize me. If this could not be done (within a reasonable amount of time), then I would find *someone* to baptize me. My other alleged option is to forego baptism altogether, but this seems far worse than the first option, given the Bible's teaching on the matter. Maybe you strongly disagree with this; maybe you were already "there" and wondered what took me so long. Regardless, it really does not matter, because I am not in that situation—and you probably are not either—and therefore neither one of us has to render a verdict here.

- ❑ A related concern that is often raised in connection with the above scenario is this: what about the *moral fitness* of the one doing the baptizing? What if *he* is insincere, or hiding some secret sin, or is a false teacher at heart (but no one has detected him yet)—does this invalidate the obedience of the one being baptized? Well, what do you think? It stands to reason that we expect men who perform baptisms to be honest, genuine, and faithful Christians. If we *know* them to be otherwise, then we should not allow them to baptize anyone. Yet, we also cannot know the heart of another man; only God knows the human heart for certain (John 2:24-25, 1 Corinthians 2:11, Hebrews 4:12-13, et al). The question, then, comes down to this: is *anyone's* obedience to God ultimately dependent upon the perfect obedience of *any* other person? If it is, then our salvation is dependent upon men and not God (and our personal faith in Him); you will not find any Scripture to support this. If it is not, then each man answers to God for his own actions; this is entirely biblical. Thus, as long as there is no good reason to believe he is deceitful, any faithful Christian man can baptize one who is prepared to become a Christian.

❑ Does this mean that a Christian does not have to be a *minister* (or, choose your favorite descriptor here) in order to baptize? Or, must a man be "ordained" or have a divinity degree or graduate from a certain "Christian university" before he can perform this sacred rite? For many, the influence of centuries-old denominationalism is difficult to ignore in this case, especially for those who had once been indoctrinated with these teachings. Many assign the act of baptism to those who have authority to do so—the so-called clergy, priests, or church officials of any given congregation. Yet, when we look into the New Testament for any support of this, we come up empty. The only "authority" to baptize is the commandments of Christ and His apostles. This authority is not given to specific men, but to *all* Christian men; it is not the exclusive right of preachers and elders, as many assume. There is no clergy-laity system described or even hinted at in the New Testament. Elders are shepherds over the congregation that appointed them; deacons are servants to the congregation that appointed them; and preachers are ministers to the Word of God. These men are not clergy, but Christians; they alone are not "priests," for all Christians are priests to God and servants of one another (1 Peter 2:9). There is no official ordination process by which one becomes specially qualified to baptize. The qualification to baptize is one's faithfulness to God and (thus) his adherence to the instructions of Christ and His apostles. It may be true that elders and ministers are frequently called upon to baptize; however, other Christian men could be called upon as well.

❑ As to the second point—namely, that no one can baptize himself (or herself)—we can also imagine a situation in which there is only *one* person who reads the gospel and wishes to obey it, yet there is no one who can or will baptize him. In my understanding, a person has to do what he (or she) believes is the best way to handle this. I think it would be highly unlikely that a person will come into contact with the gospel in such an isolated circumstance that *no one* would be able to baptize him, but this is not an impossible scenario, either. In the end, what that person does must be in agreement with the expressed will of God to the best of his ability. What we *cannot* do, however, is use that isolated, extraordinary, and rare situation and create a policy for *all* scenarios ("It's okay to baptize yourself, if you choose"). Recall the chapter on "Hypothetical Arguments": we cannot use exceptional or hypothetical situations to make new laws. The "rule" is: someone must baptize the one desiring to become a Christian, and that "someone" must himself be a Christian. Any exceptions to that, if they exist at all, must be the result of insurmountable circumstances and not personal preference, church policy, or any other subjective determination. And remember, you cannot arbitrarily create an "extraordinary circumstance" or define one *as* "extraordinary" only to uphold a certain belief or excuse yourself from what is written in Scripture.

❏ As to the third point—namely, whether women can baptize—we again must refer to the New Testament example as the precedent for what we do. In every case recorded, we see no one but male Christians baptizing; there are no exceptions. This means that, apart from extraordinary circumstances, this is the way this action is supposed to done. In a situation in which a woman needs to obey the gospel but there are no Christian men available to baptize her—if such a scenario is even possible—then she must do her best to obey God under those circumstances. (By "available," I do not mean "in the room at the time" or "physically present," but unable to be reached at all in a reasonable amount of time.)

**"Why weren't the apostles and the 120 disciples in the 'upper room' [cf. Acts 1:12-15] baptized?"**

❏ Who says they were not? It is true that we do not have a specific account of these peoples' baptisms; it is not true that this proves anything by itself. We cannot prove anything for certain based upon silence alone. What we *do* know, however, is what Peter—one of the apostles in that upper room—preached just a short time later: "Repent, and each of you be baptized in the name of Jesus Christ for the forgiveness of your sins…" (Acts 2:38). It is illogical to assume that Peter commanded the Jews to do this, yet excluded himself and certain others, when *all* parties sought the same objective. It was also Peter who wrote by inspiration, "Baptism now saves you" (1 Peter 3:21). Even though he was an apostle, Peter was not exempt from the process of salvation required of everyone else. Likewise, there is no record of Apollos being baptized into Christ (Acts 18:24-28), and yet both Peter [Cephas] and this man went about baptizing others (1 Corinthians 1:11-13). This latter action would be contradictory to these men's teaching, if indeed they were not baptized themselves.

- ❏ The above question *does* highlight one of those "I wish we had that in writing (in the Bible)" scenarios. But there are a number of things that Scripture does not reveal in actual words, but that can be answered through necessary implications and logical deductions. What we *do* have spelled out for us, however, is not negated by those situations in which the Holy Spirit has chosen to remain silent. Perhaps He wants us to use our God-given reasoning to come to a sound and sensible conclusion; or, perhaps He simply wants us *not* to know everything so that we will exercise faith in what He *has* revealed rather than doubt Him for what He has *not*. After all, faith in God requires that He does not explain everything to us (or you).

- ❏ Unfortunately, the above question is sometimes asked with an ulterior motive. In other words, some will argue, "Since the apostles were not baptized for salvation, then neither does anyone else need to do this." This assumes much and proves nothing. This assumes that the apostles (and 120 others) were *in fact* not baptized, and that the doctrine of baptism and being born of God all hinges upon this point. This *wants* to prove that baptism is not essential because some were allegedly exempted from it and were still pleasing to God anyway. Such assumptions insinuate that, despite all He *has* revealed on the subject, the Holy Spirit undermined all of this by not providing us with (what some claim is) critical information. Would God be so careless? Can we accuse Him of being careless *at all*? Once again, just because there are details that we do *not* know does not invalidate the ones we *do* know.

"What about those who had *no access* to the instruction concerning baptism—those who have lived their entire lives without ever hearing the gospel of Christ? Will they be lost because they *could not* obey?"

- ❏ First, let's assume that this is an honest question. Notice again that the person posing it does not doubt the need for baptism, but just the opposite. His question implies: "Will God hold a person responsible for a situation that is beyond his ability to control?" The short answer is: who am I (or anyone else) to say how God will judge the soul of another under circumstances that exceed human knowledge? What we *can* say is that God will be merciful and fair in His judgment of all souls, because He has proved Himself to be a merciful and fair God for thousands of years of recorded history (in the Old Testament). Thus, He will take into account a person's entire circumstance—what he knew, what he could *not* know, how he responded to what he did know, etc. The "secrets of men" will one day be exposed (cf. Romans 2:16)—not by us, but by the God who *knows* us even better than we know ourselves (Hebrews 4:12-13).

- ❏ But to understand the question and its limited answer, we need to discern between two kinds of ignorance: that which is chosen and that which is (for lack of a better word) insurmountable. Chosen ignorance is the willful rejection or suppression of knowledge even though it was available. If you live in modern America, you cannot claim that you have never heard of God, Jesus Christ, the Bible, or the gospel message *at all*. Such knowledge, however rudimentary it may be expressed, permeates our society. Or, if you have a Bible in your possession but failed to read it, you cannot claim, "I didn't know," because you *should* have known.

Insurmountable ignorance, on the other hand, is that which is *humanly impossible to know* for lack of availability (or understanding). Thus, consider the infamous example of an Aborigine tribe in the Australian interior that (many assume) has never heard the gospel of Christ. That people may be excused from having to obey Christ's gospel, since God cannot hold people accountable to what they could not know.[145] Yet, this does not mean they will not be judged *at all* by a God-given standard. God has provided sufficient physical, moral, and spiritual evidence that He *does exist*, and therefore all are accountable to Him (which is Paul's argument in Acts 14:12-17, 17:22-29, and Romans 1:18-28). *How* those people with insurmountable ignorance of His gospel will be accountable to Him is not specifically known to us. God's ability to examine fully and accurately the human heart puts Him in a unique position to determine who *could* know about this gospel and who could *not*.

❑ Now let's assume this (above) question is asked with an ulterior motive. There are some who use this line of reasoning to "prove" that baptism is not essential for salvation. (Based upon the premise they offer, however, we must conclude that the entire gospel of Christ is also not required.) In other words, if they could argue that *some* will be saved apart from baptism, then this renders baptism as unnecessary for salvation. Yet, as discussed above, the argument for baptism is based upon the revealed gospel of Christ. In the case of those who *cannot* know the gospel, they also cannot know baptism. This latter conclusion is the same by which we are to understand Mark 16:16: "He who has believed and has been baptized shall be saved; but he who has disbelieved shall be condemned." A person who does not believe in a gospel that requires baptism will certainly not be baptized into Christ. Likewise, a person who cannot know the gospel of Christ cannot believe in it (or Him) and will not be baptized.

- ❑ God does not save anyone based upon ignorance; we must never teach otherwise. To acknowledge that there might be people that *cannot* know of the gospel—assuming that this is even possible in the modern world—does not for a moment undermine any New Testament teaching on baptism. God will judge those people mercifully and fairly, by whatever moral standard they *did* know, and some of them will indeed be justified *by* grace *through* faith. This grace will still be that which comes through Christ's sacrifice, and their faith will still be in the Creator whom they acknowledge and obey, just as with us. However, they remain in a different situation than us because they are not privileged to know what we (ought to) know. They are not an *exception* to the rule; they are under an entirely different set of rules, so to speak, altogether. But as for me and you, we know too much to claim ignorance.

**"I was baptized in a denominational church. Do I need to be baptized in *your* church in order for my baptism to be legitimate?"**

- ❑ This question has been asked of me a number of times. It can be an honest question, based on several misunderstandings, or it can be asked with contempt. Let's assume the "honest question" scenario first. One's baptism in a denominational church can mean one of several different things. It may mean that a person was physically immersed in a baptistery owned by a denominational group. Or, it

*Being Born of God* 243

may mean that a person was baptized in order to become a member *of* that group, to take on its name (Baptist, Mormon, Catholic, etc.). Or, it may mean that a person was baptized for biblical reasons, but by a denominational minister (or, in a denominational context).

- In the first case, we know that baptism defined by the gospel of Christ means immersion in water. But does it really matter who owns the water, so to speak, in which you are immersed? I know that there are ultra-conservative Christians who would say "Absolutely!" They believe that if you are not immersed in a "scriptural," non-denominational tank of water, then you are not a Christian. I strongly disagree with this, simply because it is entirely indefensible *from* Scripture. But this also does not mean that all baptisms are acceptable simply because one is immersed in water. (Recall the points made in the chapter titled "The One Baptism.")

- In the second case, if a person is baptized in order to become a member of a man-made denomination—one that Christ did not authorize and His gospel does not describe—then he was not baptized into Christ; he just got wet.[146] No water baptism in the New Testament (from Acts 2 forward) was for any purpose other than putting a person "in Christ"—*not* in a congregation, a religious organization, or especially a denomination. The problem here is not merely an ineffective baptism. A baptism that serves only to conform to denominational policy is only as good as the biblical legitimacy of the denomination itself—and there is a complete absence of *any* denominational system in the New Testament. If a person thinks otherwise, then I respectfully challenge him (or her) to *find* his group defined or even mentioned in the New Testament. If he cannot, but was baptized to participate in one, then he must seriously question what he did and why he did it. (I should mention here that not all "non-denominational" or "un-denominational" groups are automatically free from the teachings and effects of denominationalism. But this is another discussion altogether.)

- ❑ In the third case, I would never recommend that someone be baptized by a denominational minister—i.e., someone who actively supports the denominational structure by the fact of his own position. If the New Testament will not support denominational-*ism*, then it will also not support those who *do*. Such teachers ought to know better. They cannot have possibly covered the New Testament without the glaringly conspicuous *absence* of anything that would legitimize the existence of their own denomination. Furthermore, the only time denominationalism (or, sectarianism) *is* mentioned in the New Testament is when it is being condemned (as in Romans 16:17-18, 1 Corinthians 1:10-13, or 11:18-19). Having said this, we also recognize that, with regard to his personal obedience to God, a person may have been baptized legitimately—for all the reasons that he *should* be baptized—yet sought out a man who in hindsight was discovered *not* to be the right person to participate in this. Once again, is one's obedience determined by the righteousness of another? It is impossible to defend a "yes" answer to that question. Yet, in this case, it remains a matter of conscience between the person who was baptized and God as to whether or not his baptism was done in factual agreement with Scripture or simply accommodated his (former) minister's agenda.
- ❑ Beyond this, we need to clear the air about another implication made in the original question above. If someone

asks, "Do I need to be baptized into *your* church?" I respond, "I don't even *own* a church! And even if I did, you would not be saved by becoming a member of it!" The only church that matters is *Christ's* church. A person needs to be baptized into *His* church, not one founded by mere men. This is not to say that Christ's *church* is the source of salvation, but that those who *are* saved must be members of it. We refer, of course, to His "body" (cf. Ephesians 1:22-23, Colossians 1:18), the spiritual sanctuary of all believers, both living and dead. I believe that the congregation I attend has the right to identify itself with Christ, but just because someone identifies with *us* does not mean he or she has necessarily identified with *Him*. Do you see the difference? The only thing that matters is one's obedience to what Christ requires. What I require—or, what "we" require—will not change your eternity.

❑ Finally, some ask the original question above in a contemptuous way, as in, "You people think you are the *only church* to be saved, and that everyone needs to comply with *your* demands! How arrogant!" Sadly, some of the people I identify with have incited such comments with their own legalistic, holier-than-thou attitude. But such comments also tend to exaggerate, misrepresent, and overgeneralize the real situation. Once again, no one—not even I—can be saved by being a member of "my" congregation. The emphasis is on Christ and *His* church, not us and "our" churches. The baptistery in my congregation's church building is not superior to another baptistery. "Our" water is not more "scriptural" than someone else's water! Compliance with *my* demands may get you wet, but compliance with Christ's demands is what obedient faith is all about. Is "my" church the only one being saved? What does that even mean, exactly? Christ does not save whole congregations, and especially not groups of them. He only saves individual souls that have obeyed His gospel and surrendered all allegiance to Him. *This* group of people—His church—is His ultimate concern. The question is: are you in *that* group? And if so, how did this happen?

**"I have sinned so much (after having become a Christian) that I have doubts about my salvation. Will my excessive sinfulness invalidate my baptism?"**

❑ The guilty conscience is a powerful thing; I speak from experience. It can convince us that we are *too unworthy* of salvation. The fact is, however, that we have *never* been "worthy" of salvation, even with our very best behavior. This notion that we are one day worthy and the next day unworthy is the result of a saved-by-works mentality. The gospel does not support it, and neither should you. Paul asked the rhetorical question this way: "Are you so foolish? Having begun by the Spirit, are you now being perfected by the flesh?" (Galatians 3:3). In other words, can we really believe that we are born again through the power of God but earn our salvation thereafter? Or, can we really believe that we were unworthy to be saved at the time of our conversion but now the situation has changed? As I understand the gospel of Christ, you—whoever you are—will *never* be worthy to receive the blood of Christ, and neither will I. So then, why do we have so much anxiety over whether we are now *un*-worthy? Our worthiness remains unchanged; the constant need for God's grace proves this. What becoming a Christian *does* change is the recourse we have by which we can *deal* with our unworthiness.

- Being born of God changes your life—and the status of your soul—forever. A congregation must sever its fellowship with those Christians who impenitently refuse to walk with Christ. But one thing we cannot do is remove someone from Christ's spiritual church. In essence, once a person becomes a "brother" in Christ, he is always a spiritual brother to us, as far as we are concerned (2 Thessalonians 3:14-15). He may be a stubborn, disobedient, blasphemous, and very worldly-minded brother, but he is still "in Christ" until Christ Himself removes him in the final cleansing of His church.[147] We must remove our fellowship from an impenitent brother in Christ, but we cannot "unbaptize" him.

- The name "Christian" does not determine faithfulness by itself; it proclaims what we *ought* to be—followers of Christ—not necessarily what we *are*. If a person has "fallen away" from the faith, he is a Christian who has not remained true to his pledge to be faithful to Christ. Is there any hope for him? If he comes to his senses, yes. He must confess his sins, repent of them, and beg God for forgiveness—just like faithful Christians do who nonetheless sin against God. However, if he sins so much that his conscience no longer feels the pang of guilt *or* the joy of divine grace, then he cannot repent because his heart is callous to any godly sorrow (cf. 2 Corinthians 7:10). This is the awful situation described in Hebrews 6:4-8, 10:26-31 and 2 Peter 2:20-22. This is not a state of being that *we* (as observers) are able to determine conclusively, but that most certainly *can* exist. In my understanding, every Christian that turns away from the Lord puts himself at terrible risk of ending up in that state; realistically, however, not all wayward Christians are in such an advanced state of moral corruption.

❑ To address the question (above) directly: the *number* of sins cannot disqualify a person from being a Christian; neither can the *grievousness* of those sins. If a person always remains a Christian, then the event which marks his having *become* a Christian—his baptism into Christ—also remains intact and legitimate. At the same time, the longer a Christian remains in defiance of the truth, the harder his heart becomes toward the grace of God. This means that he will be increasingly unresponsive to the plea of the gospel (and his brethren) *to* return (see Hebrews 3:12-15). My strong advice to any Christian reading this who has backslidden from his original allegiance to Christ: *come to your senses* and do what is right, no matter how hard or embarrassing it may be. You only have so much time and opportunity left. Every day that passes in which you remain in your present condition makes it all the more unlikely that you will ever change.

**"I've heard negative things about 'baptismal regeneration.' What is the controversy over this phrase?"**
❑ "Baptismal regeneration"—a phrase not found in Scripture—means that the very *act* of baptism is the power for or cause of one's "regeneration" to God. ("Regeneration" in this context refers to becoming alive [again] in Christ. "Made us alive" [as in Ephesians 2:4-5] is an appropriate understanding of this word.) Theologians often refer to this as *ex opere operato* [lit., "by the work performed/worked"]. According to this teaching, a person is made a Christian not only at the *time* of his baptism, but also as a *result* of it. This undermines, or completely sidesteps, God's power in regenerating the human soul. It puts the emphasis

- Baptismal regeneration, as defined above, most certainly corrupts the teaching and purpose of the gospel of Christ. If we can be saved simply by being immersed in water, then we deny the need for the blood of Christ. Or, if we can be saved through *any* method in which our action is not fully dependent upon God, then we diminish His role *in* salvation and misrepresent the message *of* salvation. No one is made a Christian simply because he is immersed in water. No one can be born of God simply by being born of water. It is the Holy Spirit who does the regenerating of the one who calls upon the Lord for salvation, but He does not do this *apart* from the "washing" of that person—i.e., his baptism in water. Baptism is necessarily involved *in* regeneration; it is not the full substance of it.
- The controversy, then, is this: many teachers and preachers who have rejected the necessity of baptism for salvation assume that anyone (like me) who thinks otherwise automatically teaches "baptismal regeneration." In other words, since I firmly maintain that baptism is required for salvation in one's response to the gospel message, therefore I must be one who believes that the *act of baptism itself* is the essence of that salvation. This is a gross misrepresentation of my own beliefs, but more importantly it is terribly misleading to anyone unfamiliar with the controversy over baptism itself in the religious world. This view also attempts to diminish the importance of baptism to the point that it is (therefore) unnecessary. They reason: since baptism is a "work"—and in fact it *is* a work!—it allegedly has no place in one's conversion to Christ, because we are not saved by

works. This distorts the meaning of and the relationship between faith and works, as if these two things are not mutually dependent. Nonetheless, those (like me) who advocate the necessity of baptism in salvation are being labeled as *false teachers*.

- I am not suggesting that everyone who *does* advocate baptism is doing so with the right teaching or for the right reason. However, I have gone to great lengths to expound upon what the New Testament teaches on baptism, and the evidence is more than compelling: a person must be baptized in order to become a Christian. This does *not* mean that his baptism by itself is what saves him, but it *does* mean that baptism is inseparable *from* his salvation. These are two very different and non-interchangeable positions.

- The controversy is also obscured in semantics and double-speak. For example, many in the denominational world loathe "baptismal regeneration," yet speak freely of the new life, being "made alive," spiritual renewal, new creation, etc. which are only made possible *through* baptism. As Beasley-Murray observes, "What is all this but 'regeneration' under different images?"[148] Another author says: "In the language of the Bible, spiritual realities such as rebirth, renewal, forgiveness, salvation, and union with Christ are intimately associated with the rite of baptism."[149] In other words, obscuring the truth about baptism behind a masquerade of word choices and misrepresentation does not make that truth go away. As it is commonly defined, "baptismal regeneration" is not a teaching of the Bible. Yet, the Bible *is* clear that spiritual regeneration in Christ begins at the time of one's baptism. Again, these are not the same positions, and we would all do well to know the difference between them.

### Being Born of God

**"Suppose I have been a Christian for years, and yet now I am convinced that I need to be baptized. What do I do?"**

- ❏ By now, the answer to this should be obvious. No one can become a Christian without being baptized into Christ. This is all we can teach, because this is all the New Testament has instructed us to teach. This sounds, of course, jarring and even offensive to the person who thought he (or she) *was already* a Christian but simply missed a step in the conversion process. All I can do is point that person back to the Bible: What does it say? How does it read to you? If Christ said that you cannot enter the kingdom of God without being born of water *and* the Spirit (John 3:5), then a person who is not yet born of water is also not born of the Spirit, and is not in this kingdom. This does *not* mean that he has purposely deceived anyone, or that everything he learned up to this point is for naught. It simply means: there is something else God requires, and until this is fulfilled, then the intended objective has not yet been reached.

- ❏ So then, what needs to be done? This person—in order to be obedient to God and submit himself to Christ—needs to be fully immersed in water. This is not to satisfy *my* expectations, but to demonstrate faith in *God's* commandments. If God has exceptions to this, then He has not told us. We cannot arbitrarily *make* exceptions, either.

**"Suppose I *was* baptized, but I was an infant at the time, or it was not for the appropriate reasons. What do I do?"**

- ❏ I have already covered these two subjects in previous chapters: "Infant Baptism" and "The One Baptism." Simply put, infant baptism is an invention of men (and man-made churches), not a teaching of Scripture. No one can become a Christian through a means that God Himself did not authorize, reveal, or prescribe. Also—and related to the first point—God only recognizes "one baptism" (Ephesians 4:5) and therefore *we* can only recognize "one." This does not mean other baptisms are not possible to perform, for they certainly are and people do perform them. It means that only *one* baptism satisfies Scripture, is acknowledged by God, and fulfills the symbolism intended by this act. The one baptism is impossible apart from faith (as in the case of infant baptism), and faith must be based upon the truth of God's Word—nothing more, nothing less. So then, the answer to this question is: Now that you know the *right* thing to do, you must be baptized into Christ in order to be born of God and enter into fellowship with Him.

**"I have come to a better understanding of baptism since I myself was baptized into Christ. Do I now need to be re-baptized?"**
- ❑ This is one of those questions that many people want to ask, but either do not have the courage to do so or believe that it is altogether *wrong* to question one's own baptism. The New Testament says nothing about "re-baptism" into Christ. There are those who were baptized more than once—most notably, in Acts 19:1-5—but these baptisms were under two different covenants and did not achieve the same objective. As far as Christian baptism is concerned—that which is directly involved in *becoming* a Christian—there is only one baptism, not several. Thus, you have either been baptized into Christ or you have not. There is no third alternative.
- ❑ Will you come to a better understanding of baptism over time? I hope so! I know that I have—over and over again—and I trust that everyone who becomes a student of

the Bible does so. But this new knowledge does not require a "new" baptism; it simply reinforces the *need* for and the powerful *symbolism* of your baptism. God always leads us from the simple to the complex, from the primary to the profound, and from child-like faith to wisdom and maturity. All of us begin on an elemental level, and *after this* we move toward greater spiritual understanding (Hebrews 6:1-3). You are growing *in* Christ, not stepping *outside* of Him in order to grow (and then needing to re-enter with better understanding). Whatever you learn *after* your baptism only adds depth and dimension *to* that baptism; it does not require you to redo it. Do you re-marry your spouse every time you come to a better understanding of marriage? Of course not. You are either married or you are not; there is no third alternative. But you can certainly become a far better husband or wife over time, and this will *enrich* your concept of marriage and your relationship with your spouse.

❑ Despite all this, every once in a while I am confronted with someone whose conscience simply cannot rest until he (or she) is "re-baptized." I go through the explanation above with them (in greater detail), but the matter still is between that person and God. If he believes that he *must* be baptized (again) in order to be saved, I do not stop him. In my understanding, this is a matter of one's level of faith, not an act of pride or rebellion. This means that "the faith which you have, have as your own conviction before God" and "whatever is not from faith is sin" (Romans 14:22-23). Personal faith must never undermine the doctrine of God. On the other hand, we must acknowledge the fact that we are not all at the same "place" in our understanding of that doctrine.

**"I have fallen away from the Lord for several years, but now I want to come back and renew my commitment to Him. Do I need to be re-baptized?"**

❏ Please see the comments on the previous question. It is true that a person can fail to live up to his original commitment to Christ and fall away from the Lord. But even this does not invalidate his baptism so as to require a "new" one. This person simply needs to confess his sins, repent of them, and ask God for forgiveness. In this context, "If we confess our sins, He is faithful and righteous to forgive us our sins and to cleanse us from all unrighteousness" (1 John 1:9). The relative simplicity of these instructions does not at all diminish the severity of one's having fallen away in the first place. At the same time, the Scripture gives no other instruction in this matter.

**"I think you are a mean, judgmental, narrow-minded, spiritual bigot [or, insert: your own favorite epithet]! How dare you call into question the faith of millions of people just because they don't conform to your [insert: favorite insulting adjective] thinking!"**

❏ Well, this is a Q&A format, and I believe that was more of a statement than a question. However, I know that some people will feel this way—but they probably never read this far into this book, so I had to anticipate their remarks. First, just because someone *thinks* that I am mean, judgmental, etc. does not mean that I am. For this person, the very fact that I dare question the faith or belief system of any sincere person makes me "judgmental" and "narrow minded" and "intolerant." What? Doesn't this person question *my* belief system—and judge *me*—when he calls me these things?

Why does this kind of argument only work for him, but apparently not for me?

❑ In any case, it is not a "hate crime" to disagree with someone's personal *or* public beliefs. It is not "judgmental" to question someone's religious convictions, especially if it is in that person's best interest to have those convictions questioned. Does someone really want to go through this life thinking that he (or she) has prepared for the life to come, only to find out—too late!—that he was terribly misinformed? Was Jesus being judgmental and narrow-minded when He told some of the Jews, "You are mistaken, not understanding the Scriptures nor the power of God" (Matthew 22:29)? Or, when He told the crowds, "Unless your righteousness surpasses that of the scribes and Pharisees, you will not enter the kingdom of heaven" (Matthew 5:19)? If I defer to His authority, appeal to His same logic, and speak with love for the human soul (like He did), why am I pegged as the monster? "Have I become your enemy by telling you the truth?" (Galatians 4:16)—or by steering someone away from his own ruinous error?

❑ Because we have been so conditioned by our overly-permissive society, few dare to question anyone for fear that we might offend someone's hypersensitive religious beliefs. Few people seem to be concerned with what is right or wrong; instead, the emphasis is on accepting without criticism whatever a person chooses to believe. This ultimately means that we will not even question our own beliefs, since it is (allegedly) the *questioning* process that is forbidden. This mentality has pervaded Christ's churches, and has poisoned the minds of many Christians. We are being told that we must be "tolerant" of everyone, regardless of a person's personal beliefs or practices. (The standard for this "tolerant" view, by the way, has no fixed point of reference. Why are people not being tolerant of my intolerance? Why must I be tolerant of everyone else, no matter how unintelligent or deviant their beliefs are, but these same people are not tolerant of my own allegedly judgmental, narrow-minded, and stupid beliefs?)

❑ Scripture *nowhere* teaches us to be tolerant of sin; we are *not* to "forbear" rebellion against God; we are *not* told to forgive those who refuse to repent and take responsibility for their actions. Tolerance and forbearance are actions that we (Christians) are to demonstrate toward those who are weak in faith—i.e., less knowledgeable, less experienced, and less spiritually mature (Romans 15:1-2). ("Weak" here does not mean "unwilling," but "unable." No one is ever given permission by God to *choose* to be or remain weak in faith.) We should also be tolerant and forbearing of those who are not *yet* Christians but are inclined to *become* Christians. Paul sums up the attitude we are to have in 2 Timothy 2:23-26:

> Refuse foolish and ignorant speculations, knowing that they produce quarrels. The Lord's bond-servant must not be quarrelsome, but be kind to all, able to teach, patient when wronged, with gentleness correcting those who are in opposition, if perhaps God may grant them repentance leading to the knowledge of the truth, and they may come to their senses and escape from the snare of the devil, having been held captive by him to do his will.
> 
> A person who thinks he is a Christian but is not, or who thinks he can become a Christian through some unbiblical, self-chosen means, is in "the snare of the

devil." He is being deceived in the worst way, and he needs to hear God's truth. But I am supposed to be politically-correct and say nothing? How Christian is *that*? If your house was burning down on top of you and I could snatch you from the fire, would you want me to act—or would you be offended that I did not allow you to remain in your perilous situation (see Jude 22-23)? I would rather err on the side of incurring your anger than to let you lose your life—and especially your soul.

- Actually, it is unimportant—to me or to God—who does or does not conform to my personal manner of thinking (see 1 Corinthians 4:3-5). What is most important—even *eternally* important—is that one conforms to God's instructions. The teaching on baptism in the New Testament is hardly obscure or difficult to understand; it is among the clearest and most frequently-mentioned subjects on conversion that have been revealed to us. Just because I embrace this teaching does not make it "mine"; just because I teach this teaching does not mean "I came up with it" or "You must answer to me." I am appealing to a person's intellect here, not his emotions. Thus, it does not matter how you "feel" about me or my beliefs, but it will be of supreme significance how you respond to God's Word. It is impossible to honor God while simultaneously refusing—for *whatever* reason—to do what He told you to do.

- Finally, it is not *me* calling into question the legitimacy of millions of so-called Christians, but God's Word. I am not in the business of consigning people to either heaven *or* hell. Are you? Will you consign a person to heaven who has no business being there? Or, will you spare someone from God's condemnation because you choose to believe that he or she should *not* receive it? Doesn't this put *you* in the Judge's seat when you ignore God's Word on the matter and make your own arbitrary decisions? My appeal is to what God says on the matter of salvation, regardless of what others say or do. What has the critic provided? If you personally disagree with all of this, what is the basis *for* your disagreement? You don't *like* me personally? You don't *like* the words I chose or the way I "talk"? You don't *like* the conclusions I have drawn? What, then, are *your* conclusions—and how did you arrive at them? God's Word trumps all personal feelings, convictions, and traditions—yours, mine, and anyone else's. If you and I will not agree to this up front and be consistent in our application of it, then neither one of us can be Christians—correct? But if we do what God says to the best of our ability and understanding, all will be well for us. God does not need us to be flawless, but He does need us to be honest, faithful, and walking "in a manner worthy of the Lord, to please Him in all respects, bearing fruit in every good work and increasing in the knowledge of God" (Colossians 1:10). Do this, and He will indeed save you in the end.

# Endnotes

1    If you were to look up "baptism" in a modern English dictionary, for example, you would find a variety of interpretations for this, including sprinkling, pouring, and figurative meanings. This is because such dictionaries define the word in its *contemporary* usage, and not what it meant and how it was used in the context of the New Testament. Thus, I have had people "prove" that baptism was *not* limited to immersion because Webster's Dictionary told them so. This is an entirely inappropriate method by which to study the Bible, yet there are many who put more faith in a modern dictionary than they do the actual Word of God.

2    *Thayer's Greek-English Lexicon* [electronic edition] (© 2005 WORDsearch Corp.), Strong's #G908.

3    For example, one author—a Reformed minister—says: "The mode of baptism in Reformed theology is largely a matter of indifference," since the emphasis is on the act itself, not how it is carried out (Richard L. Pratt, Jr., "Baptism as a Sacrament of the Covenant," *Understanding Four Views on Baptism*, ed. John H. Armstrong [Grand Rapids: Zondervan, 2007], 66). Yet, the "act" is not even accomplished if it is not performed rightly. If one is not immersed in water, then he has not been baptized *differently* than someone else; instead, he has not been baptized at all.

4    Novatian (ca. AD 251) received "emergency baptism" by having water poured upon him as he lay upon his sickbed, believing that he would not survive immersion in water. Such a mode was later referred to as "clinical baptism." Novation recovered, however, and was appointed as a priest, yet many doubted the authenticity of his baptism (John D. Castelein, *Understanding Four Views*, 140).

5    F. LaGard Smith, *Baptism: The Believer's Wedding Ceremony* (Nashville: Gospel Advocate Publishers, 1993), 90; emphases are his.

6    I am using "believer" here—and will do so through the rest of this study—with reference to a person who believes in God and is willing to act upon that belief in obedience, whether before he becomes a Christian or afterward. Others use "believer" to refer exclusively to one who has already become a Christian, and whose baptism (a "believer's baptism") is merely, as they say, "an outward sign of an inward grace." In other words, such people maintain that it is only *Christians* who are baptized instead of a person being baptized to *become* a Christian.

7    John H. Armstrong, *Understanding Four Views on Baptism*, 163.

8    The New Testament will never lead a person to become a Baptist, Catholic, Mormon, Presbyterian, or Calvinist. It will lead him to become a Christian—nothing more, but nothing less, either. Long before these denominations ever existed, people were becoming *Christians* according to the pattern revealed by Christ through His apostles. This observation is *not* intended to evaluate every person who is involved in a denominational system; however, it remains true—and no one can deny it—that no denominational system is found in the New Testament.

9    "The Bible never made a sect or a sectarian; it takes something in addition to the Bible to do it, hence in order to have Christian union we must lay down opinions and speculations, and get together on the truth and follow the Apostolic plan, and as it will produce nothing but Christians, the future Church is bound to be Christian only" (Ashley S. Johnson, L.L.D., "Debate with a Baptist," *Johnson's Speeches* [Knoxville: Ogden Bros. & Co., 1895], 162).

10    Calvinists will contend otherwise. They claim that the unregenerate soul is *completely unable* to do anything for itself, including making the decision to have faith or be saved; thus, God must make him "alive" *before* he has faith and before he decides to become a Christian. Please see a biblical response to this in the chapter on "Calvinism."

11    The New Testament refers to this as a "perishing" of the soul (John 3:16, 1 Corinthians 1:18, 2 Corinthians 4:3, et al), or the "second death" (Revelation 2:11, 21:8). In other words, one can be "dead" to God in this life, but there is still hope for him to be "made alive." Yet, once he dies in the condition of his separation from God he will be separated from Him permanently and irretrievably.

12    The word (*ouranos*) translated "of heaven" can equally be translated "of God," since whatever is "of heaven" is necessarily "of God." Matthew's Gospel emphasizes that the kingdom is "of heaven" (32 times); Luke's Gospel focuses instead on the fact that it is "of God" (31 times); both emphases are correct (*Thayer's Greek-English Lexicon* [electronic edition], Strong's #G3772).

13    "I will be their God and they [i.e., those who live by faith in Me] will be My people" is a major theme of the entire Bible. I highly recommend my book, *The Gospel of Forgiveness*, in which I expound upon this thought considerably in chapter 13, "Fellowship and Forgiveness" (Summitville, IN: Spiritbuilding Publishing, 2011); go to www.spiritbuilding.com.

*Being Born of God*

14    We must distinguish between "Christ's church" or "the church" and *your* church or *my* church. We are not talking about individual congregations here, but the universal body of believers, both living and dead, who have been saved through the blood of Christ. This church is not comprised of congregations, and certainly is not divided into various denominations, but only the blood-washed souls of those who lived by faith while here on earth. Thus, "the church" does not refer to any *group* of churches, however named or associated, but only to Christ's spiritual church.

15    This is foreshadowed—yet spoken of as a present reality—in passages like Revelation 1:6, 5:10. In these passages, those in the *church* are described as reigning (as "kings") and ministering (as "priests") within the kingdom of God. This language is idealistic, in that it assumes that all such people will be "faithful until death" (2:10), which, at the time of John's writing, had yet to be proved.

16    This explains the "Your kingdom come" phrase from Matthew 6:10. While God's kingdom has always existed, Christ has not always ruled over it as its King and (thus) our Redeemer. His ascension to the throne is the "coming" of God's kingdom with reference to bringing salvation to all men.

17    See Merrill C. Tenney's *John: The Gospel of Belief* (Grand Rapids: Eerdmans Publishing, 1948), 86-87.

18    R. C. H. Lenski, *Commentary on the New Testament: John* (Peabody, MA: Hendrickson Publishing, 1998), 235.

19    Calvinism, which underlies much of modern evangelical religion, teaches that we are born sinful creatures, and are thus helpless to do anything about this until God saves us by His own decision. There is nowhere in Scripture that teaches this, and Jesus' words to Nicodemus flatly contradicts it. We will discuss Calvinism and the Doctrine of Original Sin in later chapters in this book.

20    The "water" here cannot refer to the baptism of John. That baptism had nothing to do with entrance into the kingdom, but was merely to acknowledge a *Jews'* repentance and recommitment to God's covenant with Israel. In fact, those who were baptized according to John were later baptized into Christ (Acts 19:1-5). The baptism of which Jesus speaks in this passage (John 3:5) is directly linked to the ministerial work of the Holy Spirit, which refers to the church age. The Spirit had not yet been "given" (John 7:37-39); until Christ's church was established and then immersed in the Spirit, no one could enter into the kingdom of God in the manner in which Jesus described to Nicodemus.

21      "Born-again Christian" is a redundant phrase, and indicates an ignorance of what being "born again" really means. No one can become a Christian who is not "born again"—there is no other *kind* of Christian. Likewise, no one can be "born again" *without* becoming a Christian. In our age of denominationalism, it seems that even when it comes to the term "Christian," people are conditioned to identifying various *kinds* of Christians, as though this were possible or necessary. Yet, if one follows the New Testament, "Christian" (a Christ-follower) needs no further description. The only Christian that Christ recognizes is the person that conforms to the gospel *of* Christ.

22      "Baptism is an overt, public act that expresses inward decision and intent; since it is performed in the open [i.e., before witnesses—MY WORDS], and not in secret, it becomes by its nature a confession of faith and allegiance embraced" (G. R. Beasley-Murray, PhD, *Baptism in the New Testament* [Grand Rapids: Eerdman's Publishing Co., 1962], 101).

23      "In terms of the Great Commission in Matthew 28:19-20, baptism is something taught *before* conversion with a view to *becoming* a disciple, while 'teaching them to observe all that I commanded you' *follows* conversion and deals with the details of the Christian life" (Jack Cottrell, *Baptism: A Biblical Study* [Joplin, MO: College Press Publishing Co., 1989], 16; emphases are his).

24      Peter, for example, talks about the Christian faith, once proven through having overcome various trials, contributes directly and necessarily to one's salvation: "…obtaining as the outcome of your faith the salvation of your souls" (1 Peter 1:6-9). If this is true *after* conversion, there is no reason to believe it is not true *upon* one's conversion—and no passage in the New Testament teaches otherwise.

25      James B. Coffman, *Commentary on the Gospel of Matthew* (Austin, TX: Firm Foundation, 1968), 524.

26      Adapted from Roy E. Cogdill, *The Cogdill-Jackson Debate* (Marion, IN: Cogdill Foundation Publications, 1977), 56.

27      For what it is worth, Beasley-Murray writes: "…The authenticity of the Commission to baptize, far from being discredited by examination of the evidence, is reasonably well-supported by it" (*Baptism in the New Testament*, 88).

28      We see a similar situation in John 7:53 – 8:11, where the account of the adulterous woman apparently is not in some of the oldest and best extant manuscripts. Yet, this does not stop many preachers from teaching it, since it does not have any (Christian) doctrinal material in it. In fact, this account is far more questionable than the section in Mark 16, yet

*Being Born of God*

receives far more acceptance. Once again, such contradictory approaches indicate not a scholarly evaluation of the text, but an often deep-seated prejudice against what the text teaches—in this case, the necessity of baptism.

29 Some argue that, because Jesus did not mention "and is not baptized" in the latter clause of passage, therefore baptism is not necessary for salvation. How does that work, exactly? Why would an unbeliever *want* to be baptized as a demonstration of a belief that he clearly does not have—and for a salvation that he has clearly rejected? That person is condemned not merely because he did not get baptized, but because he failed to believe in the first place.

30 Adapted from Gareth L. Reese, *New Testament History: A Critical and Exegetical Commentary on the Book of Acts* (Joplin, MO: College Press, 1976), 74-77. This brings up an important and often overlooked point. John the Baptist's baptism was all about repentance (Luke 3:3): the *purpose* for that baptism was to demonstrate the *sincerity* of one's repentance. In fact, when certain Pharisees and Sadducees came to be baptized by him, he refused to do so because of their impenitence (Matthew 3:5-8). While the baptism that Peter required of the Jews in Acts 2:38 was for a different purpose than John's (and achieved different results), this much is the same: repentance and baptism go hand-in-hand.

31 This is notably argued by A. T. Robertson: "My view is decidedly against the idea that Peter, Paul, or any one in the New Testament taught baptism as essential to the remission of sins or the means of securing such remission. So I understand Peter to be urging baptism on each of them who had already turned (repented)...on the basis of the forgiveness of sins which they had already received" (*Word Pictures in the New Testament*, vol. 3 [Grand Rapids: Baker Book House, 1930], 36. In rebuttal to Robertson's imaginative rendition, see (for example) Gareth L. Reese, *New Testament History*, 74-77. Reese argues that Robertson's interpretation of Acts 2:38 is inconsistent with how any other passage would have been grammatically interpreted if not for a specifically-desired outcome.

32 Bob L. Ross, *Acts 2:38 and Baptismal Remission* (Pasadena, TX: Pilgrim Publications, 1976). Ross denies any grammatical link between "repentance" and "baptism" in this verse. Repentance is the "moral, spiritual act," whereas baptism is "the ceremonial, figurative act" (45-49). But no one disputes this. Ross paints those who believe that baptism is necessary as holding to the doctrine of "baptismal regeneration," which misrepresents the situation entirely. He assumes that, to advocate baptism as being essential, one must automatically reduce the emphasis of Christ's blood—another misunderstanding or misrepresentation (40-41). "The

obvious teaching of the Scripture is that faith is alive and active before baptism, and that baptism is just one of its fruits—one of the many acts of obedience that results from a loving trust in the Lord Jesus Christ as Savior" (59). Ross actually admits that baptism is an *act of obedience*; it necessarily follows that if one refuses baptism, then he is disobedient—and that is not faith. A person who comes to God *in* faith for the purpose of salvation must comply with His commandments, including the command to be baptized. To assume that a person is saved *before* this renders such commandments as being useless or expendable.

33    The word "for" in Matthew 26:38, for example—"this is My blood of the covenant, which is poured out many <u>for</u> the forgiveness of sins"—is the exact same usage and grammatical construction as the "for" in Acts 2:38 (Johnson, *Johnson's Speeches*, 127).

34    Cottrell, *Baptism: A Biblical Study*, 59; emphases are his.

35    John MacArthur, *The MacArthur New Testament Commentary: Acts 1-12* (Chicago: Moody Press, 1996), 75.

36    Adapted from F. F. Bruce, *The Book of Acts* (Grand Rapids: Eerdman's Publishing Co., 1954), 77.

37    MacArthur, *The MacArthur New Testament Commentary: Acts 13 – 28* (Chicago: Moody Press, 1996), 268.

38    For a detailed study on the subject of divine grace, I recommend my book, *The Gospel of Grace* (Louisville, KY: Religious Supply Center, 2008); go to www.booksbychad.com.

39    Being baptized in the name of Jesus Christ is not different than being baptized in the name of the Father, Son, and Holy Spirit. In either case, one appeals to God's authority. Whoever appeals to Christ's authority also must necessarily appeal to the Father's authority and the Spirit's authority. These three Personages of God maintain their separate identities and responsibilities, but they are completely united in mind, purpose, and love. "In the name of" literally refers to a transferring of money or property into the account bearing the name of its owner. Thus, baptism is performed as a legal transfer of one's allegiance into the account (so to speak) of the One who now owns him (as in 1 Corinthians 6:19-20) (Cottrell, *Baptism: A Biblical Study*, 17; Beasley-Murray, *Baptism in the New Testament*, 90-91). One who claims to "belong" to God without this legal transfer—a transaction authorized by God Himself—illegitimately assumes a status that has no reason to exist.

40    Full bathing was also required of the high priest on the Day of Atonement, both before he offered the sin offering for himself and the sin offering for the nation (Leviticus 16:4, 24). This also serves as a point of

## Being Born of God

separation: each Day of Atonement marked not only the end of one year (of the *religious* calendar), but also the beginning of a new year. The old year's sins were atoned through the sprinkled blood upon the mercy seat; the new year thus began free of sin. This was the case for the nation of Israel as well as the high priest himself.

41      Beasley-Murray notes that the Old Testament cleansings *ended* with washing in water, but (he claims that) the matter of cleansing occurred *before* this (*Baptism in the New Testament*, 28-29). In the end, this distinction does not matter. First, this is not an apples-to-apples comparison between those cleansings and baptism, but simply a foreshadow of what was to come. Second, refusal to wash (in either case) was a violation of the command, and rendered any previous compliance with the command null and void.

42      The only blood we need now is the blood of Christ; His blood offering was given "once for all" and does not need to be repeated or supplemented with any other blood offering (10:10-18).

43      Hebrews 9:13 makes a direct allusion to the red heifer ordinance that we have just discussed, and the writer shows that Christ's blood accomplishes what that (red heifer) sacrifice could never do.

44      The various instances of ritual cleansing in the Law of Moses meant that a person might be cleansed with water numerous times throughout his life. Similarly, Jewish purification rites (which were practiced during the time of Christ) required a ceremonial cleansing by water at any time a Jew became ritually unclean according to the rabbinical laws. In contrast, the one who obeys the gospel of Christ must submit to only one baptism—not just "one" in *kind*, but also "one" in *number*.

45      Baptism is itself a kind of prayer in which the believer beseeches the Lord. The believer not only confesses the name of Christ in his appeal, but also invokes His name for salvation (Beasley-Murray, *Baptism in the New Testament*, 101).

46      "What is the 'washing of water'? There can be little question that it refers to baptism. The Greek word for 'washing' is *loutron*, which can mean 'washing' or 'bath.' It is used for baptism in Titus 3:5. It is a noun form of the verb *louo*, which is used in other places for baptism. The idea that it is used here figuratively for some spiritual bath is precluded by the reference to water; it is the 'washing *of water*.' The only 'washing of water' in Christian experience is baptism" (Cottrell, *Baptism: A Biblical Study*, 121).

47      In commenting on 1 Peter 3:21, Bob Ross—a Baptist who rejects the necessity of baptism in salvation—says this: "Those in the ark

left behind the old world to live in the new; so also the believer, having risen from the waters of baptism, now goes forth to walk in newness of life" (*Acts 2:38 and Baptismal Remission*, 65). If he really believes this, then he must also believe that *no one* can experience "newness of life" *until* he has risen from the waters of his baptism. He cannot refuse the command, yet embrace a new life with God anyway—this does not make sense, and violates the message of the gospel.

48        "Baptism is only saving if there is an appeal to God for a good conscience through the resurrection of Jesus Christ. In other words, baptism saves only because it is anchored to the death and resurrection of Jesus Christ" (Thomas R. Schreiner, "Baptism in the Epistles: An Initiation Rite for Believers," *Believer's Baptism: Sign of the New Covenant in Christ*, ed. Thomas R. Schreiner and Shawn D. Wright [Nashville: Broadman & Holman Publishing Group, 2006], 70.

49        See Acts 2:17-21, 2:33. Just as Christ's blood was "poured out for many [i.e., those being saved—MY WORDS]" for the purpose of atonement (Mark 14:24), so the Holy Spirit was "poured out" upon Christ's church for the purpose of sanctification and consecration for service to God. This "pouring out" was initially manifested in the form of visible miracles, so as to prove that it (the pouring out) actually was accomplished (Hebrews 2:3-4); thereafter, it is manifested in every genuine Christian in his transformed life and the "fruit of the Spirit" produced through him (Romans 5:5, Galatians 5:22-23).

50        Cottrell, *Baptism: A Biblical Study*, 146; emphasis is his.

51        For an actual example of this point, see Haggai 2:10-14. When something that is holy comes into contact with that which is unholy (or unclean), the holy thing becomes unclean; it does not make the unclean thing holy. The reason why Jesus can "touch" our sinful souls and make *us* holy, however, is because He has offered the necessary sacrifice to *remove* our corruption, rather than Himself becoming corrupted by our own sin.

52        The Red Sea was divided in half; perpendicular to this division, God created another division between Israel and Pharaoh's army. The resulting "shape" of the two lines of division is that of a cross. Similarly, it is the cross of Christ that divides us from the world as we come through the water. It is not necessary to push such ideas too far—sometimes we "see" in Scripture what we want to see, not necessarily what God wanted us to see—but in this particular case, the implications are striking.

53        As with the case of the Flood, water can serve as an agent of *salvation* or *destruction*, depending upon the moral condition of those involved. This is the point that Peter makes: the world was made through

## Being Born of God

water, then destroyed by water (2 Peter 3:5-6); those in the ark were brought safely through water, whereas those outside of the ark were destroyed by water (1 Peter 3:20).

54    It is for this reason that God warned Israel repeatedly not to put any future trust in Egypt or its horses and chariots (Deuteronomy 17:16, et al). For Israel to look *back* upon what they had left behind would be like a Christian who returns to the world after having died to it and confessed his allegiance to Christ.

55    Remarkably, noted Baptist professor G. R. Beasley-Murray says this: "But if faith is to be taken seriously, so is baptism. In this passage [Galatians 3:26-27] the exegetes [commentators] frequently either exalt baptism at the expense of faith or faith at the expense of baptism" (*Baptism in the New Testament*, 151, bracketed words are mine). Later, he says: "…In the New Testament faith and baptism are viewed as inseparable whenever the subject of Christian initiation is made discussion, so that if one is referred to, the other is presupposed, even if not mentioned. …It is undoubtedly true that in the New Testament it is everywhere assumed that faith proceeds to baptism and the baptism is for faith" (272-273). Then later, "Baptism does not *create* faith, but faith necessarily leads one to baptism" (274).

56    In the parable (Matthew 22:1-14), the king *provided* wedding clothes for his guests, but he did not literally put these on them, since this was the guests' responsibility. Likewise, God *provides* the opportunity to be clothed with Christ, but He does not force anyone to put Him on. God *provides* the "new self" (Ephesians 4:23-24, Colossians 3:10), but He does not put it on us. God *provides* the "full armor of God," but each believer is responsible to put on that "armor" himself. In other words, there is consistency in method: God provides, but we must obey and follow through with our commitment. We do not provide what is required for salvation by ourselves, but God does not obey instead of us, either. This is true in the conversion process as much as it is in the Christian life thereafter.

57    Cottrell, *Baptism: A Biblical Study*, 81; bracketed words are mine.

58    According to Deuteronomy 5:15, the sabbath also served as a memorial of God's deliverance of His people from Egypt. But once again, the sabbath was not the same as the deliverance itself, but only a sign of it.

59    On this point, see Ezekiel 20:16. Idolatry is the sin of *misplaced worship*, as in whenever someone turns away from his covenant with God to give honor to some other god or interest. Closely linked to idolatry is adultery, which is a corruption (sexual or otherwise) of a sacred covenant between two parties. Succumbing to greed and covetousness is

idolatry (Ephesians 5:5, Colossians 3:5); yet implied in that idolatry is a violation of covenant through the introduction of someone or something into the sacred covenantal union that had no business being there, which is the essential definition of adultery (Jeremiah 3:6-9, Matthew 5:27-28, and James 4:4).

60   Anthony Lane, "Dual-Practice Baptism Response," *Baptism: Three Views*, ed. David F. Wright (Downer's Grove, IL: IVP Academic, 2009), 65.

61   The rainbow symbolizes a one-sided (or monoplueric) covenant in which a superior authority (God) makes a covenant with a lesser authority (man), but does not expect him to do anything specific in response to it except to recognize that covenant's existence. The rainbow still represents salvation—we are "saved" from another worldwide flood—and in this sense alone does the world enjoy a new relationship with God based upon new conditions, which are spelled out in Genesis 9:1-17.

62   It does not matter *which* law or *how many* laws this person breaks. "For whoever keeps the whole law and yet stumbles in one point, he has become guilty of all. For He who said, 'Do not commit adultery,' also said, 'Do not commit murder.' Now if you do not commit adultery, but do commit murder, you have become a transgressor of the law" (James 2:10-11). Once a person has stumbled, he cannot "stand" before God any longer on his own merit, but must be justified through another means—one that God alone can provide.

63   We should stress here that the *covenant itself* belongs to the Father, not to Christ. If one becomes a Christian, it is because he accepts the terms of *God's* covenant, which makes provisions for his sinful condition *and* his inability to save himself. Christ provides the *blood* required for covenant; the Holy Spirit provides the *sanctification* required for covenant; but the covenant itself is made with the *Father*.

64   This "sign of the covenant" obviously extended beyond Abraham himself. Later, this sign was given to the entire nation of Israel—descendants of Abraham through Isaac and Jacob—and not to any other nation. In the 400 years between Abraham's day and Israel's exodus from Egypt, it appears that the sign had been neglected because the covenant itself had been virtually forgotten. When Jehovah commissioned Moses to deliver His people from Egypt, Moses responded that the Hebrews will not know who He is (Exodus 3:13). Before the Israelites could participate in the Passover, they had to be circumcised in order to identify with God's promise with Abraham (Exodus 12:48). Before the new generation of Israel entered into the land of Canaan, every male had to be circumcised (Joshua

*Being Born of God*

5:1-8), since possession of that land was a key stipulation of God's promise to Abraham.

65    Obviously, the responsibility and accountability of his citizenship did not begin when the male was eight days old. It was not until the child became of age—in essence, a son of the law (or *bar mitzvah*)—that he was obligated to the Law and its requirements. And it was not until he was 20 years of age that he could be counted as a male (or, man of war) for that nation (Numbers 1:2ff). In other words, the sign was rich with symbolism, but did not serve to qualify a male to represent Israel in every respect until he became an adult.

66    By change of "law," we must understand this to be a change of a *body* of laws, but not necessarily a change of every *single* law, either. Moral laws—those laws which directly reflect that nature of God Himself (e.g., "You shall not murder")—are constants in *every* covenant that God makes with men. It is not as though these moral laws "carry over" from an older covenant, but that they are a mainstay of the new covenant for the same reason they were a mainstay of the old. Ritual and ceremonial laws, as well as laws of specific responsibilities under a given covenant (e.g., "Do this [memorial] in remembrance of Me"), will change from covenant to covenant.

67    Some scholars believe that we (American Christians) are "westernizing" the burial process, since we are accustomed to a body being buried *underground*, whereas in many cultures this was not the case. Personally, I am willing to concede the point, since it is an irrelevant one. "Burial" does not necessarily mean "six feet under," as is common to the Western mind, but simply *separated from the realm of the living*. This is Jesus' meaning when He refers to His own burial (John 12:24) and is Paul's meaning when he refers to that burial (1 Corinthians 15:3-4). Thus, whether one is buried in the ground, in a mausoleum, in a tomb, or in any other manner, it is understood that he is *dead* and thus disconnected from those who are *alive*. In the case of baptism, however, it is impossible to achieve a burial without lowering someone into the water, regardless of any Western-burial implications.

68    "More than one exegete [commentator—MY WORD] has pointed out that the most likely point of contact between circumcision as a rite and baptism is their joint character of being rites of initiation; circumcision was the mode of (male) entry into the Israel of the old covenant, baptism the mode of entry into the Israel of the new covenant" (Beasley-Murray, *Baptism in the New Testament*, 160).

69    "Paul does not establish a connection between physical circumcision and baptism, but *spiritual circumcision and baptism*" (Schreiner,

"Baptism in the Epistles," 78; emphasis is his).

70    "The parallel, then, between circumcision and baptism in the new covenant is not between physical circumcision and infant baptism; rather, the parallel is between spiritual circumcision of the heart and baptism which signifies regeneration, faith, and union with Christ" (Bruce A. Ware, "Believer's Baptism View," *Baptism: Three Views*, 46.

71    For a much more detailed explanation of this, I recommend my book, *The Holy Spirit of God: A Biblical Perspective* (Summitville, IN: Spiritbuilding Publishing, 2010); go to www.spiritbuilding.com.

72    It is more accurate to say "baptism *with* the Spirit" (rather than "Holy Spirit baptism") since this corresponds to the actual language of the biblical text, *and* because this baptism is something the Father does *with* His Spirit upon Christ having taken His rightful place at His right hand (Acts 2:33-34).

73    The NASB reads that these men were "coming for baptism"; some translations read "coming to his [John's] baptism." This begs the question: did these men come to *be* baptized, or just to see what John was doing? My firm understanding of this is that they came to *be* baptized, since John's words to them do not make sense otherwise. He would not tell them to "bear fruit in keeping with repentance" unless they were about to participate in a procedure that *necessarily implied* repentance. See also Luke 3:7-8, where John addresses "the crowds who were going out to be baptized by him" as before—and *this* language is consistent across numerous translations.

74    Dave Miller, *Piloting the Strait* (Pulaski, TN: Sain Publications, 1996), 292; emphases are his.

75    For a detailed study on fellowship with and worship of God, I recommend my book, *Seeking the Sacred* (Summitville, IN: Spiritbuilding Publishing, 2009); go to www.spiritbuilding.com.

76    F. LaGard Smith writes, "The thief on the cross was an exception" (*Baptism: The Believer's Wedding Ceremony*, 83), but this is not accurate. The thief's situation was not an "exception" to the rule; he was under an entirely different set of rules or expectations altogether. A person's situation cannot be an "exception" to a context to which he does not even belong.

77    http://www.gty.org/resources/questions/QA79/is-baptism-necessary-for-salvation; dated May 11, 2007.

78    This subject is re-addressed in the chapter titled "Common Questions about Baptism."

79    In fact, the apostle Paul said that, in his lifetime, the gospel had been "proclaimed in all creation under heaven" (Colossians 1:23).

*Being Born of God*

Yet whether Paul was being literal or figurative becomes a moot point in determining one's appropriate response to Christ's gospel.

80     Adapted from a scenario posed by Thomas J. Scirghi, *Everything Is Sacred: An Introduction to the Sacrament of Baptism* (Brewster, MA: Paraclete Press, 2012), 120-121.

81     Anthony Lane, for example, appeals to a "seismological approach" to justify the baptism of children. In other words, just as seismologists in New York can detect an earthquake in California from the effects from the epicenter, so we can tell what New Testament writers *really* meant or implied by what "the church" did and taught in the next several centuries ("Dual-Practice Baptism View," *Baptism: Three Views*, 144ff). With such reasoning, we can justify all sorts of subjective traditions, superstitions, adopted pagan practices, and spurious beliefs collected by those closer in time to the apostles than ourselves. Yet, this proves nothing in itself, and is a poor attempt to prove anything. Paul warned that men would turn away from the truth (2 Timothy 4:3-4); how do we separate those who turned away from those who did not? The only standard worth citing is that of the New Testament itself (see footnote 109).

82     This remains, in my opinion, a glaring contradiction among the so-called Protestant churches that vehemently denounce baptism as *necessary* for salvation, yet baptize their infants so that they will not be lost because of "original sin" (to be discussed shortly). Martin Luther, for example, preached passionately in favor of infant baptism, but then claimed that we are saved by faith *only* (Philip Schaff, *History of the Christian Church*, vol. VII [Grand Rapids: Eerdmans Publishing Co., 1995], 610-611; Luther, "The Babylonian Captivity of the Church," 197-198; "The Freedom of a Christian," 280-284, *Three Treatises*, 2nd revised ed., trans. by A. T. W. Steinhäuser [Philadelphia: Fortress Press, 1970] ). It cannot be both ways. If faith *only* is necessary for salvation, then *no* baptism can be required, including infant baptism. Furthermore, no infant can possibly have the kind of faith required for discipleship, yet Luther insisted otherwise based upon his own authority.

83     "In the end, they [Reformed and Presbyterian theologies] contend that the silence of the NT concerning the baptizing of infants must be interpreted as endorsing the practice" (Castelein, *Understanding Four Views on Baptism*, 84; bracketed words are mine). With such an open-ended method of interpretation, we can make the New Testament endorse *anything* that is not specifically mentioned in it ("God didn't say we *couldn't*...!").

84     Beasley-Murray, *Baptism in the New Testament*, 315; bracketed words are mine. Consider also 1 Corinthians 16:15-16, in which

the "household of Stephanas" had devoted themselves to the ministry of the Word. This speaks of an adult action that would never be applied to an infant or child in the context of Paul's words. Christians are never told to "be in subjection" to children of any age.

85    *Thayer's Greek-English Lexicon* (electronic edition), Strong's #G3623 and #G3624.

86    Matthew A. C. Newsome, "On Infant Baptism…" © 2001 Turris Fortis (www.turrisfortis.com/baptism.html). Another author states: "The Gospel periscope of Christ blessing the children…further confirms our general approach to the status of children in the covenant community" (Sinclair B. Ferguson, "Infant Baptism View," *Baptism: Three Views*, 107).

87    In John 4:2, it specifically says that Jesus did not baptize *anyone* Himself. Nonetheless, H. J. Evander suggests that the laying on of hands by Jesus constituted a kind of baptism, "a consecration, an initiation to become Christians—it might be said, baptism without water" (quoted in Beasley-Murray, *Baptism in the New Testament*, 321). This is absurd reasoning, yet emphasizes the desperate attempts to defend the doctrine of infant baptism.

88    Dr. Richard P. Bucher, "Why We Baptize Babies (The Case for Infant Baptism)" (http://www.orlutheran.com/html/trinfbap.html); cited Sept., 2012.

89    Martin Luther, for example, supported the baptism of infants because it could not be proved that they do *not* have faith. Yet, no one can prove that infants *do* have faith, either. This makes Luther's position not only biblically and logically untenable, but also fanciful.

90    "In effect what is said [during the sponsorship—MY WORDS] is this: 'I promise that when this child can understand sacred truth I shall educate him and shall rise him up by my teaching in such a way that he will renounce all temptations of the devil, that he will bind himself to the sacred promises and will bring them to fruit'" (Scirghi, *Everything Is Sacred*, 70).

91    This scenario originated with M. M. Davis, *How to Be Saved* (Joplin, MO: College Press, [no date]), 192.

92    Martin Luther's reasoning has become the accepted answer to this problem: "For Luther, as for Augustine, faith was no human work, but the gift of the grace of God. And the faith which Luther insisted was necessary in baptism was faith granted, created, and bestowed through the Word itself, specifically, the gospel Word spoken in the baptismal ceremony. That an infant cannot reasonably understand the Word is no obstacle to the Word; the Word performs its work of creating faith without our cooperation. In baptism the infant comes under the hearing of the Word, which penetrates

his heart and creates faith; he answers the baptismal questions through the mouths of his sponsors" (Jonathan H. Rainbow, "'Confessor Baptism': The Baptismal Doctrine of the Early Anabaptists," *Believer's Baptism*, 192). In other words, God is responsible for creating an infant's "faith," even though the child is oblivious to this, which contradicts every biblical and logical definition for or description of faith that we know. Luther said directly: "Infants are aided by the faith of others, namely, those who bring them for baptism. For the Word of God is powerful enough, when uttered, to change even a godless heart, which is no less unresponsive and helpless than any infant. So through the prayer of the believing church which presents it, a prayer to which all things are possible, the infant is changed, cleansed, and renewed by inpoured faith" (*Three Treatises*, 197). This is entirely without Scripture, and is even in defiance of it (Hebrews 11:1). Ironically, Luther also wrote, "Whatever has not been commanded and is done beyond what God commands is certainly the devil's doing"; and also, in his condemnation of the Pope, "You force and twist the Scriptures to suit your fancy" (ibid., 76, 85).

93    Smith, *Baptism: The Believer's Wedding Ceremony*, 216.

94    This assumes that God's covenant with Abraham was to be *continued* in Christian believers rather than being *fulfilled* in Christ. "By God's appointment, infants share in the benefits of the Abrahamic covenant and therefore received circumcision as a sign and seal. Since the 'new covenant' is essentially identical with the Abrahamic covenant, infants of believing parents who receive the sign of the covenant are not excluded from covenant or church membership" (Louis Berkhof, quoted in Wellum, "Baptism and the Relationship between the Covenants," *Believer's Baptism*, 100). This "unified covenant of grace" essentially teaches that if circumcision was good enough for eight-day-old Israelite boys, then baptism is good enough for eight-day-old children of Christians. Likewise, if these Israelite babies were inducted into God's covenant with Israel, then babies can be inducted into God's covenant with Christians.

95    In Matthew 27:25, the Jews who sought Jesus' crucifixion cried out, "His blood shall be on us and on our children!" The same conclusion applies as in Acts 2:39: the Jews did not mean, "We will assume full responsibility for this action, and so will our little ones at home," but, "We take responsibility for this action—and we are confident that every generation that follows will agree with us."

96    Smith, *Baptism: The Believer's Wedding Ceremony*, 157.

97    William Hendriksen, *New Testament Commentary: Romans* (Grand Rapids: Baker Book House, 1981), 178; *Catechism of the*

*Catholic Church* (Liguori, MO: Liguori Publications, 1994), 105 (para. 416).

98    David expresses an inward feeling of spiritual inadequacy in the presence of God's unquestionable righteousness. This is how he sees himself: from the very beginning of his existence, he has been a transgressor. This is evident in the full context of this passage (51:1-9): "my transgressions," "my sin," "I have sinned," "[I have] done what is evil," "my sins," "my iniquities." Never does David attribute the responsibility for *his* guilt to anyone but himself. Yet, this is a personal and even poetic reflection, not a basis for theological doctrine; if anything, his "conceived in sin" expression exposes the guilt of his mother, not himself. Conspicuously, not once does he bring Adam or "original sin" into the picture. To force this passage into an argument in support of "original sin" is to corrupt its context *and* impose a man-made doctrine into holy Scripture.

99    Nearly every reputable scholar agrees that Romans 5:13-17 is a parenthetical explanation of 5:12, and that the thought began in 5:12 is resumed in 5:18.

100    Jim McGuiggan, *The Book of Romans* (Lubbock, TX: Montex Publishing Co., 1982), 168.

101    R. L. Whiteside, *Commentary on Romans* (Denton, TX: Inys Whiteside, 1945), 125.

102    *Catechism of the Catholic Church*, 102 (para. 404).

103    Ibid., 319 (para. 1250).

104    The concept of "limbo" (from *limbus*, "edge" or "border") describes the state of being of an unbaptized baby that dies and is stuck on the borders of heaven and hell. While this has never been officially its teaching, the Catholic Church still offers prayers for these dead children (Scirghi, *Everything Is Sacred*, 114, 118-119). This begs the question: what do these prayers hope to accomplish? And where did this teaching come from? Certainly it was not from Scripture.

105    Scirghi, a Catholic priest, says this: "A young child cannot commit sin. Nonetheless, while one may not be capable of committing a sinful act, the stain of original sin blots the souls of the newborn and aged alike" (*Everything Is Sacred*,115).

106    Beasley-Murray, *Baptism in the New Testament*, 368.

107    I realize that the Catholic Church cites papal authority and church traditions to legitimize their teachings. However, papal authority itself is inconsistent with New Testament doctrine. A religion that contradicts the New Testament cannot at the same time appeal to the New Testament as the basis for its legitimacy. But it is not my intention here to critique the Catholic Church, except for its teachings on baptism.

108    James B. Coffman, *Commentary on Romans* (Austin, TX: Firm Foundation, 1973), 212.

109    "Since…we are committed finally and ultimately to biblical authority, we all recognize that whatever conclusions can be drawn from the practice of the church in its earliest centuries, while instructive and important, can only rightly be viewed as secondary and under both the critique and correction of Scripture itself. …Appeals to early church theology and/or practice on any given issue are no guarantee that one is directed rightly in accord with the teaching of Scripture" (Anthony Lane, *Baptism: Three Views*, 70-71). This is an excellent response to those who cite "early church history" as an authoritative argument for deciding how or when baptism is to be carried out. The only thing I would add is that not only is "early church theology" trumped by biblical authority, but so is any modern teaching.

110    Some information on Calvinism in this article is from: *Amazing Grace: The History and Theology of Calvinism* (DVD), Apologetics Group, © 2004; David N. Steele and Curtis Thomas, www.the-highway.com/compare.html (2010).

111    Summaries are from "Five Points of Calvinism" by Matthew J. Slick, © 1998-2006 (www.calvinistcorner.com/tulip.htm), cited April, 2010.

112    A doctrine that makes God responsible for human decisions cannot escape making Him also responsible for human sin. If He is responsible for good choices, then He must also be responsible for evil choices, since in either case man's free will to determine his own future is removed. The truth is, every decision of man will be accounted for on the Day of Judgment, whether it is good or evil (2 Corinthians 5:10). This accounting is useless if in fact God has already overridden man's ability to make his own decisions.

113    Slick, "Five Points of Calvinism," www.calvinistcorner.com.

114    Slick, "Five Points of Calvinism," www.calvinistcorner.com.

115    *Amazing Grace* (DVD), on "Perseverance of the Saints."

116    The fact is, however, that God's sovereignty *is* overruled (albeit in a limited context) in every case of sin. To transgress or violate God's law—*any* law—is a usurpation of His authority. Calvinism cannot deny this in the case of human sin, including Adam's sin, but wants to make this an absolute in the case of salvation. This begs the question: if a person can—by his own choice—reject God's authority in order to sin, then why can't he reject God's salvation in order to make him—again, by his own choice—a sinner who has forfeited what God offered him?

117    The "born again" process in Calvinism defies logical explanation. Imagine a baby being "born" without coming out of its mother's womb—its movement through the amniotic fluid in the birth canal being considered an "outward" sign of a "birth" that was supposed to have already occurred! This is the kind of reasoning that must be used in order to explain this doctrine, yet it is clear that it simply does not work.

118    In the previous chapter, I brought up this point with relation to infant baptism: how can a Calvinist baptize a baby (or a young child, or anyone else) without knowing for certain if it is God's will that this child one of the predestined elect? Furthermore, *how does anyone know for certain* who belongs to which group—even the Calvinist himself? The Bible, on the other hand, teaches that we *know* who have eternal life based on their obedience to God's commandments, their imitation of Christ, and their Christian love for one another (1 John 2:3-6, 3:23-24, 5:13). Whoever *does* these things is saved—not because of God's sovereign decree made before he was born, but because he accepted the terms of God's salvation. Whoever does *not* do these things is condemned—not because of God's sovereign decree, but because of his rejection of God's offer of salvation.

119    The Canons of Dort (1618), as cited in *Amazing Grace* (DVD).

120    Philip Schaff, *History of the Christian Church*, vol. VIII (Grand Rapids: Eerdmans Publishing Co., 1995), 571.

121    Johnson, *Johnson's Speeches*, 29; bracketed words are mine.

122    Ironically, even "asking Jesus into [one's] heart" is a work of human effort, and not a mere intellectual agreement to God's power. If God is not doing the "asking," yet such asking is required for salvation, then even to "ask" God for anything constitutes an action on the part of the believer that exceeds the so-called "faith only" condition.

123    "Philadelphia Confession of Faith" (1689), x.3, page 10; bracketed word is mine.

124    Cogdill, *The Cogdill-Jackson Debate*, 67.

125    This illustration is adapted from Davis, *How to Be Saved*, 178.

126    It should be noted that the Greek noun often translated "faith" and the Greek verb translated "believe" come from the same root word (*pistis*). This makes the two words ("faith" and "believe") inherently related to each other. To "have faith" is "to believe"; to follow through on one's beliefs is to demonstrate one's faith.

127    D. N. Jackson (on John 3:18), *The Cogdill-Jackson Debate*, 3-4. But if demons "believe" and are still condemned (James 2:19), then it

*Being Born of God*

is clear that "(to) believe" requires something more than just an intellectual agreement to something or someone. And if demons *do* believe and are still condemned, then what is different with a human being who "believes" and remains condemned?

128     Cogdill, *The Cogdill-Jackson Debate,* 12-13.

129     Adapted from Cogdill, *The Cogdill-Jackson Debate,* 49. Furthermore, any argument that necessarily implies, but does not mention, the word "faith" can also be used for any passage that necessarily implies but does not mention "baptism." The argument, in other words, works both ways; and it often contradicts the very argument by which "faith only" proponents hope to defeat the necessity of baptism.

130     John MacArthur, as quoted in: http://www.gty.org/resources/questions/QA79/is-baptism-necessary-for-salvation; dated May 11, 2007. © 2012 Grace to You.

131     If the rejection of John the Baptist's baptism was a rejection of God's will (Luke 7:29-30), how much more will be the rejection of (what is called) Christian baptism? The command of a prophet is not greater than the commandment of the Son of God.

132     Edward T. Hiscox, D.D., *The Standard Manual for Baptist Churches* (The American Baptist Society, 1965), 22.

133     Ibid., 20.

134     This does not mean to say that if a church claims to be "non-denominational," it automatically agrees with the New Testament pattern. The point being made is that there exists no biblical instruction or example of denominationalism among the early Christians—except when it is being condemned (as in 1 Corinthians 1:11-13).

135     We could also note that while faith, repentance, confession, self-denial, etc. all accompany a person's new birth in Christ, these other actions must continue to be demonstrated throughout that person's Christian life. Baptism, on the other hand, is a one-time accomplished action that does not need to be repeated but is perpetually *remembered* in each of these other actions, since without this baptism these actions lack meaning and context.

136     Richard L. Pratt, Jr., *Understanding Four Views on Baptism,* 44.

137     For a detailed study of "forgiveness," I recommend my book, *The Gospel of Forgiveness* (Summitville, IN: Spiritbuilding Publishing, 2011); go to www.spiritbuilding.com.

138     Beasley-Murray, *Baptism in the New Testament,* 265.

139     Some will no doubt cite Cornelius' experience of "receiving" the Holy Spirit prior to his baptism as a point of refutation here (Acts 10:44-48). There is no contradiction, however. The Spirit did not perform miracles

through Cornelius in order to *save* him—no one has ever been saved by a miracle alone—but to show that he (a Gentile) was an acceptable candidate *for* salvation. Both Peter *and* Cornelius had to be instructed by God that Gentiles were now welcome to receive salvation in Christ just as the Jews did. This is the purpose for Cornelius' speaking in tongues, not to save his soul. After the Spirit had made His point, Peter knew what to do from there: Cornelius needed to be baptized into Christ, just like Peter had commanded the Jews (Acts 2:38ff). Cornelius' situation is exceptional in what *God* did for him that he did not request; it is not exceptional in the manner in which he became a Christian. "It is a serious mistake…to see these events [i.e., of speaking in tongues by the apostles in Acts 2 and Cornelius in Acts 10—MY WORDS] as typical and as representative conversion experiences. In fact, they are intended to be just the opposite" (Cottrell, *Baptism: A Biblical Study*, 62).

140    We cannot teach that immersion in water replaces other required demonstrations of faith, or that it is just as effective with the insincere person as it is with the sincere. Thus, I want to underscore again that baptism *as an isolated action* does nothing, but baptism *when accompanied by genuine faith* does all of the things mentioned in this paragraph. No one is saved only because he is baptized, but neither can we divorce baptism from salvation.

141    An example of tweaking the Scriptures to fit a contemporary mindset is evident in the following quote: "Theology by nature is somewhat fluid rather than solid. This is what it means to follow 'a tradition.' … In the process of handing over these cultural artifacts [beliefs, teachings, and customs—MY WORDS], some evolution occurs as we adapt the cultural wisdom to the current context. This does not mean that we change core beliefs and doctrine. Rather, the task of theology is to present these beliefs and doctrines in such a way that renders them pertinent to the current age" (Scirghi, *Everything Is Sacred*, 108). But theology *is* "core beliefs" and "doctrine"; how can these be "fluid" and at the same time not be changed? Such doublespeak is popular—and necessary in order to support sectarian religion—but it is foreign to the New Testament. You would *never* hear the apostle Paul, for example, say such things.

142    Bob L. Ross, *Campbellism: Its History and Heresies* (Pasadena, TX: Pilgrim Publications, 1976), 61.

143    Smith, *Baptism: The Believer's Wedding Ceremony*, 204.

144    Martin Luther has something important to consider on this point: "We ought to receive baptism at human hands just as if Christ himself, indeed, God himself, were baptizing us with his own hands. For it is not man's baptism, but Christ's and God's baptism, which we receive by

the hand of a man, just as everything else that we have through the hand of somebody else is God's alone" (Luther, *Three Treatises*, 184). I believe this thought can be easily misunderstood or taken to unwarranted extremes, but it does help clarify the believer's perspective in his baptism.

145 This would also apply to those who are born mentally incapacitated to make a responsible, adult decision of this magnitude. God knows who these people are, and He will deal with them in a righteous manner.

146 Amazingly, one can allegedly get into heaven by simply asking Jesus into his heart; yet in order to become a member of a certain congregation, he must be baptized (!). "According to Baptist usage and doctrine it is more difficult to get into the Church than it is to get into heaven. Or to put it still stranger, it is easier to become a Christian than it is to become a Baptist" (Johnson, *Johnson's Speeches*, 33).

147 In my understanding, passages like Matthew 13:47-50 and 25:31-46 provide not the exact *description* of this cleansing, but the *pattern* for it. In the Final Judgment, Christ will determine who remains in or who will be expelled from His church. The church, as the bride of Christ, will not enter into glory with wayward, impenitent, or rebellious souls within it; these must be removed before then. My point here is: we are not to take Christ's place in making that decision for Him ahead of time (see Romans 14:10-12, James 4:11-12, et al).

148 Beasley-Murray, *Baptism in the New Testament*, 278.

149 Pratt, *Understanding Four Views on Baptism*, 61.

More Bible Study workbooks that you can order from Spiritbuilding.com or your favorite Christian bookstore.

---

**Inside Out (Carl McMurray)**
*Studying spiritual growth in bite-sized pieces*

**Night and Day (Andrew Roberts)**
*Comparing New Testament Christianity and Islam*

**Church Discipline (Royce DeBerry)**
*A study on an important responsibility for the Lord's church*

**Exercising Authority (John Baughn)**
*How we use and understand authority on a daily basis*

**Compass Points (Carl McMurray)**
*22 foundation lessons for home studies, prospects, or new Christians*

**We're Different Because... (Carl McMurray)**
*A workbook on authority and recent church history*

**Communing with the Lord (Matthew Allen)**
*A study of the Lord's Supper & issues surrounding it*

**Parenting Through the Ages (Royce & Cindy DeBerry)**
*Bible principles tested & explained by successful parents*

**Marriage Through the Ages (Royce & Cindy DeBerry)**
*A quarter's study of God's design for this part of our life*

**What Should I Do? (Dennis Tucker)**
*A study that seeks Bible answers to life's important questions*

**How To Study the Bible (Jeff Archer)**
*25 lessons on how to study & understand the Bible*

**From Fear to Faith (Matthew Allen)**
*Coming to grips with the doctrine of grace*

**The Messiah's Misfits (Bryan Nash)**
*A study of the apostles of Jesus Christ*

**Living a Spirit Filled Life (Matthew Allen)**
*A study of Galatians & Ephesians with practical applications*

**The Lion Is the Lamb (Andrew Roberts)**
*A study of the King of Kings, His glorious kingdom, & His promised return*

**When Opportunity Knocks (Matthew Allen)**
*Lessons on how to meet the J.W./Mormon who knocks on your door*

**The Last Mile of the Way (Kipp Campbell)**
*A workbook study of the last week of the Messiah's life*

**Ancient Choices for Modern Dilemmas (John Baughn)**
*Biblical view of the modern family, current culture, and American politics*

**In Search of Christian Confidence (John Baughn)**
*A study to help one find the confidence God intended for His people*

More Bible Study workbooks that you can order from Spiritbuilding.com or your favorite Christian bookstore.

## Textual Studies

**The Parables, Taking a Deeper Look (Kipp Campbell)**
*A detailed look at our Lord's teaching stories*
**That I May Know Him (Aaron Kemple) Vol. 1 & 2**
*A chronological study of the life of Christ in a harmony of the gospels*
**1st Corinthians study guide (Chad Sychtysz)**
*Studies to take the student through this important letter*
**2nd Corinthians study guide (Chad Sychtysz)**
*Studies to take the student through this important letter*
**Hebrews study guide (Chad Sychtysz)**
*Studies to take the student through this important letter*
**Romans study guide (Chad Sychtysz)**
*Studies to take the student through this important letter*
**Galatians study guide (Chad Sychtysz)**
*Studies to take the student through this important letter*
**Ephesian study guide (Chad Sychtysz)**
*Studies to take the student through this important letter*
**Philippian, Colossians, Philemon study guide (Chad Sychtysz)**
*Studies to take the student through these important letters*
**1 & 2 Timothy and Titus (Matthew Allen)**
*A commentary workbook on these letters from Paul*
**Faith in Action: Studies in James (Mike Wilson)**
*Bible class workbook and commentary on James*
**From Beneath the Altar (Carl McMurray)**
*A workbook commentary on the Book of Revelation*

**1 Samuel & 2 Samuel (Matthew Allen)**
*Studying the life and times of this prophet, priest, & judge*
**Proverbs, Wisdom for Dummies (Carl McMurray)**
*A workbook study including every verse in Proverbs, divided into topics*
**An Overview of Isaiah (Chad Sychtysz)**
*A workbook study of this messianic prophet*
**An Overview of Jeremiah (Chad Sychtysz)**
*A workbook study of this prophet*
**Esteemed of God, Studying the Book of Daniel (Carl McMurray)**
*Covering the man as well as the time between the testaments*
**The Minor Prophets, Vol. 1 & 2 (Matthew Allen)**
*Old lessons that speak directly to us today*

## Special Interest

**The AD 70 Doctrine (Morris Bowers)**
*The truth about Realized Eschatology*
**The Holy Spirit of God (Chad Sychtysz)**
*A diligent, thorough study of this important subject*
**The Gospel of Forgiveness (Chad Sychtysz)**
*A presentation of this subject from different biblical angles*
**Letters to Young Preachers (Warren Berkley)**
*Letters from older preachers to younger on what they face*
**Behind the Preacher's Door (Warren Berkley and Mark Roberts)**
*Issues that preachers will have to deal with*
**Seeking the Sacred (Chad Sychtysz)**
*How to know God the way that HE wants us to know Him*
**Will You Wipe My Tears? (Joyce Jamerson)**
*Wisdom & resources to teach us how to help others through sorrow*

## Studies for Women

**I Will NOT Be Lukewarm (Dana Burk)**
*A ladies study on defeating mediocrity*
**Reveal in Me... (Jeanne Sullivan)**
*A study to assist ladies in discovering and developing their talents*
**Will You Wipe My Tears? (Joyce Jamerson)**
*Wisdom & resources to teach us how to help others through sorrow*
**Bridges or Barriers (Cindy DeBerry & Angie Kmitta)**
*Study encouraging harmony with younger/older sisters-in-Christ*
**Learning to Sing at Midnight (Joanne Beckley)**
*A study book about spiritual growth benefiting women of all ages*
**Re-charging Your Prayer Life (Lonnie Cruse)**
*Workbook for any woman wanting a richer prayer life*
**Does This Armor Make Me Look Fat? (Lonnie Cruse)**
*A study of the Christian armor and how it fits women*
**Heading for Harvest (Joyce Jamerson)**
*A study of the fruit of the Spirit*
**Behind Every Good Man (Joyce Jamerson)**
*Studying the women that stand behind faithful men of today*
**Forgotten Womanhood (Joanne Beckley)**
*Studying the traits of godly womanhood*
**Look Into Your Heart (Joyce Jamerson)**
*Studying how to calm one's heart, to develop one that is God approved*

## Studies for Young People

**The Purity Pursuit (Andrew Roberts)**
*Helping teens achieve purity in all aspects of life*
**Paul's Letter to the Romans (Matthew Allen)**
*Putting righteousness by faith on a young person's level*
**Snapshots, Defining Moments in a Girl's Life (Nicole Sardinas)**
*How to make godly decisions when it really matters*
**The Path of Peace (Cassondra Givans)**
*Relevant and important topics of study for teens*
**Transitions (Ken Weliever)**
*A relevant life study for this changing age group*
**A Christian's Approach to... (Cougan Collins)**
*Studies that deal with the issues of life*
**God's Plan for Dating and Marriage (Dennis Tucker)**
*Considering God's directions in this vital area*
**Back to the Beginning (Cougan Collins)**
*Studying the book of Genesis*
**A Christian's Approach to... (Cougan Collins)**
*Dealing with the issues of this life*
**Compass Points (Carl McMurray)**
*22 foundation lessons for home studies or new Christians*
**Eye to Eye with Women of the Bible (Joanne Beckley)**
*Studies for girls of biblical women, good and bad*
**The Gospel and You (Andrew Roberts)**
*Helping teens achieve and possess their own saving faith*
**We're Different Because... (Carl McMurray)**
*A workbook on authority and recent church history*

**Try any of these study workbooks in the
LIVING LETTER SERIES by Frank Jamerson**

The Gospel of Mark / The Gospel of John / Acts
The Letter to the Romans / 1 Corinthians / 2 Corinthians
The Letter to the Galatians / The Letter to the Ephesians
Philippians and Colossians / 1 & 2 Timothy & Titus
1 & 2 Thessalonians / The Letter to the Hebrews
The Letter of James /1 Peter / 2 Peter and Jude / 1-2-3 John

**Other Bible Study Workbooks by Frank Jamerson**
The Godhead / Lord, Please Teach Us to Give!
A Study of the New Testament Church
Bible Authority, How Established How Applied
Elders & Deacons...and Their Wives